I0641647

Keinen Vater, keine Tante
In Amerika er hat,
Trotzdem fand dort Violante
Beifall gleich der toten Stadt.

# Erich Wolfgang Korngold

*by* Jessica Duchen

Φ

Phaidon Press Limited
Regent's Wharf
All Saints Street
London N1 9PA

First published 1996
© 1996 Phaidon Press Limited

ISBN 0 7148 3155 7

A CIP catalogue record for this book is
available from the British Library

Printed in Singapore

*Frontispiece*, 'He has no
father or aunt in America;
even so, *Violanta* was met
there with applause as was
*Die tote Stadt.*' A caricature
of Korngold from
*Amerikaerfolg.* Korngold, as
an immigrant in Hollywood,
was ultimately to find his
music celebrated more in
the USA than in his home city
– and in a very different
context.

# Contents

# Preface

Erich Wolfgang Korngold (1897–1957) first entered my life indirectly, in the same way that he entered many thousands of other lives. When I was about ten years old, Sunday afternoon was the best time for sitting in front of the television because that was when the Hollywood blockbusters of the 1930s and 1940s were shown. I became aware of an image of a ship in full sail, the handsome Errol Flynn as a self-appointed pirate hero, Flora Robson with her wry smile as Queen Elizabeth I, and, over it all, some of the loveliest music I had ever heard: a glorious melody with a broad, generous sweep and weird, fascinating harmonies. *The Sea Hawk* was always a treat – 'Oh that's the one with that *wonderful* music!'

The name of its composer was unfamiliar – a funny, long-winded, Germanic name that did not stick in the memory easily after its brief moment splayed across the screen. It was only many years later that the penny dropped. A friend who adored historical recordings said to me, 'Haven't you heard of Korngold?' and put on the turntable a recording of the 'Pierrot Tanzlied' from Korngold's opera *Die tote Stadt* ('The Dead City'). At once I was mesmerized. There was a 'voice' within this music which spoke directly to me – a voice that was warm, tender, regretful, idealistic, fully human. I rushed off to hunt down a recording of the complete opera (which fortunately existed) and found in it that voice magnified many times over, filling every spectrum of emotion from that deeply nostalgic sentiment to the hero's murderous and self-destructive passion for Marietta. Korngold, I realized, had it all. And he was the composer of not only my favourite *Sea Hawk*, but also *The Adventures of Robin Hood*, *Deception*, *The Constant Nymph* and many other films. I then found out that Korngold had been probably the greatest composing *wunderkind* since Mozart and subsequently went on to become the most privileged and influential film composer in Hollywood. Why should such an exceptional figure have been forgotten in the world of serious classical music? I began rooting about in libraries looking for clues.

The reasons are manifold and range from the ebb and flow of musical fashion to the rather more sinister effects of Korngold's own family.

*'I hear you are playing young Korngold's sonata. Is it grateful?'*
*'No, but his father is.'*

Such were the jokes that circulated in Vienna around 1913, when the boy composer was a source of endless gossip. Erich Wolfgang Korngold was the son of Julius Korngold, the most powerful music critic in Vienna. Given the naturally uneasy relationship of critics and composers, for the one to have been the father of the other seems quite extraordinary – and quite extraordinarily bad luck.

The life and work of Korngold is bound up inextricably with his father's personality and outlook. Julius's musical preferences were extremely conservative and he did his best to iron out his son's early tendencies towards modernistic writing and to keep him well away from circles in which such new music was encouraged. Erich, sunny and non-combative in personality, was not strong enough to rebel outright against this overwhelmingly possessive figure – except on one significant occasion, when he insisted on marrying the girl he loved, against the wishes of his father. The result of his father's influence is that Korngold's musical style changed barely a jot from the age of ten to the age of sixty. Julius Korngold seems to have wanted to hold back the waves of the new by himself; since this was impossible, Erich's probably unconscious assimilation of many of his father's views may have led to what many regarded as the composer's downfall. But nevertheless, he was possessed of great personal integrity and always refused to be swayed from his ideals – a conviction which belongs to the true artist.

After his early runaway successes, and many scandals and fiascos largely of his father's creation, Korngold was forced into Nazi-induced exile in Hollywood, where Warner Brothers had cleverly won him over to movie music, with high fees and ideal terms which at that time were never normally awarded to film composers. But although he approached the job at first with his customary optimism and idealism, he became gradually disillusioned. He went back to Vienna in 1950, planning a comeback, but found that the musical world no longer valued beauty in music for its own sake and that as a 'film composer' he was snobbishly snubbed in the concert hall.

Korngold's child-prodigy works were referred to again and again by eminent musicians of the time with such words as 'daring' and 'modernity'. It was the very lack of perceived and accepted modernity in his music forty years later that led to his being largely forgotten. In that time the world had changed beyond recognition, while Korngold inhabited a sort of musical never-never land. In 1911 the boy Korngold's music was regarded as wholly contemporary. One can only speculate on how Korngold's compositions might have developed had the pressure upon him been less intense and especially if it had been of a less conservative nature. If he had had the courage and the drive to follow Beethoven's example and 'seize Fate by the throat', his position in musical history might have been very different.

Looking at the wider picture of his work, Korngold is one of the hardest composers of all to force into a convenient pigeon-hole. He forms an unusual bridge between the serious and the light-hearted, his work ranging from vast, psychologically fascinating operas through masterly arrangements of Johann Strauss's operettas to the equally masterly film scores for Warner Brothers.

In the film world, Korngold's influence cannot be overestimated. Today, when audiences pile into cinemas to see such films as *ET* and *Raiders of the Lost Ark*, the music they hear is a direct descendant of the passionate melodies and chromatic harmonies, the dramatic fanfares and atmospheric mood painting in the music of Korngold. And since this modern film music is known to far more people the world over than the vast majority of contemporary classical music, that, paradoxically, makes Korngold one of the most influential composers of the twentieth century.

In the world of the concert hall, however, the swing in fashion, which formed a large part of the reason for Korngold's disappearance, was perhaps the tip of a more traumatic iceberg. After Auschwitz and Hiroshima, the twentieth century somehow had to come to terms with its self-made horrors. Beauty and sentiment had no place in a shocked universe. For many years, overtly emotional and aurally pleasant elements – other than those designed solely for an initiated few – disappeared from accepted contemporary composition; something that Korngold believed would result in 'ultimate disaster for the art of music'. Admittedly it was the critics, not the public, who rejected Korngold; nevertheless, he was morally destroyed.

In taking as his gods inspiration, beauty and the elevation of the human soul, Korngold was merely following in the footsteps of most of his compositional predecessors for many centuries. He happened to live at a time when such qualities, despite fulfilling a basic human need, were subjected to a critical rejection which almost amounts to psychological denial. If Korngold was out of step with his times, that is not his fault; if twentieth-century humanity has been scared of the heart-on-sleeve emotion in his music, that is not his fault either. But now that the stranglehold of 'atonality' and serialism has run its course in contemporary music, many tonal composers who happened to live at the same point of history – and many were destroyed by World War II – finally have a chance to be heard and appreciated. Korngold is at the forefront of these.

My aim in writing this book is to encourage its readers to go and hear Korngold's music. His life is a fascinating one, divided between pre-war Vienna, Hollywood in the 1930s and 40s and the shattered world of post-war Europe. But his music stands perfectly well by itself and there is no substitute for hearing it. Performances today are sadly still few and far between, but there is an increasing number of fine recordings – and, of course, those glorious films which still crop up regularly on television screens on Sunday afternoons.

I would like to express my warmest thanks to the very many people who have helped to make this book possible. My special thanks, first, to Ernst and Helen Korngold and their family and to Bernd O. Rachold of the Erich Wolfgang Korngold Society – without whose assistance I simply couldn't have written this book; to Esther and Henry Roth, for their support and hospitality in Los Angeles: if it wasn't for them, I would still be rambling around on the freeways trying to find my way home; to Carl F. Flesch and Johanna Maier for their invaluable help in translating complex German texts (the translated texts which are quoted in the course of the book are in some cases theirs, in some cases my own and in some cases quoted from translated sources by Brendan Carroll and others, such as notes to recordings).

I would also like to thank Dr Rudolf Bletschacher, dramaturg of the Vienna Staatsoper; Norman Lebrecht in London; Schott's and Weinberger's publishing houses in Mainz and London respectively, and Andrew Knowles of Kalmus, which now holds Korngold's Universal Edition works; the staff of UCLA and USC in Los Angeles for making research material available; Sonja Blickensdorfer of the University of Vienna for access to her unpublished thesis *Erich Wolfgang Korngold Opern und Filmmusik* (1993); the conductor Charles Gerhardt; and Brendan Carroll, the eminent Korngold scholar, whose devotion to the composer and promotion of his music for the past two decades has been instrumental in the current revival of interest in Korngold's work, and to whose published articles I am strongly indebted, especially his notes to the Decca recording of *Das Wunder der Heliane.*

And finally, thanks to my family and friends for their support and supplies of chocolate; Eric Wen (now of Biddulph Recordings) for playing me that fateful record; and Dr Derrick Puffett of Cambridge University for encouraging me to begin my formal Korngold studies in 1986.

Jessica Duchen
London, 1996

# I

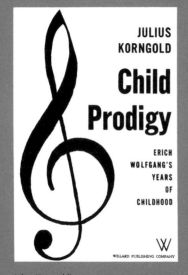

JULIUS
KORNGOLD

## Child
## Prodigy

ERICH
WOLFGANG'S
YEARS
OF
CHILDHOOD

W
WILLARD PUBLISHING COMPANY

Julius Korngold's
reminiscences of his genius
son's childhood were
published in the USA in
1945.

*This child ... changed in a strange manner
when carried away by his music. Then his
childish features were suddenly transformed by
an expression of deep absorption, a strong
assertiveness and tense energy. He seemed to be
burning with a hidden flame, betraying a
temperament that might rise to the heights of
ecstasy ...*

Julius Korngold, *Child Prodigy*, 1945

# Father and Son 1897-1910

*'I never wanted to compose. I only did it to please my father.'*

This was one of Erich Wolfgang Korngold's favourite little jokes. He had begun composing at such an early age and with such ease, fluency and sophistication that he was quickly declared a *wunderkind*, an infant genius. But the humour has an uncomfortable undercurrent. It is impossible to understand Korngold and his progress without understanding the nature of his extremely complex and difficult relationship with his father, which dominated not only the composer's childhood but his adult life as well.

The Korngolds came from Brünn, the capital of Moravia (today in the Czech Republic and called Brno). This city was sometimes nicknamed 'The Austrian Manchester'; it was a small, industrial satellite to Vienna with a strong bourgeoisie and a reasonable but provincial cultural life in the form of a thriving theatre and some operatic interest. Emanuel Schikaneder, the librettist of Mozart's *Die Zauberflöte* and its original Papageno, had for a few years been director of the Brünn opera house. Maria Jeritza, the soprano who inspired some of Erich Wolfgang Korngold's best operatic music, was also born there.

The wine merchant Simon Korngold was part of the Brünn bourgeoisie. The Korngold family was Jewish; but, like the vast majority of families of similar origin and social standing, they did not practise their native religion and saw themselves first and foremost as Austrians. The long period of political stability under the rule of the Emperor Franz Josef had allowed most of the empire's Jewish population to become thoroughly assimilated, despite the presence of popular and widespread anti-Semitic feeling. The security of the late nineteenth century in the Austro-Hungarian Empire was described by the Austrian Jewish writer Stefan Zweig in his autobiography *The World of Yesterday*: 'In this vast empire everything stood firmly and immovably in its appointed place, and at its head was the aged emperor; and were he to die, one knew (or believed) another

Brünn (now Brno): the
Moravian capital was the
birthplace of both Erich
Wolfgang Korngold and
his future muse, the singer
Maria Jeritza.

would come and take his place, and nothing would change in the
well-regulated order. No one thought of wars, of revolution or revolts'.

The Jewish bourgeoisie held typically traditional Austrian values:
security, financial and familial; and considerable ambition on behalf of
their children. Thus Simon Korngold's son, Julius (born in 1860), who
possessed an unusual gift for music, departed for university in Vienna
– his Mecca – to study law. His intention, however, was not merely to
stick to 'safe' legal studies but to enter the music conservatory part-
time. He had saved up the fees for his first year so as not to raise
parental opposition.

Vienna, capital of the empire, provided a cultural banquet for
Julius and his student colleagues. Under Franz Josef's reign the arts
had blossomed extraordinarily in this city. In 1858 the emperor had
set about creating its famous Ringstrasse, building along it the monu-
mental structures which house the national museums, the parliament,
the town hall, the Burgtheater, lush and spacious parks and the great

A Viennese coffee house around 1900. Café society was, and arguably still is, central to Viennese lifestyle and culture.

Vienna Hofoper, a splendid opera house (today known as the Staats-oper) with vast chandeliers, ornate stairways and glittering foyers. In the society that surrounded these architectural transformations, artists, musicians and writers enjoyed an unprecedented degree of privilege and respect.

The students stood in the 'fourth gallery' through innumerable performances at the Hofoper and frequented Sunday lunchtime concerts by the Vienna Philharmonic Orchestra. The sound of this orchestra, warm and velvety in its golden-clad home at the great hall of the Musikverein, deeply influenced virtually every composer who ever wrote for it, including the day's most famous symphonists, Johannes Brahms, Gustav Mahler and Anton Bruckner; Erich Wolfgang Korngold would be no exception.

Julius Korngold spent Tuesdays, Thursdays and Saturdays in his precious studies at the conservatory. Here his harmony professor was Anton Bruckner himself and his fellow students included the violinist Arnold Rosé (later concertmaster of the Vienna Philharmonic), the Lieder composer Hugo Wolf, and two brothers named Franz and Josef Schalk. Franz Schalk became a conductor; he would later co-direct the Vienna Hofoper alongside Richard Strauss, and was to be an important figure in helping to bring Erich Wolfgang Korngold's music to the public. Julius was a fine pianist and possessed a pleasant tenor singing voice; his youthful musical gods were Schumann, whose 'magically romantic vision' made a deep impact upon him, and, of course, Wolfgang Amadeus Mozart. His greatest dreams were of conducting *Don Giovanni* or the Schumann symphonies.

Perhaps because he had to fight so hard to pursue his musical gifts at all, he developed ideals powerful to the point of exaggeration, in which music was 'the Sacred Art', which he was duty bound to serve. A strong moral sense went with these ideals, a responsibility to his own instinctive though somewhat subjective 'sense of justice'; this, thanks to his 'impulsive and fanatical' temperament, tended to sweep other considerations aside in its path, eventually including his composer son.

When his Viennese student days were over, Julius Korngold returned reluctantly to Brünn and continued to pursue his 'respectable' studies. But the young lawyer needed to find an outlet for his musical leanings, and an opportunity presented itself when an article in the local paper about Brahms's new Fourth Symphony annoyed him and prompted him to write a reply, examining the new symphony, which he greatly admired, in considerable detail. The article appeared anonymously in the *Deutschen Blattes*. And the newspaper fell into the hands of the symphony's composer.

The office passed Julius a letter addressed to the unknown author. 'You will be pleased to hear how Johannes Brahms has reacted to your article …' he read. 'Brahms brought the article to me specially and expressed genuine pleasure in the review.' This was all the more special, went on the correspondent, since Brahms habitually took little notice of reviews of his works, especially the good ones. 'I should be delighted to hear the name of my esteemed Brünn colleague who thinks of music as I do myself,' closed the letter. It was signed 'Eduard Hanslick'. Hanslick was music critic for the powerful Vienna paper *Die Neue Freie Presse*, and was already famous for his stance against Richard Wagner's operatic excesses in favour of the more traditional, 'absolute music' approach to composition represented by Brahms.

Deeply flattered by the attention of such prominent men, Julius Korngold wrote to thank Hanslick, with whose musical attitudes he was very much in sympathy, and declared himself the critic's pupil in matters of musical criticism. But it was not until a year later that he gathered the courage to visit Hanslick in Vienna. Warmly welcomed by the diminuitive and shy Hanslick, the young man found himself

The music critic Eduard Hanslick (1825–1904) who groomed Julius Korngold to take on his mantle at Vienna's influential *Neue Freie Presse*

This caricature shows Hanslick waving incense at the feet of Brahms, whose music he championed against the onslaught of Wagner.

being rigorously tested on his musical knowledge and opinions of contemporary composers, and even being asked to play piano duets to demonstrate his practical skills. ('In Vienna we are glad if a critic can play the piano with one finger,' commented Hanslick.) Julius felt that he must have made a good impression since his host, who was partial to snuff, began to encourage him to take snuff himself.

Hanslick had another assignation for Julius: this time to visit Brahms. The gruff composer cordially received the overawed would-be critic in his Karlsgasse apartment and took him out for a meal at his favourite inn, finally asking him to send him copies of some more of his articles and to stay in touch. The meeting soon bore fruit: Brahms's recommendation was instrumental in helping Julius to get his first appointment as a music critic, on the *Brünner Tagesboten*.

Julius Korngold's flair for music itself was surpassed only by his flair for the written word. He was a perfectionist in his writing as well as in his, and other people's, music-making; his reviews were vivid, stylish, pictorial and pertinent. His strong views over the ethics of musical criticism led him from the beginning to avoid personal contact with performing artists as far as possible, so that his judgement could remain objective. Even when the Korngolds later lived in the same house in Vienna as the young pianist and conductor Bruno Walter, critic and musician maintained a cool and respectful distance.

In 1888 Julius Korngold married the daughter of a business contact of his father. Josephine Witrofsky, whose family owned a spirits manufacturing firm, was a lively, outgoing and pretty young woman with a soft, round face and dark eyes. Her temperament both complemented and contrasted with that of her husband, whose persona displayed two distinct and confusingly different strands. He could be charming and lively, with a quick wit that made him excellent and popular company; but in his own study he could become a darker being, with a sombre and pessimistic outlook and an overwhelming ethical severity which could cause his family considerable discomfort. Josephine was prey to the conformity and moral strictness that prevailed, and subordinated her own mischievous sense of humour to her husband's dour temperament. After his death in 1945 her grandchildren were astonished to find a fondness for unmistakeably 'naughty' jokes breaking forth in the venerable lady.

Julius and Josephine's first son was born in Brünn in 1891 and was named Hans Robert – Robert after Schumann, who was the musical god and major influence of Julius's young years. On 29 May 1897, Josephine gave birth to a second son, named Erich at her wish and Wolfgang at Julius's – this time, none too fortunately for the baby, after Mozart.

Hanslick by now needed an assistant, a younger critic to cover the events which he was unable to attend himself; Julius Korngold, his self-confessed disciple with the recommendation of the composer whom Hanslick admired the most, was the obvious choice. And so, in November 1901, the Korngold household packed their belongings and moved to Vienna. Three years later, Hanslick died and Julius was appointed as his successor. This post gave him the mantle of the most influential critic in Austria.

Julius Korngold was feared both because of his newspaper's influence and because of his own exceptional abilities as a writer. Even his victims admired him. The conductor Felix Weingartner wrote: 'He was a brilliant writer, of cultivated aesthetic tastes and thoroughly well educated in musical matters; he wielded his pen much as Hanslick did, with an ease which conjured up prismatic colourings, making the reading of his articles and criticisms a thing of joy, even when the subject was of no interest to the reader, nay even when the content of the article constituted an attack upon him.'

The Vienna to which the Korngolds made their triumphant entry was widely accepted as the centre of the musical universe. At the opera house Gustav Mahler was director; the works of Richard Strauss, Bruckner and Mahler were still new as the Vienna Philharmonic performed them in the rich acoustics of the Musikverein. And an intelligent and intense young man in his late twenties, named Arnold Schoenberg, had begun to draw critical notice and public and critical curiosity alike with the power and 'strangeness' of his music. Artistically gigantic, Vienna was nevertheless a small town in that its musical figures for the most part knew one another well, even if they had personal enmities; in some cases they were related by marriage; and their public were passionately partisan in the coffee houses. There was an intimate, intense, hothouse atmosphere, which produced not only great music but also controversies blown out of all proportion to their real significance.

Gustav Mahler: the composer was also celebrated as director of the Vienna Hofoper, where he raised standards to new heights.

It was not only in music that Vienna was enjoying a golden age. The Burgtheater was the focal point of Viennese serious drama, and here the great actor Adolf von Sonnenthal had, during his long directorship from the mid-nineteenth century, raised the level of the theatre to the greatest heights it had known. Sonnenthal, another artistic jewel of the Viennese Jewish bourgeoisie, was a favourite with the Emperor Franz Josef who granted him his title and gave him the occasional precious gift or a coveted invitation to dine at court. His fiftieth-anniversary performance at the Burgtheater drew an adulatory response from its audience, which moved the revered man to tears as he stood on stage acknowledging the response. In one of the boxes, his four-year-old granddaughter, Luzi von Sonnenthal, was watching.

The city was also the home of great artists. This too was a small world, interwoven to some extent with the musical circle. Gustav

A self-portrait from 1910 by Oskar Kokoschka: the bleak image demonstrates the despair which lay beneath the superficial Viennese *Lebenslust*.

Klimt, a close friend of Gustav Mahler, was working there, creating art of vivid sensuality with rich colours and gold paint. He apparently spent some time running after Mahler's wife, the young man-eater Alma, who subsequently had a turbulent affair – also in Vienna – with the Expressionist painter Oskar Kokoschka. (It is the Expressionist movement which relates most closely to the psychological and harmonic adventures in Korngold's music, as well as the music of Berg and the early works of Schoenberg.) Egon Schiele, who died tragically young in 1918 aged twenty-eight, would through the second decade of the century counter Klimt's lushly Viennese *Lebenslust* (lust for life) with its counterpart, *Weltschmerz* (worldly anguish), bypassing superficial glamour to depict a darker, pessimistic and degenerate side of life and perhaps foreshadowing the fate of Vienna itself. The pianist Artur Schnabel was experiencing there at this time an underlying sense of 'decadence' in the city, an atmosphere of 'defeatism'.

The Viennese-born writer George Clare, in his autobiography *Last Waltz in Vienna*, described the *Zeitgeist* of these times: '... all the glory of the Empire … was nothing but elegant futility and … underneath that sparkling surface was hiding the decay of the nineteenth century and of the Austro-Hungarian monarchy.' What started among artistic intellectuals as an idealistic 'death wish' for their flawed and over-ripe society led ultimately to the disaster of war and dissolution through the first half of the twentieth century.

Eduard Hanslick had found in Julius Korngold an assistant after his own heart; and Julius Korngold continued to be deeply influenced by his controversial mentor. Hanslick's musical outlook was supremely conservative. In a musical world divided between admirers of the 'pure', structured, symphonic music of Brahms and the theatrical, exploratory and explosive works of Wagner, Hanslick was a staunch partisan for Brahms, losing no opportunity to launch the most caustic invective against Wagner (and finding himself heavily caricatured by the composer in the opera *Die Meistersinger von Nürnberg* in which the character of the fussy juror, Beckmesser, was in the composer's early sketches named 'Hans Lich'). Korngold followed his senior staunchly, not only in points of writing style, but in his musical taste which also fell strongly on the side of conservatism. However, a generation on, Julius Korngold's battle was not to be against Wagner for the sake of Brahms – indeed, he admired Wagner – but against the Second Viennese School's atonal musical revolution for the sake of his own son.

While the Korngold's first son, bearing Schumann's name, grew into an unremarkable little boy, Erich Wolfgang was another matter. A docile, happy, tractable child with huge, deep dark eyes and a sweet tooth, he was beating time with a wooden spoon by the age of three. Julius, delighted, encouraged him, and was startled to see the rapidity with which his son got to grips with music. At five years old, Erich was picking out melodies at the piano and could sit happily side by side with his adoring father to play tunes on the keyboard, which Julius accompanied. Julius decided to send the child for lessons with a distant relation, Emil Lamm, who would teach him piano and also the rudiments of musical theory. One day the boy played for Hanslick. The great critic took a pinch of snuff and remarked, 'The little Mozart!'

By the age of six Erich was composing his own music. When he had the chickenpox he wanted the piano pushed up to his bed so that he could improvise. He kept a music notebook from which he was quite inseparable; it went with him everywhere and grew steadily fuller, even on family holidays to the Tyrol, the summer haven of much Viennese society. When his father was away, the little boy composed a whole cantata for soloists, choir and piano, to a text that one of his schoolmates had made up for him. Its title was *Nixe, Gold.*

Julius Korngold received the score from the boy while he was holidaying, without his family, in Abbazia, playing four-hand piano music with a famous lady singer named Karoline Gomperz-Bettelheim (he gives no explanation of why he was there in the first place!). He held the opinion that the cantata was inspired by Wagner's *Das Rheingold.* One quality leapt out at him – 'The excesses, acerbities and violent sounds of this immature product announced an individual note of abruptly emerging "modernism".' This distressed Julius, whose paragraph concludes with the reminder that 'Later, however, this artist, endowed with the healthy imagination of a thoroughbred musician, was to find his way back easily and spontaneously to the inner laws of tonal art.' Julius was ignoring, and continued to ignore, one important and irreversible law of nature: nothing ever goes *back.*

For the time being, there was nothing for it but to make sure that Erich was given a good grounding of music theory and traditional compositional techniques. The elderly Robert Fuchs was himself a conservative composer and a superb theoretician with particular expertise in the teaching of counterpoint, and it was to him that Julius Korngold decided to entrust the next stage of Erich's formal musical education. The lad went for his first lesson, sat down at the piano and began to play, and years later he recollected how Fuchs's expression darkened, 'he seized my hand from the keyboard and exclaimed, "But you cannot do that!"'

Far from resenting the shackling of his musical gifts, the nine-year-old was soon making progress in theory and counterpoint which, Fuchs reported, would overshadow that of a student of twenty. Julius was beginning to feel worried. Evidently the child had no ordinary talent for his own beloved 'sacred art' and it was vitally important that he should make the right decisions on Erich's behalf.

If there was anyone in Vienna whom Julius trusted and admired, it was Gustav Mahler. Mahler had in that same year (1907) been forced to resign as director of the Vienna Hofoper, in which post Julius had been one of his staunchest supporters. They were on good terms personally, and the great composer would occasionally visit the home of the critic and his family. So great a supporter of Mahler was Julius that when the composer's departure from the Court Opera was announced, the new director had to start his new job with a serious handicap: the hostility of the *Neue Freie Presse*. That new director was Felix Weingartner, who remembered in his memoirs that 'Dr Korngold was by no means a personal opponent of mine, he was not even actually opposed to me as an artist. He was the opponent of Gustav Mahler's successor.' Johann Strauss's brother-in-law, Josef Simon, had happened to see Julius on the day of Mahler's resignation, and recounted to Weingartner that 'Korngold ... clenching his fist, exclaimed, "His successor will have a nice job, we'll show him something ..."'

When father and son, the latter fetchingly attired in a sailor hat, arrived at the Mahler household a few weeks after Erich's tenth birthday, it would seem that Mahler had nothing to lose by giving an encouraging and positive assessment of the little boy's musicality. But it has passed into the realms of musical legend (via Alma Mahler's autobiography) that the restless and candid composer paced about as Erich performed his entire cantata from memory, declared him 'a genius', and gave an immediate recommendation that he should be sent to study with Alexander von Zemlinsky. 'Zemlinsky will give him all he needs,' he told the proud father.

The *wunderkind*, in the meantime, was not particularly interested in the burgeoning plans for his future. Unlike the precocious prodigy figure so often portrayed as a little adult with no true childhood, Erich underwent, if anything, the opposite process. He was a real child; and in some ways, in his natural generosity and innocent outlook, even naïvety, he never really grew up. On one visit to Mahler's house with his parents, when he had finished his dutiful piano performance he promptly escaped outside to play with the Mahlers' little daughter Anna (who later became a successful sculptress and included him among her subjects). Alma Mahler recalled in her autobiography that when she went to call the children in to tea Erich did not want to come in because he said he 'didn't eat nicely'. But even on the first, famous visit, Mahler was no stranger to him; about two years earlier he had been allowed into a dress rehearsal at the opera house where he had had his first impression of Mahler at the conductor's podium. He

A drawing of Alexander von Zemlinsky, the teacher from whom young Korngold is said to have concealed some of his best early works

sat quietly, taking in every detail and every remark the conductor made to the singers.

Julius Korngold was well pleased with Mahler's advice. He had great respect for Zemlinsky, whose works, including the operas *Es war einmal*, *Kleider machen Leute* and *Der Zwerg*, showed a wonderful melodic fluidity and fantasy. Zemlinsky had taught most of the talented young musicians in Vienna, counting among his pupils Arnold Schoenberg, who was now his brother-in-law, and the young Alma Schindler before she married Mahler and abandoned composition (Zemlinsky had also had an affair with her). He was a lush late romantic, writing music of considerable chromatic complexity that was, however, not too experimental – someone of whom Julius could certainly approve.

*Following page*, the manuscript of a waltz which Korngold, aged ten, composed for his grandmother in June 1908

As a composer, Zemlinsky often seemed not to have fulfilled the promise of his prodigious talent. Some thought that he was lazy,

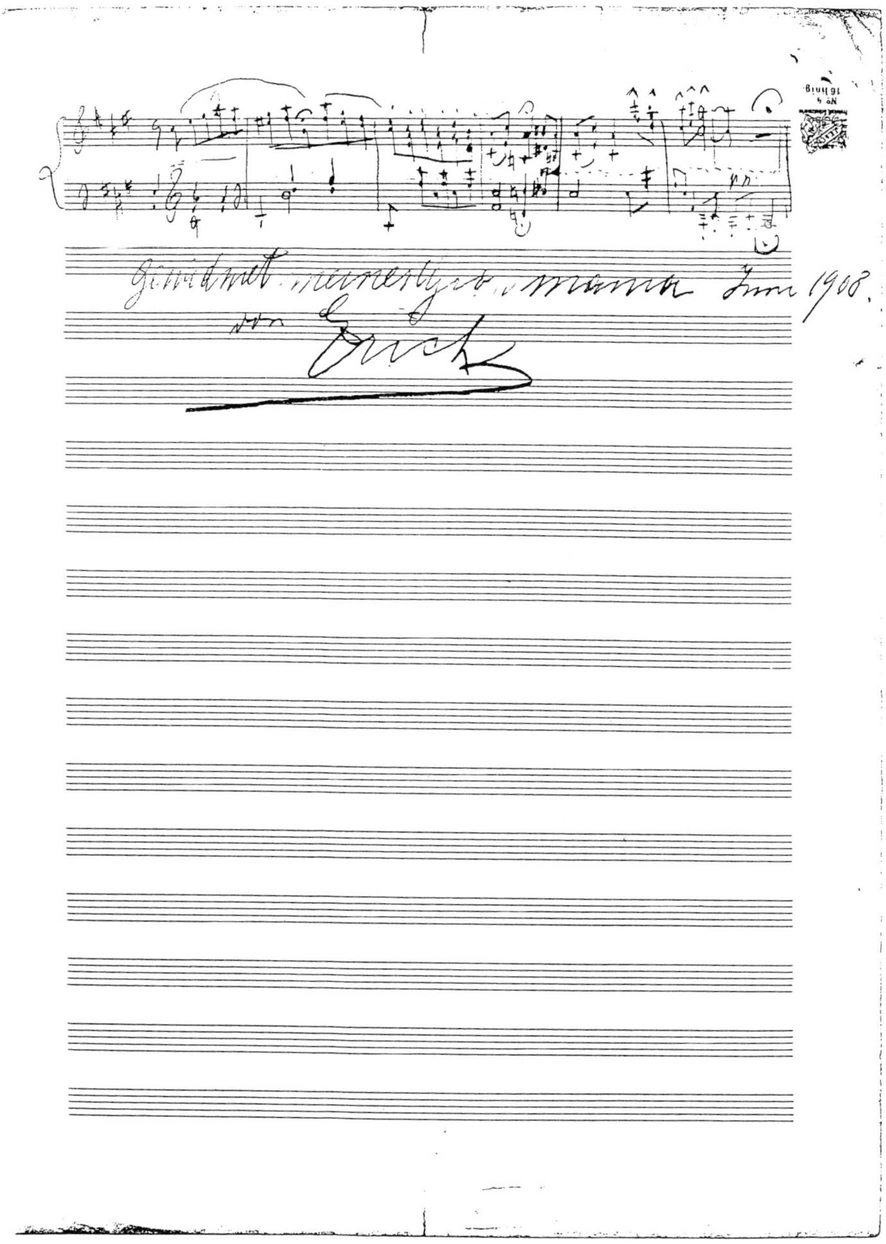
Juni 1908.
von Erich

others that he was simply too busy. Schoenberg described Zemlinsky's way of dealing with his tightly-packed schedule:

> *He had a peculiar method of using his time rationally, since he was forced to give many piano lessons in order to earn a living. He would alternately compose and practise the piano. Writing in ink one page of music, he had to wait for the page to dry. This interval of time only could he spare for practice. A busy life!*

For Erich the results could not have been better. He and Zemlinsky developed an instant mutual liking and respect. Writing about the relationship in the *Prager Musikzeitung*'s 'Auftakt' (Upbeat) column in 1921, the by then successful young composer remembered how Zemlinsky's teaching had been 'free of all systematic shackles, fascinating teaching … My youthful fantasy soon came under the impression of his legendary musicality, the originality of his opinions and his convictions, the light irony in the pronouncements and the communication of absolute authority pouring forth from the teacher, which my young heart listened to'.

But Zemlinsky's 'absolute authority' did not prevent Erich from harbouring some ambitious plans which he undertook to realize without his teacher's knowledge. Underneath the placid and loving exterior of the little musician there already lay a strong-minded wilfulness, even stubborness, a certain determination to have things his own way. Perhaps he was a little spoilt, musically; perhaps he simply knew the extent of his own talent. But the quality stayed with him all his life, and when faced with situations where he felt himself poorly treated he could react with incomprehension, hotheadedness or downright anger. Even when apparently seeking the advice of others he would probably have made up his mind already on his course of action. As a young composer with an interventionist critic for a father, however, that was also one of a number of traits which would lead him into some very uncomfortable family conflicts.

At the same time, music was fun for him. He would compose little pieces as presents for his family and friends on birthdays and at Christmas, some so striking, Julius tells us, that Erich was able to incorporate the ideas into his later serious works. And music effected an astonishing transformation in the child. Julius Korngold wrote: 'This child, so dependent and docile that he seemed to lack will power

– a state partly caused by his indifference to everyday life, changed in a strange manner when carried away by his music. Then his childish features were suddenly transformed by an expression of deep absorption, a strong assertiveness and tense energy. He seemed to be burning with a hidden flame, betraying a temperament that might rise to the heights of ecstasy'.

One of Erich's first lasting compositions did come into being directly via Zemlinsky's teaching. The professor provided his pupil with a theme on which to compose a Passacaglia for piano. The piece turned out so well that the boy later – at the suggestion of Mahler – incorporated it into his D minor piano sonata, of which it forms the final movement. The powerful, slow, serious theme which Zemlinsky wrote has more than a few features in common with the Passacaglia theme for the last movement of Brahms's Fourth Symphony – the very work which helped to provide Korngold's father with his role as music critic. Erich responded to it with both originality and pianistic adeptness. Julius must have been pleased to see his son composing what might be an indirect homage from the teacher to the father's background.

More frequently, however, Erich played his compositions to Zemlinsky, who said to him, 'You are an outrage!' So instead of ceasing to be outrageous, the little composer simply hid his compositions. And indeed Zemlinsky knew nothing of Erich Korngold's eventual Op. 1, a trio for piano, violin and cello, until it was finished (1910). But the pair maintained a happy relationship until Zemlinsky was appointed to a post to conduct opera in Prague in 1911. Erich was sad to lose his much-loved professor and was sent instead to study counterpoint with a teacher named Hermann Grädener. He received a postcard from Zemlinsky: 'Dear Erich! I hear you are studying with Grädener. Is he making progress?'

Despite Zemlinsky's own oddly-determined practice schedule, he had insisted that his young charge should practise the piano religiously. Erich did so, and here his talent was as strong as his bent for composition. His pianistic ability would allow him, while still a young teenager, to compose piano music of astonishing technical wizardry – almost more orchestral than pianistic in quality. He was a superb improviser and his father loved to hear him experimenting on the instrument late into the evening after the parents had retired to bed. Years later, his playing would be preserved in certain of the Hollywood films he scored and in the rare recordings in which he plays his own works: the touch is unmistakable, arrestingly powerful, both deep-toned and glittering, coloured with the richness of an entire orchestra.

Most of Erich's first compositions were for the piano. Encouraged by his father, he developed a precocious interest in the story of *Don Quixote* and decided to write a set of six short piano pieces based on episodes in the book. The family was on holiday at the time, in the Dolomites. In the Toblach Hotel, the boy would close himself up in a room with a piano to work, and here one day his mother found him, emerging later than usual, red-eyed. The child had been crying, afraid that he would not fulfil his father's expectations.

Julius, in his turn, was astonished by Erich's instinctive ability to relate his musical imagination to dramatic episodes and characters. Entitled 'Dreams of heroic deeds', 'Sancho Panza and his grey donkey', 'Don Quixote goes forth', 'Dulcinea von Toboso', 'Adventure' and 'Don Quixote's Conversion and Death', the pieces are exceptionally sensitive to the mood, excitement, idealism and innocence that they interpret. Here too are the first signs of Korngold's predilection for tales of fantastic adventures – a gift for interpreting and filling out stories with character, atmosphere and sympathy – which would be best shown when he composed music to accompany adventures like *Robin Hood* or *The Sea Hawk* on the screen.

The first Piano Sonata in D minor is an extraordinary work for a child to have composed. Sombre, intense, highly chromatic, it falls into three movements with a dramatic Allegro, a fleeting scherzo with a more peaceful trio and finally the already-composed Passacaglia. The harmonic daring and chromatic dissonances which the little boy produced so easily were better suited to someone two or three times his age. (The rather older Alban Berg wrote his own Op. 1 Piano Sonata at about the same time, 1908–9 – another piano sonata that stretches harmony to its limits.) According to Julius Korngold's somewhat over-dramatic memoirs, the precocious darkness in the sonata stemmed from a horrible episode when Erich accidentally injured a playmate who nearly bled to death as a result; fortunately the child survived, but there could meanwhile have been some

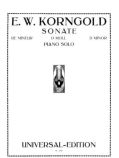

The cover of Korngold's First Piano Sonata, published in 1910 by Universal Edition in agreement with the prodigy's father

terrifying moments for the conscience-ridden Erich. In more recent times, the great Canadian pianist Glenn Gould found this sonata more symphonic than pianistic, writing that he felt it could have been a blueprint for one of that age's better symphonic efforts. There was another work that had remained hidden from Zemlinsky: a ballet-pantomime, a *commedia dell'arte* creation, named *Der Schneemann* ('The Snowman'). Erich wrote the first part during the Christmas holidays of 1908 and the second in the Easter holidays of 1909.

Korngold *père* felt that he could not ignore his responsibilities as father of a genius. Erich had finished three superb works – the pantomime *Der Schneemann*, the Piano Sonata and the *Don Quixote* character pieces. The decision his father needed to make was: should the world now be told about his son's talent?

Julius Korngold went to the music publishers Universal Edition in Vienna and organized a strictly limited, private printing of his son's

The libretto of Korngold's first stage work, the ballet-pantomime *Der Schneemann*. This was the composition that first demonstrated his natural instinct for the theatre.

first completed compositions. The edition carried a foreword announcing: 'It is not intended to release them [these three works] for general publication, but solely for private distribution in numbered copies to musicians, musicologists and others interested in music. The sole purpose of printing them is to 'make a statement'. They have been composed by a boy who at the time was eleven to twelve years old.'

The critic's 'sense of justice' forbade him at this stage to make his son's gifts known in Vienna. It was safer to send them to musical luminaries in Germany and the provinces rather than allow them to fall into the hands of his own powerful and potentially prejudiced Viennese colleagues and adversaries. But he could reach musicians of the stature of the composers Richard Strauss and Engelbert Humperdinck, the conductor Artur Nikisch, and the professor Arthur Seidl. The response was instant and overwhelming; and then there could be no turning back. Julius Korngold had begun what his daughter-in-law Luzi von Sonnenthal later described somewhat generously as his *Passionweg* (way of the Cross).

Richard Strauss's reply read: 'The first reaction on learning that this has been written by a boy of eleven is something of a shock mingled with apprehension, that such a precocious genius may not experience the normal development one sincerely hopes for him. The stylistic assurance, mastery of form, individuality of expression in the sonata, these harmonies – they all are really astonishing.' The distinguished musicologist Hermann Kretschmar, professor at Berlin University, proclaimed: 'Your son is phenomenal even among the exceptional cases of early musical development. His modernity and virility are, to my mind, comparable only to that of the young Handel.'

Artur Nikisch, the conductor of the Berlin Philharmonic Orchestra, who would later champion the young man's orchestral works, made the judgement: 'But this is phenomenal! I am excited about these pieces! I mean the compositions as such, not the fact that they were written by an eleven-year-old boy. What radiant imagination, inventiveness, what daring harmonic innovations! One really does not know what to admire most! Dear God, what precious gifts can we look forward to from the genius of this boy if it develops normally. May God grant health to this chosen being – then there is nothing to fear'. Engelbert Humperdinck, composer of the magical operas *Hänsel und Gretel* and *Königskinder*, found in Erich an infant prodigy 'from fairyland' but expressed reservations about his 'dubious modernity'. And Arthur Seidl discussed the compositions in his seminars at the Leipzig Conservatory.

A more disturbing response came from the composer Karl Goldmark in Vienna itself, when he was shown the pieces at his express wish. 'I have one objection … It is a daily occurrence that youth becomes avid for every new thing. Yet the newest isn't new enough. Youth … tries to reach even further. This has been demonstrated and proven by the development from Haydn up to the present. But have we reached a point where the question is justified: where to? Picture to yourself that, just as Beethoven left behind Mozart's and Haydn's formal structure, Erich Wolfgang Korngold might leave behind Strauss, Debussy and others in the course of his development. Then it might well be justified to ask: where to? Probably my worries are unfounded, because I am addressing a careful father whose rich, mature and artistically clarified judgement will be on guard lest this glorious blossom might come to harm.'

Julius was evidently pleased with Goldmark's comments and seems to have been wholly in agreement with him. Heaven forfend that his son should leave behind the well-established conservative style of the day. It seems to have escaped his notice that looking forwards rather than backwards and exploring new musical frontiers to find his own voice had done Beethoven no harm whatsoever and indeed was the very thing which made him the towering figure he is today. Heaven forfend that Erich should change, develop, rebel or *grow up*.

The conductor Bruno Walter referred to similar 'daring' traits in Erich Wolfgang Korngold's first officially published work, the Piano Trio Op. 1, in the première of which Walter was the pianist (with violinist Arnold Rosé and cellist Friedrich Buxbaum). Walter became a great champion of the young composer's early operas. Like Julius Korngold, he opposed the rising atonalists and enjoyed reading the critic's *Neue Freie Presse* reviews with 'the masterly treatment of his themes and the force of his formulation and … his clever and high-spirited attack upon atonality and atonal composers and his struggle against those symptoms of a musical disease'. Remembering the Piano Trio, Walter wrote in his autobiography that the work was 'very

*Following page, changing the guard in Vienna's Franzenplatz: imperial influence was still strong in the early years of the twentieth century.*

interesting and harmonically daring'. This outset did not look like the first steps of a composer who would later be considered conservative and unexperimental. Erich upset his teachers, played with modulation, indeed developed a sound world that was entirely his own – and all apparently effortlessly. Interestingly, Julius was to write in his memoirs that at the age of thirteen his son had actually heard very little music, other than that which Julius played at home on the piano. He had been to fewer than ten concerts and about five operas and showed limited interest in listening to music that was not his own.

The *Neue Freie Presse*, Julius's own paper, demanded a report on the *wunderkind*, which the musicologist Ernest Decsey duly wrote. Julius protested strongly, but Moritz Benedikt, the editor, declared that the paper could not bypass such an unusual business. 'Even this suspicious man, knowing human nature only too well,' wrote Julius in his memoirs, 'did not anticipate the stigma which the son of the *Neue Freie Presse* music critic would have to carry from the very beginning. And how the father was never to be forgiven for having brought such a son into the world.'

For the young Erich Korngold this was the beginning not of a *Passionweg* but of a long period – more than twenty years – in which he and his music fell victim and even scapegoat to the enmities of his father and the gossip-laden Viennese. And Julius had many enemies, partly through jealousy of his powerful job (he named the critic Max Graf 'Iago' in his memoirs), partly through the difficult extremes of his personality, and partly through his clever writing. As Weingartner found, for instance, Julius Korngold, 'apparently full of good will and strictly impartial, knew how to slip poison with deadly accuracy into his accounts of whatever I undertook'. The news of the critic's prodigy of a son spread like wildfire through the close-knit city centre and the sceptical populace came to one natural conclusion: these pieces of music could not have been written by an eleven-year-old boy. They must be the work of someone else.

Julius found much amusement in the accusation that he himself was the author of little Erich's music. 'If I could write such music, I would not be a critic,' he replied. And at the same time accusations began to fly around that the father had tagged on 'Wolfgang' to his son's name after the *wunderkind*'s talent emerged, to highlight the obvious similarity to Mozart – it was too much of a coincidence. Father and son nevertheless did not see fit to downplay Erich's Wolfgang; it was always included, rather proudly and unlike most middle names, in print; and throughout his life the composer's signature remained the full 'Erich Wolfgang Korngold'.

Did the great and good musicians of the day offer positive reactions and take up little Korngold's works simply because of the power held by his father and the *Neue Freie Presse*, which could otherwise have been used against them? Certainly as Erich's career progressed there were rumblings and accusations and manipulations aplenty where it was alleged that Julius's reviews were affected by whether the artist in question played or sang Erich's music. But at the outset this

Julius, Josephine and Erich Wolfgang Korngold in 1911. Erich's older brother, Hans, is not included in this family group.

can scarcely have been the case. The little boy's music was so spont-aneous, sophisticated and personal that he could not have been mistaken for anything other than a true prodigy – once it was accept-ed that he, and not his father, was the author of his music. His con-temporaries, when not blinded by jealousy, regarded him as nothing less than a miracle.

Young Erich led a sheltered life, usually left, along with his elder brother, in the care of servants while their father worked, writing or studying scores in his solitary music room, and their mother went out to tea parties and coffee houses. When they were at home, he was not excessively spoilt; his mother wisely cared for him 'like any boy who had not written sonatas'. Perhaps that very shelter and distance was what protected him and allowed him to grow up into a relatively undisturbed personality with good common sense and a marvellous sense of humour. He was, however, overprotected to the extent that his father wrote, with distressing pride, 'Erich's first unaccompanied walk was actually the one to the barracks when the First World War in 1914 tore the eighteen-year-old from the side of his parents.' (In fact, Erich turned eighteen in 1915.)

But throughout his life he hated to have his music interfered with, and that included the interference of his father. If Julius made some throwaway criticism while Erich was working or improvising at the piano, the otherwise docile boy proved himself willing to defend his work furiously. In the meantime, probably unconsciously, Erich was absorbing those same attitudes to music that his father was fighting for.

That is not to say that Julius did not help and advise his son from his wealth of musical understanding. One area where he felt he really had influenced Erich was in melodic thinking: 'by always admon-ishing him to "continue". Not to be satisfied with beginnings, but to breathe out any melodic phrase he had started and to follow up, as if anwering a question, an anterior period with a posterior one.' It was good advice, for Korngold's melodic writing always remained one of the strongest features of his music.

One visitor to whom Erich was required to play his pantomime *Der Schneemann* was Dr Ludwig Winter, the general intendant of the Vienna Court Theatre. He happened to let slip an enthusiastic remark about the piece in front of the prime minister's wife, Baronin

Bienerth, who decided to arrange the first performance of the work in the ministry at a special charity evening. The city was curious; the little genius could no longer be kept under wraps. From this occasion stemmed Erich's determination to have thorough control over the performance of his own music, for he was able to direct the rehearsals himself, along with the pianist-conductor Richard Pahlen; and the cast included the prima ballerina of the day, Louise Wopalensky, as Columbine and the Hofoper's ballet master, Godlewsky, as Pierrot 'the snowman'. The assembled Viennese glitterati watched the pantomime in its original two-piano instrumentation, enchanted by the melodious outpouring of a child with the gifts of a grown man.

The touching tale showed Pierrot painting himself white and standing disguised as a snowman in front of Pantalon's house where Columbine is being kept under lock and key. Pantalon is tricked into submission when the 'snowman' terrifies him by beginning to move, and thus Pierrot wins his beloved Columbine.

Today, *Der Schneemann* is remembered mainly through extracts such as the prelude, interlude and serenade. The music has the lightness, melodiousness and danceability, as well as the sweetness, of ballet music by such composers as Glazunov; but already some of the Korngold hallmarks are firmly in place. The gift for flowing melody and incisive, strongly-marked dance-like rhythm is evident here; the glistening chromatic harmonies that enliven the musical textures, and the exceptional ability that Korngold always displayed to capture the atmosphere of his story to perfection. There is an icy crispness and delicacy in the prelude which is exquisitely suggestive of the snowy setting.

The private première was to lead directly to the public one. Julius Korngold was alarmed to find matters out of his control. The pantomime had been heard and enjoyed by an emissary of the emperor Franz Josef, for one thing; and for another, Universal Edition seemed quite unconcerned about ignoring its contract with Julius Korngold, which included a small clause stipulating that the pantomime might only be performed on a Viennese stage with his special permission.

The publishing house's director Emil Hertzka offered the one-act ballet to Felix Weingartner for performance at the Hofoper, and the conductor was so impressed when he examined the score that he agreed at once to take it on. Julius Korngold heard of the breach of contract from Josef Simon, who was president of Universal Edition. The critic opposed to Mahler's successor found himself with the embarrassing necessity of visiting that successor's office to ask him not to produce the ballet, as it would put Julius, as critic, in a difficult professional position. Weingartner was not prepared to relinquish the opportunity, however – which provided him with an occasion not only to give the première of the work of a new Mozart but also to get back at the new Mozart's father. In his autobiography, he wrote: 'I could only give him the same answer as I had given Direktor Hertzka, namely that father and son were for me two entirely distinct personalities.' And Weingartner, though no great friend of the critic, really liked the young composer – a situation that was the first of many of its type. He found him 'jolly, often exuberant, clever but in no way precocious; affectionate and grateful but never submissive; of frank and sure judgement and with a goodly portion of humour'. As for his music, Weingartner felt: 'He gives one an impression as though Nature had the caprice to sum up everything the art of music had produced in the last decades in order to give the sum to a child in his cradle, who now plays with it.'

For public performance the pantomime had to be orchestrated – a task which was not entrusted to the boy composer but to his former teacher, Zemlinsky, Julius having refused even to consider the more experimental composer Franz Schreker for the job. Julius's erstwhile conservatory companion Franz Schalk was to conduct the evening, and here was something else for Julius to worry about. Schalk was possessor of a sharp wit and had been an opponent of Mahler's directorship, which immediately put him in the opposing camp to the *Neue Freie Presse* critic; his eagerness to conduct *Der Schneeman* made Julius worry about his motives. But, like Weingartner, Schalk was able to rise above personal partisanship and to distinguish between cantankerous father and gifted, likeable son. *Der Schneeman* received its successful public première at the Vienna Hofoper on the Emperor's name day, 4 October 1910, with Arnold Rosé as violin soloist and King Albert of Belgium as guest of honour. Julius was 'as stunned as if a brick had dropped on my head'.

# 2

A photograph of the sixteen-
year-old Korngold. One
newspaper described him as
'a Richard Strauss in knickers'.

*If we had a little boy of twelve who preferred
writing this sort of music to hearing a good folk
tune or going out and playing in the park, we
should consult a specialist.*

W. J. Henderson in the *New York Sun*,
reviewing Korngold's Piano Trio Op. 1, 1910

# Adolescence among the Stars 1910–16

Julius, Josephine and Erich Korngold attended together a rehearsal of
Erich's Piano Trio. 'Too fast!' exclaimed Josephine as the three
eminent musicians launched forth. 'No, too slow!' Julius contradicted.
'I say it's too fast,' insisted his wife. 'And I say it's too slow,' the critic
proclaimed. Between them, Erich – whose trio it was, after all –
ventured to remark that in his opinion the ensemble had got it just
about right. 'You shut up!' retorted both grown-ups. The trio's printed
score bore the inscription: 'Dedicated to my dear Papa'.

    The Piano Trio was Korngold's first officially published work and
its luscious score, although influenced strongly by the likes of Richard

The decorative front page of
Korngold's Piano Trio
(1910), a piece that reveals
both Korngold's deep roots
in Romanticism and the
distinctively personal
harmonic language that
helped to establish his own
'voice'.

Strauss and Brahms, shows many traits that became Korngold hallmarks as the years went by. The opening bears a strong resemblance to the opening of Brahms's Trio in B major, Op. 8, starting with a romantic, songlike theme played quietly on the piano alone, then growing and blossoming in the full forces of the trio. The tender counterpoint, especially in the second leading melody of the first movement, is Brahmsian in its use of thirds and sixths (i.e., pitch distances of three notes and six notes apart). It is the various harmonizations of the first theme, discordant and tortuous within a comfortable tonal framework, and certain dramatic and expressionistic developmental moments, which are Korngold's stylistic giveaways. The second movement, the Scherzo, is even more characteristic, constantly switching time, inflections of tempo and tonal centres before finding its way triumphantly home. Its Viennese bounce and syncopated swings, the sharply rhythmic closing theme and the warm, sorrowful contrast provided by the trio are a wonderful example of the young Korngold's inborn lightness of touch, which stayed with him all his life. The third movement's mysterious chromaticism, circulating freely in a very slow Adagio, is desperately adventurous by anyone's standards – here little Korngold really moves, within one work, from the nineteenth century firmly into the twentieth, with echoes of composers as contemporary as Debussy and Berg. But however gymnastic Korngold's musical adventures are, there are always moments when they come home to rest in a friendly tonic anchor. The final movement's opening is motivically related to the Adagio; the declamatory start leads into a beautifully lyrical and lengthy melody, again Brahmsian in its motivic but songful nature, which draws out and develops the triplet motif of its first phrase. The main theme of the first movement puts in a reappearance in counterpoint with a theme from the Scherzo – such 'cyclic' elements often came into Korngold's works. This glorious movement contains all Korngold's warmth, technical virtuosity, malleability and idiosyncrasy – in far more than embryo.

How pressurized was Erich? The answer appears to be *exceptionally and unrelentingly.* His father's attitude combined, none too comfortably, encouragement, bullying and proprietorial control. The conductor Karl Böhm spent several holidays with the Korngold family in Velden am Wörthersee, where Böhm's sister-in-law ran the

Schlosshotel. 'I remember that young Korngold's father, Dr Julius Korngold … constantly encouraged his son to compose,' recalled Böhm, 'so much so that on one occasion when we all went to bathe in the lake he shouted after him: "Erich! Don't bathe – compose!"'

On another occasion, father and son went to a matinée (an afternoon musical party) in the house of a rich Viennese industrialist. Erich performed some of his own music, and 'as usual,' wrote one contemporary, Marcel Prawy (dramaturg of the Vienna State Opera for the greater part of the twentieth century), 'Julius Korngold acted "the boss".' When it was suggested to the industrialist that next time he might have a matinée featuring the music of the eighteenth-century composer Pergolesi he answered, 'All right, but only on one condition – Papa Pergolesi stays at home!'

A strict father was yet another factor that Erich Wolfgang had in common with his namesake Wolfgang Amadeus. Leopold Mozart and Julius Korngold both pushed their gifted sons in the extreme – Mozart even more than Korngold, given the child Wolfgang's tours and performances at the great courts of Europe. Julius Korngold's emphasis for his son differed in that he sought not so much upwardly-mobile social situations for him to perform in as those where the greatest musicians of the day would be present. A reverence towards music as Art had come into being during the Romantic era which was strongly characteristic of its day, and which is not as relevant when considering Leopold Mozart's attitude towards his son.

As a teenager Erich Wolfgang Korngold took mainly after his mother in appearance and temperament. He had her round face, her large, deep eyes, and her cheerfulness. But in other respects he resembled his father. His standards were extreme; he hated compromise; and he was harshly critical and intolerant of poor performance. After a performance of *Der Schneemann* conducted by Franz Schalk on 24 February 1911, when the composer was thirteen years old, he wrote a letter to the opera house's director: 'I am sorry to say that I did not know my own music. The melodies could not be heard, the tempi were rushed … Schalk considers an orchestral rehearsal for the work extremely necessary, as has been considered from the start. Alternatively, may I ask you not to perform this work any more.' Here the influence of his father is more than evident.

But as Erich set about composing a second piano sonata, a new topic of conversation was sweeping through the Vienna coffee houses:

'the little Korngold'. Of course opinion split into 'pros' and 'cons', the cons deciding this time that it was not Julius Korngold but the orchestrator Zemlinsky who was the real author of *Der Schneemann*. And that he had been hired for the job by the boy's father. Even Zemlinsky could not quite believe his ears when he heard what his young charge had written. Several years later, at the first performance in Prague of the first orchestral work fully completed by Erich, the *Schauspiel Overtüre*, Zemlinsky asked his ex-pupil, 'Erich, did you really orchestrate it by yourself?'

Julius decided that it was time for his son to 'tread on sacred soil'. In August 1910 he and Erich boarded a train for Salzburg, Mozart's home town, a well-loved meeting place for the great and good of the music world, and the nobility, even before the founding of the Salzburg Festival by Max Reinhardt in 1919. The arrival of the prodigy caused a stir, and Archduke Eugen himself expressed his wish to hear Erich Korngold play his own music. A small but select crowd gathered around a piano in the Österreichischer Hof hotel – in a room that was currently occupied by the great piano pedagogue Theodor Leschetizky. Also present was the composer Paul Dukas, composer of *L'Apprenti Sorcier* ('The Sorcerer's Apprentice'), and several eminent critics from France. At the next day's concert, the audience rose to honour the Archduke as he entered; but on his way to his seat he paused by the child composer and his father, asked Erich how he felt after his performance and thanked Julius for sending him the piano score of *Der Schneemann*. The Korngolds felt themselves honoured indeed. Erich dedicated his next piano work, the *Märchenbilder* ('Fairy Tales'), to the Archduke.

Later the same year, the young composer travelled twice to Munich. On the first occasion he and his father sat in on rehearsals of Mahler's gigantic Eighth Symphony ('Symphony of a Thousand'), while the composer conducted. Mahler had already made a deep impression upon Erich – so much so that Julius would later remember that whenever Erich was asked what he wanted to be when he grew up, he would reply 'Direktor Mahler'. Julius also reported a remark by an elderly inspector at the opera house watching Erich on stage at the rehearsals for *Der Schneemann*: 'There's a little Mahler inside that boy.' Perhaps neither remark should be taken as a clue to the sort of music that Erich Korngold hoped to write. From his early works onwards,

Korngold's music possessed a *joie de vivre* and optimism that is notably absent from the neurotic and anguished music of the older master. It is also worth remembering that in his lifetime Gustav Mahler was far better known as a conductor and as the director who pulled the Vienna Opera kicking and screaming into the twentieth century; his own music took second place in the public eye. Given the degree of control which Erich liked to have over his own works, Mahler the autocrat was an unsurprising ideal.

This caricature from a *Neues Wiener Tagblatt* of 1911 shows the child prodigy Korngold surrounded by the astonished musical luminaries of the day: from left to right, Siegfried Wagner (the composer's son), Max Reger, Artur Nikisch, Richard Strauss and Eugen d'Albert.

The second trip to Munich involved a three-day festival of French music under the auspices of the Société Française des Amis de la Musique, whose general secretary Jules Ecorcheville had been present at Erich's impromptu recital in Salzburg. The festival, to Julius's relief, included 'no radically new modernists', but boasted the presence of such composers as Charles Widor, César Franck, Vincent D'Indy, Emmanuel Chabrier and Édouard Lalo. Camille Saint-Saëns, by then seventy-five, was the dominant figure. When Erich performed his

Second Piano Sonata in E major at a soirée organized by the festival committee for the visiting celebrities, the venerable composer came up to the piano and, wrote Julius, 'His searching glances rested on the boy as if trying to find out whether this music could really be credited to him. Then, clasping his hand, he held it for a long time.' But Julius also had his moment of glory in Munich. At a reception given by the owner of the *Münchner Neuste Nachrichten* newspaper, Richard Strauss went to the piano and played from his new opera *Der Rosenkavalier* for the first time. Julius turned the pages for him.

A caricature in the *Neues Wiener Tageblatt* around 1911 pictured Erich as an infant bald, bespectacled professor surrounded by these amazed older musicians: Siegfried Wagner, Max Reger, Artur Nikisch, Richard Strauss and Eugen d'Albert. But what did the boy think of it all himself? 'It seemed funny to me at the time,' he told his wife. 'I, a little boy, cool and cheerful, recklessly playing the piano and beside me all the bearded, worthy men with their faces becoming more and more astonished.'

And well they might have been, given the complexity and strong personality evident in the Second Piano Sonata, which became the best known of Korngold's three. The opening fanfare figure, declaimed in octaves, seizes the attention by plunging through at least three bizarre implied modulations (suggested, but not actual, changes of key) in a matter of a few bars; the second subject of the first movement is a complete contrast, gloriously melodic and lyrical, set in a pianistic texture fit for an orchestra. The second movement combines dance elements with the idea of a scherzo, the swing and lilt of Viennese waltzes interwoven with piano fireworks including fiendish chordal leaps. The slow movement is weighty and sensual and the fourth and final movement scarcely lets up its challenge to the pianist for a moment, bringing the sonata to a close with a triumphant restatement of the opening fanfare. 'Publishers, performances – the boy has everything!' wrote Anton Webern jealously to his teacher, Arnold Schoenberg, in November 1910. 'I will become old before that!' The sonata had performances too, its première being given in Berlin on 13 October 1911.

Korngold's next trip to Germany, this time Berlin, was instigated by a formidable lady impresario, Louise Wolf, whose late husband had been impresario to the important conductor Hans von Bülow.

The modern edition of Korngold's 'Fairy Tales' for solo piano retains the romantic illustration of the original.

ERICH WOLFGANG
KORNGOLD
MÄRCHENBILDER
7 STÜCKE FÜR PIANOFORTE
OPUS 3

1 DIE VERZAUBERTE PRINZESSIN
2 DIE PRINZESSIN AUF DER ERBSE
3 RÜBEZAHL
4 WICHTELMÄNNCHEN
5 BALL BEIM MÄRCHENKÖNIG
6 DAS TAPFERE SCHNEIDERLEIN
7 DAS MÄRCHEN SPRICHT DEN EPILOG

ED 7580

SCHOTT

Moving in high society, she was able to advance her artists through her many influential contacts who came to her frequent dinner parties and soirées. 'What have you ever done for art, Louise?' ran a popular ditty of the *cognoscenti*, sung to the famous second theme of Tchaikovsky's *Pathétique* Symphony. But her musical knowledge was sound and lively. 'Wherever interesting new music could be heard … the corpulent lady with her clumsy, wobbling gait appeared,' wrote Julius.

Wolf devised a Berlin performance of the Piano Trio, but the event somewhat backfired. Erich had to take over the piano part from Bruno Walter, who cancelled at the last moment. And Korngold and his father found Berlin a difficult city to break into: cold, critical and suspicious of the warm young Viennese talent. The reviews were unwelcoming. This was even before Berlin's heyday as a major centre for modernist, experimental new music, which came into its own in the 1920s.

Erich made some good contacts in the city through Louise Wolf, including the composer Engelbert Humperdinck, who had termed him 'a wonder child from fairy land'. (Julius's opinion of Humperdinck was mixed. 'How marvellous to be the composer of *Hänsel und Gretel*! But how less marvellous, nay, even oppressive, to remain just that for all times!') There were also two conductors, Leo Blech and Artur Nikisch. Nikisch, one of the most respected maestros of the day, was struck by Korngold's music and agreed he would instantly 'subscribe' to the first orchestral work of the young composer – and he was as good as his word.

Meanwhile the Piano Trio had been heard in the USA. The Margulies Trio had given its New York première on 17 November 1910, though the critic W. J. Henderson in the *New York Sun* the next day was no more favourable in his response than the Berlin critics had been. 'Maybe his papa is trying to bring him up to be a real modern composer,' he wrote (Julius was not), 'but if he is not, then something ought to be done. If we had a little boy of twelve who preferred writing this sort of music to hearing a good folk tune or going out and playing in the park, we should consult a specialist.'

At an invitation from the Frankfurt Society for Aesthetic Culture, Erich travelled with his mother to Frankfurt, where he himself performed both his piano sonatas and the trio with members of the Arthur Rebner Quartet. Following the concert they visited Dr Ludwig Strecker, the director of B. Schott's Söhne in Mainz, now Erich's publishers. Erich's earliest works had, of course, been published by Universal Edition, but the Vienna première of *Der Schneemann*, lacking Julius Korngold's authorization, had (ironically, given its success) caused a breakdown in relations between firm and family. Strecker and his two sons, who also worked for Schott's as editors, became close and loyal friends of the young composer, which Erich, utterly in character, repaid with his own loyalty, once at some financial cost to himself.

Erich's own compositions now included the seven *Märchenbilder* for piano solo, delightful miniatures containing some of the best and most characteristic music he had yet composed. They had their première in Berlin on 30 March 1912, preceded by the première of a version for violin and piano (27 June 1911). Each piece is named after a different story or image ('The Enchanted Princess'; 'The Princess and the Pea'; 'Rübezahl', literally 'Cream stealer'; 'Wichtelmännchen', 'Goblin'; 'The Fairy King's Ball'; 'The Brave Little Tailor' and 'Epilogue'). Again, Korngold's pianistic textures are quasi-orchestral, with strongly accented rhythms in full chords and a plethora of dramatic effects. The first piece, 'The Enchanted Princess', opens at the lowest C on the piano keyboard, marked *p misterioso* (quiet, mysterious) and in just twelve bars has worked its way up to the highest C sharp, marked *sffz* (very loud, very strongly marked); later, open-sounding fourths and fifths, a striking element of Korngold's personal harmonic language, become a feature of both melody and accompaniment while glissandos (rapid slides) across the black keys add atmosphere and magical coloration. 'The Fairy King's Ball' opens with a motif of linked rising fourths that Korngold later made his personal musical signature, the 'Motif of the Cheerful Heart'.

The tender epilogue recalls Schubert's favourite 'Rosamunde' motif and features a 'foreshortening' of the phrase structure, where the rhythm of the theme, which could be expected to proceed in a four-square, regular manner, is 'distorted' by a form of written-out rubato (rhythmic ebb and flow – not frequently indicated by composers, it is usually a matter for the performer to adjust according to his or her interpretation). It shifts the structure back a notch so that the melody apparently finishes before the end of the phrase, and there pauses before its continuation. This alteration of predictable phrase patterns in melody is a powerful Korngold trait, whether he stretches them out or shortens them, as here (other examples are Marietta's Lute Song in *Die tote Stadt* – lengthening – and the closing phrase, in some renderings, of the march theme in *The Adventures of Robin Hood* – shortening). Throughout his works we find that his time signatures change with exceptional frequency: what he is actually doing is writing out with great precision the sense of rubato that he wishes the performer to achieve. Interpreters of Korngold's music need do very little other than exactly what he tells them in order to project a sense of total musical freedom. He liked to leave nothing to chance.

Each of the *Märchenbilder* is preceeded in the score by a couple of lines of verse from the poet and dramatist Hans Müller. The epilogue is given the lines:

*'Es war einmal …' Ein letztes Raunen,*
*Dann zitterst die Sonne hell durch den Hag.*
*Nun, Menschen, auf von Träumen und Staunen –*
*Geht frischen Muts in euren Tag!*

The little poem exquisitely sums up the value of fairy tales –
'"Once upon a time …" A final whisper, then the sun sparkles clearly
through the grove. Now, everyone, from dreams and wonders – draw
fresh courage in your day!' It seems exceptionally in tune with
Korngold's own idealistic attitudes (not to mention foreshadowing the
less subtle approach of Hollywood in the 1940s, which encouraged its
audiences by asserting the rights and values that were being flouted by
the Nazis in Europe and the Japanese in the Pacific). For Erich the
epilogue to his opus 3 was anything but a tender farewell to boyhood
fairy tales. Time and again in Hollywood he would refuse to score a
film until he actually saw the movie – upon which, drawn in and
enchanted by the story and the drama, he would capitulate.

But who was Hans Müller? A poet, dramatist and hypochondriac,
brother of the better-known poet Ernest Lothar; the librettist of two
of Korngold's most intense operas; apparently a homosexual; and a
native of Brünn, where he had been a newspaper colleague of Julius
Korngold. He became a friend of the family, as he was also of the von
Sonnethals', and stayed a close and lifelong friend of Erich's. He
always wore a woollen scarf, even in warm weather, so afraid was he
of catching cold. In the group photograph of the creative team at the
dress rehearsal of Müller and Korngold's greatest (if ill-fated) collaboration, *Das Wunder der Heliane*, Müller stands aloof, bald and
unsmiling in his spectacles, behind the seated and apparently worried
composer. After the Anschluss, Müller escaped to Switzerland, where
he changed his name to Hans Müller Einigen; later he was one of the
librettists of the popular musical *White Horse Inn*. His work with
Korngold shows him to have possessed a powerful imagination, and
not only about his health: *Violanta*, the Renaissance drama which
became one of Korngold's best-known operas, is an original story with
dark, psychological undercurrents and *Heliane* shares with it a sense
of overripe dramatic effect on the grand scale.

In the summer of 1911 Erich went to Karlsbad, where one member
of his audience was the theatre director Max Reinhardt. This was

Artur Schnabel, the pianist who performed Korngold's Second Piano Sonata throughout Europe – a man of fascinating but contradictory personality

Korngold's first encounter with the man who would later effectively save his life. From there he went on to Prague where *Der Schneemann* was to be given at the National Theatre. A short stop in Salzburg en route from Prague to the Tyrol gave Erich and his father the chance to meet a young pianist named Artur Schnabel, who today is remembered as one of the greatest interpreters of the Viennese classics. Erich's Second Piano Sonata, with its grand, orchestral scale, its tortuous chromaticism and its generous exuberance, quickly drew his attention. In Schnabel's lecture series *My Life and Music* he speaks of the piece enthusiastically: 'The work was really amazing; of course this is a relative judgement, for you cannot help but automatically judge a work by a twelve-year-old boy differently from that of a sixty-year-old. Yet I think even today, if one can see it in this perspective, it is still a most amazing piece.' Schnabel championed the work, playing it on many occasions across Europe. He and Korngold became close friends

despite the discrepancy in their ages – indeed, for many years
Korngold found his friendships were primarily with people up to
twenty years older than himself, probably thanks to the somewhat
'older' circles he had to move in thanks to his unusual gifts. 'I'll be
that age myself one day, so I have started young,' he remarked once
when, in his twenties, someone raised the issue. Schnabel was the
long-standing duo partner of the great violinist Carl Flesch, and the
two of them gave the first performance of Korngold's Violin Sonata
Op. 6 a few years later.

In fact Schnabel's friendship with Korngold was not without its
difficult undercurrents. But then, few things were simple where
Schnabel was concerned. His was a difficult, temperamental, unpre-
dictable personality; as Flesch described him, 'A man whom one has to
love and hate at the same time, full of the most hair-raising contra-
dictions, idealist and materialist, naïve and wily, impulsive and finicky
… he will mount an attack on any view expressed by someone else,
even if (or just because) it agrees with his own.' He was himself a
composer, and a frustrated one; his approach was avant-garde, which
made his music dense and inaccessible, and he seems to have had
little obvious success with it. Korngold, from his securely successful
viewpoint, seems to have admired his friend's music; he wrote to
Flesch in an undated letter that one piece had left him 'over the
moon'. But in 1928, when Flesch suggested that the duo should revive
Korngold's Violin Sonata, Schnabel referred to it scathingly: 'Under
no circumstances do I want to play the Korngold Sonata; altogether
no piece whose value is based solely on the composer's youthful age
and whose novelty can be likened to that of a freshly minted penny.'
Perhaps Schnabel was undergoing a fit of pique, but his jealousy of the
younger man is quite understandable. Whether jealousy was entirely
to blame for this attitude is not clear – the Violin Sonata is by no
means Korngold's greatest work. Either way, their friendship was not
adversely affected.

Around this time Erich went to a ballet performance with his
grandmother and heard a new piece of music which greatly excited
him. At the end he began to applaud enthusiastically. 'Stop it! Do
you want to compromise your father's position?' demanded the
elderly lady. The work was Igor Stravinsky's *Petrushka*, the characterful rhythms and timbres of which often seem to be straining to get

through the glistening surface of Korngold's music. Clapping or none, Korngold brought his enthusiasm home with him and persuaded his father to go to a performance and write about a ballet for the first time.

The peace of the Tyrol, this time Grundlsee, gave Erich time to work on his first orchestral piece, the *Schauspiel Overtüre* ('Dramatic Overture'); and, declared Julius in his memoir, Erich composed the whole orchestral score (and later that of the Sinfonietta) without making a preliminary piano version. Family friends renting a noble-man's mansion nearby gave him a room with a piano to work in. The Korngolds themselves were staying in a wooden cottage. 'When we returned at night,' Julius affectionately remembered, 'Erich – still thinking of his fiddles and horns – lighted us home in the dark, merrily swinging his small lantern, as if he were beating time.'

A signed photograph (taken c. 1920) of the conductor Artur Nikisch, who brought the work of the fourteen-year-old Korngold into the Leipzig Gewandhaus

The first performance of the *Schauspiel Overtüre* had been promised to Artur Nikisch, who had asked for the score 'hot from the stove'. The Korngolds obligingly sent the new piece and received a prompt telegram informing them that the work had been accepted for performance at the Leipzig Gewandhaus, one of the most famous halls in Germany, where Nikisch had been chief conductor since around 1895, in addition to his post at the Berlin Philharmonic. The overture's première was given there on 14 December 1911.

This work was another landmark in Korngold's career. Despite the inevitable accusations that it had been orchestrated by someone else, probably Zemlinsky, it established the fourteen-year-old boy as a composer of more than chamber and instrumental musical forms and more than fairy-tale drama. There was some argument about which play 'Schauspiel' referred to. By this age Korngold was already passionate about literature and drama and a keen admirer of Shakespeare. Fearful in case the unspecified source would be filled out with the imaginative falsehoods of his enemies, Julius put it about that the overture was based on Shakespeare's *The Winter's Tale*. There is no evidence of this in the music and, while Korngold's elder son Ernst later offered the opinion that *The Tempest* was a more likely inspira-tion for a boy of that age, it seems equally probable that the work relates to no one particular play but to the general dramatic atmos-phere and stage-magic which so appealed to the young composer. *The Tempest*, however, is not impossible: the overture opens with a mood of great tension, the high, repetitive string patterns almost suggestive of a burgeoning rain storm while mysterious brass chords rich in colourful harmonies build magically up against it – the fiddles and horns which Julius referred to in his memory of the swinging lantern. The grandeur of the closing pages fulfils the sense of declamation, serious dramatic power and well-crafted development that fill this incredibly mature work. The overture again foreshadows Korngold's excellence in providing a dramatic musical backdrop for the stage and screen.

Julius had quickly learned not to attend performances of his son's works. He became too nervous. Even for the Vienna première of *Der Schneeman* he had stayed home, waiting for a phone call to tell him how the piece was going. But for the *Schauspiel Overtüre* he plucked up courage and travelled to Leipzig with his son. He was delighted with the rehearsal – 'The Overture's tempi, accents, expression: all constituted a surprise growing almost into bewilderment. Nikisch virtually conducted the work *against* the composer. But what marvellous results came out *for* the composer! Nikisch, the most ingenious of tempo modifiers, understood balance. Everywhere the sound was deepened, invisible scenes were conjured up by the music …'

For the performance Julius was invited to sit in the director's box. But here he was addressed by a gentleman who clearly did not know who he was: 'A sixteen-year-old performed in the Gewandhaus concerts! That is unheard of! We can only hope the thing will be a flop.' 'A fourteen-year old,' Julius corrected him, 'and one who has been performed already at thirteen in the Vienna Court Opera!' But the damage was done. Julius slunk out of the hall and wandered around outside until the performance was over, swearing to himself that he would never expose his nerves to such an ordeal again.

Despite the snide comment, the piece was a great success. The British critic Ernest Newman wrote of it in *The Nation* in 1912: 'Mozart and Korngold are two geniuses who began to write music in their earliest childhood. Why does Mozart spontaneously lisp music in the simple idiom of his own day, while Korngold lisps in the complex idiom of his? Korngold can hardly have derived his harmonic system from the study of other composers, for in what composer's work could he have found it? It is the spontaneous product of a most

The Vienna State Opera
House (originally the Court
Opera), here pictured
around 1910, is one of the
imposing Renaissance-style
institutions that Emperor
Franz Josef built on the city's
new Ringstrasse. Others
included the Art History
Museum, the Natural History
Museum and the Burgtheater.

subtly organised brain which at the first span embraces practically all we know and feel today in the way of harmonic relation.'

Opinion was not always so favourable. An American critic, Philip Hale, wrote a couple of years later (in the *Boston Herald*, 16 May 1914): 'Korngold's Overture deserves an honorable place in the Museum of Infant Prodigies. If Master Korngold could make such a noise at fourteen, what will he not do when he is twenty-eight? The thought is appalling!' Fortunately for his own peace of mind, Mr Hale could not have imagined the sort of noise that Korngold would indeed be making at twenty-eight, when he would be hard at work on his most immense work, the opera *Das Wunder der Heliane*.

Earlier in the autumn of 1911, young Korngold had received his best response yet in a German town – in Hamburg. Hamburg was to be his most loyal town: he and his family saw it as 'his' town. Here he had not only the support of the audience but also of the powerful critic Ferdinand Pfohl, sometimes called the North German Hanslick. Today Hamburg is the home of a society dedicated to the study, preservation and promotion of Korngold's works.

A caricature of the conductor Felix Weingartner, the dedicatee of Korngold's Sinfonietta

Encouraged by the *Schauspiel Overtüre*, Korngold began another orchestral work as he approached his fifteenth birthday – in effect, a symphony, although it bears the modest title Sinfonietta. He dedicated it to the conductor Felix Weingartner and it had its first performance in Vienna on 30 November 1913. In four movements, scored for an immense orchestra and lasting some forty-five minutes, it introduced a 'signature' motif for Korngold – a motif which had in fact appeared in several of his works already (notably the *Märchenbilder* and *Der Schneemann*). It is an undulating, upward-striving group of notes, based on a melodic pattern of rising fourths; it is written on the title page and referred to as the 'Motiv des Fröhlichen Herzens' ('Motif of the Cheerful Heart'). Korngold was to use this theme in the majority of his works from then on and it was this motif that caused his first biographer to call him 'an upward-soaring composer in Major'.

The theme recurs throughout the Sinfonietta and lends its own character to the music itself, which is, in typical Korngold fashion, sweepingly generous, uplifting, tender, richly coloured and full of melody. The first movement, *Fliessend, mit heiteren Schwunge* (flowing, with happy swing), takes wing with the Cheerful Heart motif and features some extraordinary rhythmic manipulations during its balletic, waltz-like flight. It closes in ecstasy with shimmeringly orchestrated chromatic harmonies. The Scherzo, *molto agitato, rasch und feurig* (very agitated, swift and fiery), is essentially symphonic, grand in scale, traditional in form; the slow movement, marked *träumerisch* (dreaming), is built around a tender and simple melody heard on the cor anglais, surrounded by the most sensitive and subtly coloured accompaniment; and the final movement opens with a tense, dramatic flourish and fugato marked *patetico* (solemn) and proceeds as a lively, terse, duple-time variation on the main waltz theme from the first movement, recalling elements of the other movements as it goes along.

While it abounds in a youthfully unaware sensuality, the Sinfonietta is not emotionally weighty, which may account for the choice of title – 'Symphony' might have aroused expectations of less cheerful content. The enrichment of the orchestra with extra percussion, piano and celesta was to become a hallmark of Korngold's orchestral colouring and burnishes the dancing, rhythmic propulsion of his music ideally. (So danceable are the rhythms that the Sinfonietta was chosen, years later, by the American choreographer Glen Tetley as music for a ballet, *La Ronde*, based on Schnitzler's play about 'decadent' *fin de siècle* Vienna.)

The use of a signature motif is not unusual in music. What is unusual about Korngold's Cheerful Heart is first that it goes unaltered through his entire oeuvre from the age of fourteen; and second, its happy nature. Composers, in public opinion, are apparently not *meant* to be happy. They suffer in love, grapple with emotional, financial and spiritual problems, seize fate by the throat, but do not generally dance along loving life the way Korngold was doing at fifteen. Music abounds in 'fate' motifs (Beethoven and Tchaikovsky); J. S. Bach had written fugues on his own name translated into music; there are the encoded musical love messages of Robert Schumann to Clara Wieck; Shostakovich used his initials as the basis of themes in many painful and personal works; and Brahms was particularly fond of musical ciphers and used a recurring 'FAF' motif, standing for 'Frei aber froh' (free – i.e., single, unattached – but happy) which expressed his emotional condition. But the idea of a 'cheerful heart' was unheard of. One composer who seems to have had a happy life

but retained his musical vision and sensitivity was Mendelssohn –
with whom Korngold seems to have had not only many personal
factors in common but also a strong musical affinity, judging from his
arrangements of the *Midsummer Night's Dream* music. Not that
Korngold or his music are universally happy – far from it. Perhaps the
young composer was helping himself to maintain his cheerful heart
in the midst of his already overcomplicated life.

At the Sinfonietta's first performance Korngold sat beside no less
a personage than Richard Strauss, to whom he looked up with 'shy
respect' and who was now persuaded to take a serious interest in
Korngold's works, adopting him – for the time being – as a sort of
protégé. Two years later Strauss conducted the Sinfonietta himself in
the Berlin Opera.

Of the première at the Musikverein on 28 November 1913 under
Weingartner's direction, the *Musical Courier* in New York painted a
colourful portrait: 'Occasion: the third Philharmonic concert. Scene:
the great concert hall of the Musikverein in Vienna. Prophets to the
right, prophets to the left, and the wonder child, young Korngold, in
the middle … His Sinfonietta performed for the first time before what
is perhaps the most critical audience in the world went the way of
most productions destined to outlive the praise and blame of the day:
it evoked storms of applause and protests.'

Korngold had also been finishing his Sonata for Violin and Piano,
another large work in four movements. It has many aspects in
common with the Sinfonietta, notably a distinctive way of exploring
'decorative' chromatic harmonies (i.e., harmonies using notes outside
the remit of the key) to create colourful effects, only to resolve
triumphantly onto a blazing major triad. Energy and challenges are
plentiful; the rhythmically complex melodies and intense contrapuntal
interweavings give the entire sonata a sense that the composer is somehow striving against the limitations of his instruments. The influence
of Brahms comes to the fore in the slow movement, where the figura-
tions of both violin and piano recall that composer's violin sonatas,
although the rhythmic manipulations, stretching bars into five-four
from the basic four-four is a typically Korngoldian written-rubato
device; as is the graceful mood of the final movement, with its dense
chords in dotted rhythms (alternating longer and shorter notes)
demanding the lightest of playing, and the undulating melody full of

rising fourths. But at this stage, Korngold does appear to have been most in his element writing for a very large orchestra, or a piano alone that simulated an orchestra.

Carl Flesch was pleased to find that Korngold, despite his success, had not allowed himself to become conceited. As he and Artur Schnabel worked on the sonata for its première, they consulted frequently with the young composer by letter. Korngold's instructions to them in a letter dated 15 October 1913 contain ample evidence of how precisely he knew how he wanted his own music played, but also show that he had a reassuring bent for practicality – and humming.

*Please take the 'g' in the 14th bar of the final movement flageolet as you suggest, I myself have in fact always hummed this note in falsetto …*

*As regards the quavers to be repeated, please note: the accel. starts in the 11th bar before Tempo 1 (minim sign = 100 is maintained up to that*

Artur Schnabel (left) and Carl Flesch, the piano and violin duo for which Korngold wrote his Violin Sonata

*bar). 4 1⁄2 bars on but before Tempo 1 there begins a big ritardando, so
that the accel cannot be particularly substantial. If it is too difficult to
repeat the quavers … then please play simple eighths. But in that case
please let me know so that I can rearrange the printing accordingly …*

After its première in Berlin on 21 October 1913, Flesch and
Schnabel would play the work a number of times, although the
pianist, as mentioned, later refused to revive it. And the Violin Sonata
was the work which Korngold offered in 1918 for performance in a
new Society for Private Musical Performances in Vienna, started
up specifically to provide a platform for new composition. Arnold
Schoenberg himself was the founder; he magnanimously invited
his school's young rival, and adversary's son, to submit work for
performance. Another Korngold work from that time, written in
1913, was a setting of Heine's *Der Sturm* for choir and large orchestra;
this piece, however, never reached publication.

So what of the young man himself? Surrounded by success, what
was he really like? 'At fifteen, following his vocation, Erich Korngold
was already a man,' wrote Luzi von Sonnenthal. 'He was working
twelve hours a day, sitting alternately over his schoolwork or over a
new score. Then, in the evening hours, often late into the night, he
gave his imagination free rein at the piano.' In congenial
surroundings, she tells us, he would be clear-minded and good-
humoured and deal easily with his day's work. He was also becoming a
strong critic of his own pieces: 'The child soon worked with the
artistic conscience and seriousness of a man – and experienced in
earliest youth not only happiness but also creative pangs.' Musically,
Korngold was as precocious as could be imagined. But his protective
parents had left him little room to grow emotionally. 'At fifteen he was
more childish than his contemporaries, untouched by the problems of
puberty,' wrote Luzi.

Luzi von Sonnenthal, at this time, had heard much of the infant
prodigy and was curious to catch a glimpse of him. The glimpse took
place in an unlikely setting – an orthopaedic doctor's gymnasium,
where Viennese children assembled to do exercises. He was standing
on a sloping board with handgrips – 'a somewhat stout, corpulent
and even flabby boy, dutifully and lazily pulling the grips'. And,
ignoring the presence of the other children, he was singing to himself,

sometimes quietly, sometimes quite loudly. His mind was clearly not on his exercises.

Erich was certainly innocent and overprotected, but 'untouched by puberty' is rather too extreme a term. He was becoming interested in girls. Already in 1911–12 he had composed four 'little, happy waltzes' for piano duet, which he called opus 5, each bearing the name of a girl: Gretl, Margit, Gisi and Mitzi. Mitzi was his first major crush. He was fourteen; she was two years his senior. She was the eldest daughter of a Viennese doctor, Rudolf Kolisch, a family friend of the Korngolds. A dark-haired beauty, she scorned the plump little boy, genius or not. Her brother, Rudi, was a violinist and later founded the famous Kolisch Quartet which often performed Korngold's string quartets; their younger sister, Trudi (Gertrude), whom Korngold always referred to as the 'Fratz' ('little rascal') and with whom he later had a brief romance, became the second wife of Arnold Schoenberg.

Did the young composer bewail his fate and pour out his sorrow in soulful works full of the bitter disappointment of youth? Not a bit of it. He kept his cool and turned elsewhere. Another friend of his father's, Dr Rudolf Ganz, the Frankfurt correspondent of the *Neue Freie Presse*, had a very attractive daughter named Margit, or Manzi for short. She was four years older than Erich, cut her hair short

The Kolisch String Quartet: its leader, Rudolf Kolisch, is seated on the right, unusually for a quartet. He held his bow in his left hand and violin in his right due to a childhood injury. The Kolisch Quartet gave the world premières of a number of significant twentieth-century quartets.

according to the latest fashion, and had clever, sparkling grey eyes. She had numerous admirers – even a jealous fiancé who later married Luzi's sister Susi – but she assured the younger boy that she was only interested in him. The friendship lasted for four years.

Julius was not happy. He felt that girlfriends would distract Erich from his work. His ideals told him that a composer should have heart only for art. His pessimistic predictions and mistrust of 'the crafty girl' began to make his son's life extremely difficult. And the ceaseless chaperoning cannot have helped either. Erich began to champ at the bit. His father was 'embittering the innocent joys of his youth' and so, naturally, the relationship of father and son became increasingly strained. Erich might happily follow the conservative path in music, but in his personal life he was suddenly, after his peaceful childhood, obstinate and rebellious. But Julius could be obstinate too. Even after Erich's marriage to Luzi he could never accept his son's right to have a happy, normal, independent personal life and he caused the young couple inordinate suffering.

What happens to suppressed sexuality? Often it finds another way into expression (in Freudian terms, 'sublimation'). In Korngold's case, it appears to have found its way into his music and also his choices of dramatic subject. In his three greatest operas, sexual conflict, and especially the conflict of the spiritual and the corporeal, is a recurring theme which is treated musically in the most heady and sensual manner.

Korngold was looking for an opera story. When he wrote *Der Schneemann* he was already fascinated by the theatre and loved to read dramatic works. He greatly enjoyed browsing about and buying in Vienna's second-hand bookshops, and in 1913, aged not quite sixteen, he bought a copy of a comic play by Heinrich Teweles entitled *Der Ring des Polykrates*. The story was based on a slightly tortuous analogy with a Greek legend in which King Polykrates throws his ring into the sea to appease the gods and finds it returned to him inside a fish. Schiller had turned the legend into a ballad. The play's action is set in a little house in Saxony in 1797 and concerns the involvements of two couples, in the best light-opera tradition: a kapellmeister, Wilhelm, and his wife Laura; the drummer Florian Döblinger and his girlfriend Lieserl. Julius and Erich Korngold travelled together to Prague to meet Teweles, who was at that time director of the Prague German Theatre,

Berlin's Royal Opera House staged Korngold's first opera, *Der Ring des Polykrates*, in 1917. This scene from the production shows Claire Dux and Gustav Bergman.

and they gained his approval for the project based on his 'long-forgotten comedy'.

For this story, set in the eighteenth century, Erich slimmed down his lavish style and wrote quasi-Mozartian music of much charm and beauty, in which his lightness of touch is particularly clear. The opera's most famous aria is a 'diary song', 'Kann's heut nicht fassen' ('Today I cannot understand'), in which Laura takes an ironic look at her romantic involvements. The lovely melody, waltz-like and quintes-sentially Viennese, is a pointer towards Korngold's later success in the world of operetta and is exquisitely accompanied by a celesta. Little else from the opera is commonly heard.

But there are other reasons for the overshadowing of *Polykrates*: namely, the overwhelming power of its companion piece, and the personality of the soprano who took its leading role. *Polykrates* was a one-act opera, too short to be performed alone. Korngold needed to write a second work that could take the stage alongside it. It therefore needed to offer a contrast to the unaffected ironies of the first piece, both to keep the audience well entertained and to show the range of compositional talent in the young composer. The two needed to complement one another well enough to prevent one being performed alongside a less suitable opera by someone else.

Erich, at the instigation of Julius, turned to Hans Müller, the family's friendly hypochondriac dramatist, for a story – and he got perhaps more than he bargained for. Müller offered two librettos: one based on the life of Savonarola; the other, which the Korngolds accepted, an original text set in sixteenth-century Venice. It told the story of a young wife whose sister has thrown herself into the sea after being seduced and abandoned. Obsessed with revenge upon the evil seducer, the woman entices him into her house, intending that her husband should murder him. But before the murder can take place, she realizes that she herself is desperately in love with her sister's killer. As her husband arrives to stab his victim, she throws herself in the dagger's path and receives the fatal blow. She dies in her husband's arms, singing of the purity she will now attain. Her name, and the name of the opera, is *Violanta*.

Vienna was, of course, the city of Sigmund Freud, whose work must by that time have been well known, but there is little to suggest that Korngold and his circle were interested in it. (Although Direktor

Mahler had had a famous psychoanalytic encounter with Freud, the founder of psychoanalysis is not even mentioned in Julius's memoirs.) Renaissance tales, on the other hand, were very much in vogue in Germany: other operas were written on Italian sixteenth-century stories around the same time, including Schreker's *Die Gezeichreten* and *Die Florentinische Tragödie* by Erich's former teacher Zemlinsky. *Violanta* can roughly be classed as 'verismo' opera, sharing with Puccini the exploration of 'real' human behaviour in a specific and colourful setting.

Perhaps Hans Müller had spent some time in Vienna's marvellous Kunsthistorisches Museum – the immense art gallery on the city's Ringstrasse. The gallery's collection, which opened to the public in 1895, was based upon the works collected by the Habsburg monarchs and contained a number of works by such artists as Titian and Rubens. One exquisite portrait by Titian is entitled *Violante*. It shows

Titian's *Portrait of a Young Woman (Violante)* of 1515-18 is on display in Vienna's Kunsthistorisches Museum. Name, era, city and personality could match Korngold and Müller's complex heroine.

a sixteenth-century Venetian woman, apparently a courtesan, with glowing golden hair and a small, beautiful but somewhat unpleasant face. Before earning its name 'Violante' from the violets she wears on her dress, the portrait had been known as 'the little cat'. The character fascinates. Who is she? What is her story? The main difference between Titian's courtesan and Korngold's Violanta is that a stipulation of the latter is that she is dark-haired. Not far away hang two immense canvases by Rubens, displaying, in timeless, dramatic yet classical scenes, saints working miracles. One is called *Das Wunder der Franz Xaver*. Müller's other opera for Korngold (based on Kaltneker's play *Die Heilige*) was called *Das Wunder der Heliane* and shares with Rubens's paintings not only a timeless, mythical setting but an atmosphere of conflict, more than slight hysteria and transcendental striving.

*Violanta* gave Korngold the opportunity to write his most ambitious work yet – seventy minutes of claustrophobic intensity, with a huge orchestra including bells, harps and keyboards, complex double choruses and a towering role for the lead soprano. The historical setting and local colour – Venice at carnival time – seems to have inspired Korngold to reach new heights of musical depiction. Perhaps it is no coincidence that his most successful film scores would also be for tales with historical settings in which he could give his imagination great freedom to create new and picturesque atmospheres. He had plenty of say in the dramatic structure, working closely with Müller to achieve the effects he wanted. Julius reported that the idea of having a lull before the storm, in which Violanta is de-robed by her maid, Barbara, was Erich's own idea: 'Erich … improved motivation, increased intensity and rearranged scenes to tighten the plot. It was Erich who insisted on a "breather", a quiet episode, after the passionate duet … This break increases the tension, creates the stillness before the storm and propels the action towards the tragic climax.' Korngold may well have been emulating the Willow Song in Verdi's *Otello*, which achieves a similar effect.

A photograph of Korngold in 1916, autographed with a phrase from *Violanta*. Above, a scene from the Venetian-set melodrama as staged in Hamburg in 1931

In *Violanta*, as in his later operas, Korngold uses the Wagnerian device of Leitmotiv – a melodic fragment which becomes associated with a particular character or underlying theme of the opera. Violanta's hatred, for instance, has its own ascending, shuddering theme, and the astonishing chord with which the work begins recurs, like a sharp pang of mingled anguish, longing and fury, throughout the opera, mirroring the psychological distress and confusion of the heroine. The atmosphere set by that chord in the prelude pervades the opera and lends the necessary inevitability to the melodramatic tragedy that ensues. There is little happiness to be found in the Venetian carnival which is taking place in the background – the carnival song, which is heard near the beginning of the work, itself becomes a symbol of doom.

Erich began work on *Violanta* in 1914 and finished it in the summer of 1915, when he was just eighteen. During the family's summer retreat to the Tyrol he worked on the orchestration and performed extracts to hotel guests on the piano. Fortuitously, the guests included the Baron Clemens von Franckenstein, the director of the Munich Opera. It did not take long for him to guarantee the performance of Korngold's double bill. The young Korngold's performance must have made a vast impression. Bruno Walter, who was to conduct the première, compared hearing the composer performing his score to 'the eruption of a musico-dramatic volcano'.

The double-bill received its world première in Munich under Walter's baton on 28 March 1916 and a couple of weeks later, on 10 April, Leopold Reichwein conducted the Viennese première at the Hofoper. The casting was extremely successful, Laura in *Polykrates* being sung in Munich by Maria Ivögun and in Vienna by Selma Kurz, two of the loveliest high soprano voices of the day; in Vienna the lyrical Alfred Piccaver sang the tenor lead. But *Violanta* was the opera which stunned the public, not least because of the dramatic and sensual power of its leading lady, Maria Jeritza. This tall, beautiful and dynamic soprano, with a voice as clear and accurate as a bell, had made a great impact in roles calling for high drama and sexual presence – Carmen, or Salome, for instance – and her magnetism as Violanta inspired Korngold to write his two great full-scale operas with her in mind. He had first seen 'Mizzi' Jeritza, who was, like him,

A portrait of Bruno Walter, who in 1916 conducted the world première of Korngold's double bill - *Der Ring des Polykrates* and *Violanta* - in Munich. He became a long-standing champion of Korngold's music.

a native of Brünn, in March 1911 when she took the lead in an operetta, directed by Max Reinhardt: Offenbach's *La Belle Hélène*.

In his preface to the first complete recording of *Violanta* (CBS, 1980), Marcel Prawy, executive producer of the Vienna State Opera, recalled the première: '… seventeen-year-old Korngold was already a "cause célèbre" and a sceptical Viennese opera public attended the première of *Violanta* in 1916 with a defiant attitude. The surrender was complete. Sold out performances and standing ovations accompanied *Violanta* during its twenty years in the repertoire of the Vienna State Opera.'

The reviews were overwhelming. 'As Violanta Maria Jeritza has reached the peak of her art,' wrote Richard Specht. Richard Strauss himself talked about 'the unbelievable many-sidedness of Korngold's genius'. In the *Neuen Tag* (30 March 1916) Egon Wellesz wrote: 'The powerful sensuality fascinates with its magical orchestral sounds.'

Maria Jeritza, pictured here in New York in 1922. The striking soprano took Vienna by storm when she sang the part of Violanta and became the inspiration for all Korngold's later operatic heroines.

There was something fascinating about the opera's sensuality quite apart from its magical orchestral sounds. This was the work of a sheltered, well-chaperoned, innocent seventeen-year-old lad who had done little in his life other than write music, read books and argue with his father. Where in the world did he find such sexual power? How did he know about it?

Korngold himself seems to have been a little surprised. Julius tells in his memoirs of how his perplexed son said to him that 'one can write about love without having experienced it'. Julius's high-flown explanation was this: 'Hearing and listening can directly release intuition and vision … the metaphysical element immanent in the child's tone creations – like in all other tone creations – enables him to independently attain the adult's spiritual plane.' Metaphysical or not, Korngold had an infallible instinct for creating the atmosphere of a story – on the piano, orchestra, stage or film – but his emotional directness always sings through his music and he possessed a very rich imagination. Who knows what may have passed through the silent dreams of a busy seventeen-year-old genius? Although he had not apparently *experienced* sexual passion, that does not necessarily mean that he had not *felt* its urgings in their purest, most ideal and distilled form – fantasy. As the musicologist Christopher Palmer commented many years later,

*Somehow Korngold* knew*: knew how to compose, how to play the piano, how to score, all brilliantly and all apparently without any untoward expenditure of effort. We should remember however that genius often contrives to grasp instantly and intuitively what mediocrity may spend year after year laboriously laying up … how Korngold found, evolved or summoned his style into being is a question which can never properly be answered in terms which the scientific mind would find satisfactory.*

The *wunderkind* had now proved himself as a serious, adult opera composer. The double bill was taken up and performed in many centres around Europe, although in Vienna itself it would have a slightly more traumatic life as a result of Julius Korngold's disputes with the opera house management. Its success was consolidated by another triumph for Korngold in a different field: that of chamber music, with a string sextet in D major, Op. 10, which he had written in 1914–15 and which received its first performance on 2 May 1917 in Vienna, led by the violinist Arnold Rosé, concertmaster of the Vienna Philharmonic. The sextet is often programmed together with its predecessor in the medium, Schoenberg's *Verklärte Nacht*. Each work is immensely successful in its own way; and Korngold's is probably the best of his chamber works.

The opening is warm and glowing, developing with dramatic pizzicato and accelerando into a lyrical second subject, accompanied with tremolandos and proceeding in a dramatic development full of contrasts that could have come straight out of *Violanta*. So could the opening of the second movement, a plunging chord that shifts from major to minor and leads into a powerful, melancholy adagio. The lighter third-movement Intermezzo, graceful and rich in portamento (simulating a smooth singing style), provides a relaxation of mood after the intensity of all that has gone before. Julius Korngold suggests that the Sextet is one example of the chamber works that his son liked to write after finishing an opera, to 'cleanse' himself.

Later the same year, Erich Wolfgang Korngold was called up for military service and, according to his father, was allowed to walk down the street alone for the first time on his way to the barracks.

*3*

*The Kiss* by Klimt epitomizes
the heavy, luscious beauty of
Viennese late-Romanticism
and the age of art nouveau.

*He has so much talent that he could easily give
us half – and still have enough left for himself!*

Giacomo Puccini on Korngold, 1916

# The Dead City 1916-22

World War I, anticipated by so many with a sense of idealistic optimism, soon proved itself a horrific and bloody tragedy. Hundreds of thousands of lives were lost, from every nation involved in the conflict. And for the Austro-Hungarians it marked not only the end of an era but the end of an empire. The Habsburg dynasty was in its death throes, in-bred and mentally unstable; the family had never truly recovered from the suicide of the crown prince, Rudolf, with his mistress Marie Vetsera at the Mayerling hunting lodge in 1889. The war and the political revolution that followed it transformed Austria, after so many years of near-absolute monarchic rule, into a country searching desperately for its lost sense of identity. In the words of George Clare, it was 'a rump of its former self'.

Korngold was lucky enough to be recognized by the doctor who conducted his medical examination for military service. The doctor arranged for a 'B' classification to be given which meant that Korngold would not be sent to the front. Instead he was given a 'fitting' position as musical director of an infantry regiment. Although he was preoccupied with his newest operatic project, army service was an important experience for him, not only because it granted him new independence but also because it considerably broadened his range of experience and emotion. The young composer was deeply sympathetic to and moved by the plight of the young soldiers who were his colleagues and the suffering of the country at war. In his new post he wrote an *Österreichischer Soldatenabschied* ('Austrian Soldier's Farewell'), a tender song for voice and piano which he may have started as early as 1915, inspired by the departing troops around him; another song, *Zita-Hymne*, to a text by Baroness Hedda von Skoda, was a celebration of the last Habsburg Empress and was later orchestrated (both versions were performed in Vienna in 1917); and there was one military march in B flat. These patriotic pieces served to raise money for the Austrian War Relief Fund.

Whatever darker impressions were made on the young Korngold
from his army days, he never lost his sense of humour. He was
constantly asked to play the piano in the officers' mess. And when he
played the colonel the march he had written for the regiment and was
asked, 'Isn't it a little fast?' he promptly replied, 'Yes, but this is for the
retreat.' Korngold's duties gave him ample time to continue composing and arranging; at this time he also made an arrangement of
Mendelssohn's B minor Scherzo and of some marches by Schubert
and wrote a *Tanz im alten Stil* ('Dance in the Old Style') for small
orchestra. But, more importantly, he was working on a new opera.

Julius Korngold had by chance met the playwright Siegfried
Trebitsch in the street. Trebitsch, best known as the German translator
of the works of George Bernard Shaw, was one of the poets whose
work Erich had set in his *Einfache Lieder* ('Simple Songs'), Op. 9, in
1911–13 (the others being Eichendorff and Elizabeth Honold). Now
Trebitsch was working on a German translation of a play by the
Belgian symbolist writer Georges Rodenbach, called *Le Mirage* ('Das
Trugbild' in German), which in turn was based on his novella *Bruges-*

A scene from *Die tote Stadt*
as first produced in
Hamburg, 1920. This cast
shows, from left to right,
Walter Diehl (Graf Albert),
Josef Degler (Fritz), Anny
Münchow (Marietta), Felix
Rodemund (Gaston), Paul
Schwarz (Victorin).

*la-Morte*. Trebitsch was convinced that the story would make a good opera. Julius recounted that the operetta composer Leo Fall had also been interested in the tale (odd, as the gruesome tale is hardly operetta material); and, more convincingly, even Puccini had had a look at it. Erich duly read it and was struck immediately by its dramatic possibilities. Its central theme was the conflict of body and soul, of living sensuality versus dead purity, and the impossibility of recapturing the past.

The book is an icily-written horror story in which parallels are constantly drawn between the 'dead' city of Bruges – the ancient Belgian town set among atmospheric waterways – and the hero's dead wife. The man, Hugues, is devoted religiously to her memory and has turned his house into a shrine around her portrait and a long plait of her hair. Then he meets a dancer, Jane, with whom he similarly becomes obsessed, for she is the living physical image of his wife. But their characters differ, and Hugues undergoes the painful process of realizing that Jane's coarse, licentious nature is far indeed from the saintly spirituality he saw in his wife. Ultimately he murders the dancer with the lock of his dead wife's hair, so that the two women are finally exactly the same – dead. The book closes with him murmuring 'Bruges la Morte' over the corpse.

Korngold was particularly attracted by the atmosphere of the little book. He was at his dramatic best when translating a rich setting into music – as he did for *Violanta* – and years later, in a programme note to a piano recording of his own improvisation on themes from the opera, he wrote that the opera had been inspired by the atmosphere of Bruges. Whether he meant this literally, or in the sense of the fictional portrayal of Bruges, is uncertain. His father wrote that they had visited Bruges together; Luzi contradicts this, saying that Erich had never been there; and their children never knew the truth. One way or another, the atmosphere, full of dark canals, a cloister of Beguine nuns and the pealing of innumerable church bells, made a powerful impression. Erich decided that this would be his next opera. It was to be named *Die tote Stadt* ('The Dead City'). Coming to its composer during the days of war and the death of the empire, *Die tote Stadt* was a work very much of its time.

*Opposite, the cover to Schott's publication of extracts from Die tote Stadt, arranged for piano duet, captures something of the atmosphere which Korngold sought to portray: the medieval city of Bruges with its dark streets, canals and church bells.*

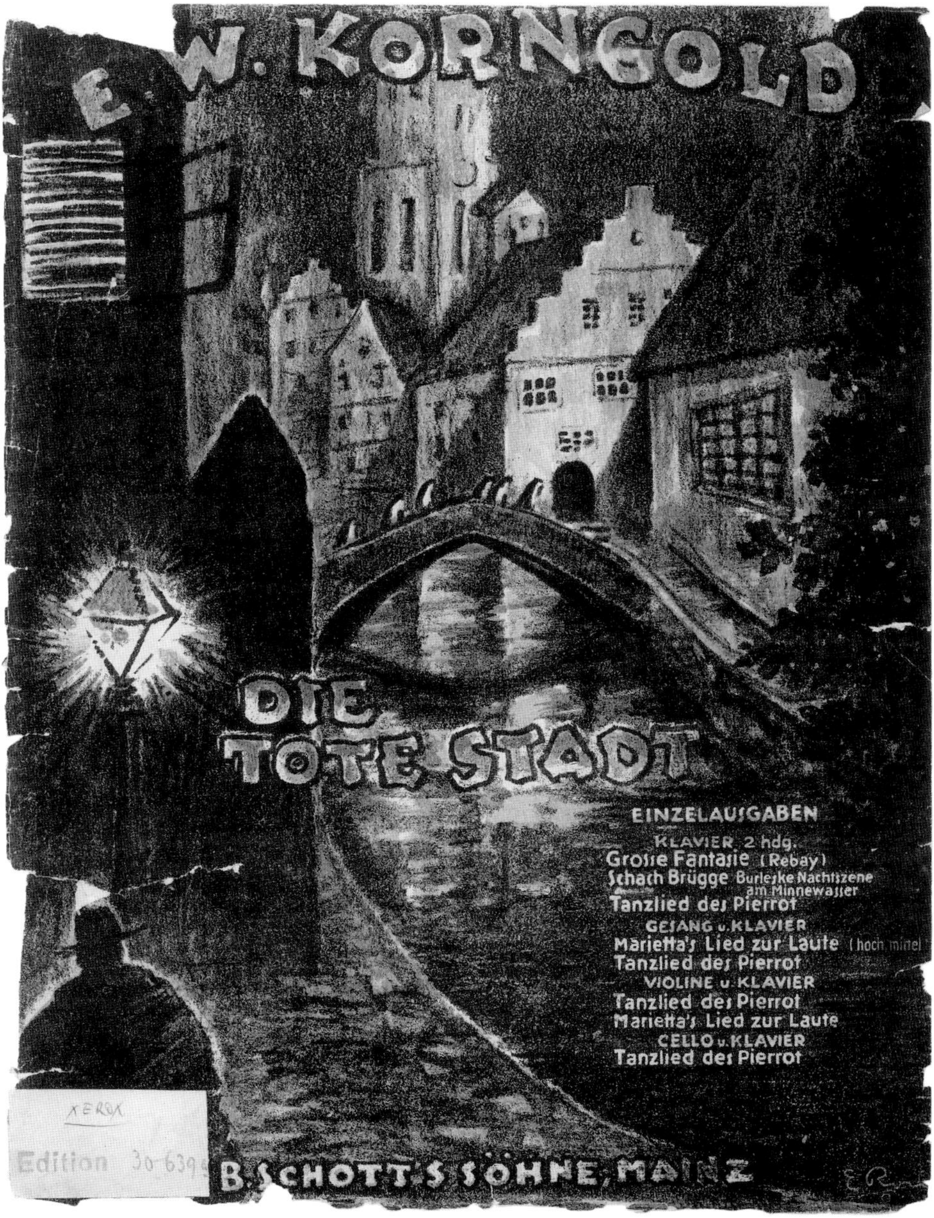

E.W. KORNGOLD

DIE TOTE STADT

EINZELAUSGABEN

KLAVIER 2 hdg.
Grosse Fantasie (Rebay)
Schach Brügge Burleske Nachtszene
am Minnewasser
Tanzlied des Pierrot

GESANG u. KLAVIER
Marietta's Lied zur Laute (hoch mittel)
Tanzlied des Pierrot

VIOLINE u. KLAVIER
Tanzlied des Pierrot
Marietta's Lied zur Laute

CELLO u. KLAVIER
Tanzlied des Pierrot

B.SCHOTT'S SÖHNE, MAINZ

The cover for the completed
score of the opera,
conveying a suitably Gothic
image

Korngold approached his *Violanta* librettist, Hans Müller, and
asked him if he would begin the preparation of a one-act libretto
based on Rodenbach's text. Müller began, but soon abandoned the
task. Erich and his father were not particularly happy with his efforts,
which tended to be too wordy; and Müller himself was busy with
his own stage works, with which he was now achieving some success.
But he did give Erich a valuable piece of advice: to get away from the
one-act trap and compose a full-length opera.

Julius and Erich were about to collaborate directly. Both were
possessed of a sound dramatic sense; they would prepare the libretto
themselves. But as Julius's involvement with a major work by his son
would be a certain kiss of death with the critical fraternity and the
musical establishment, they credited the libretto to one Paul Schott –
the name being an amalgamation of the opera's hero's name (which
they had changed to the more singable 'Paul' from the original
'Hugues') and the name of its publisher. Paul Schott was generally
assumed to be one of the younger members of the esteemed publishing house. So successful were Julius and Erich at keeping the
truth hidden that it did not come to light until 1975, when the opera
was revived (after a long absence from the stage) in New York.

Julius had more persuading to do. He was unhappy with the
impression that the tale in its original form would create – it is
undoubtedly grim and would hardly send people home happy. He put
forward the idea that the events in the book leading up to the murder
should be couched in the form of a dream sequence. At the end the
hero awakes wiser for his dream of killing the dancer and is able
finally to bury the past, accept that his dead wife cannot return, and
leave Bruges, the dead city, behind forever.

The alteration of the original Rodenbach/Trebitsch work had both
its strengths and weaknesses. On one hand, direct action is rather
sapped by its protagonist waking up and finding it was all a dream.
On the other hand, the opera glows with a warmth and sympathy
which is notably absent from the original book. Marietta, the dancer,
whose name is a trivialization of the saintly wife's name, Marie, is not
coarse and vulgar, but warm, cheerful, flirtatious and full of lust for
life. The audience is able to sympathize better with the hero Paul if he
does not in reality commit a murder; and at the end there is a sense
that a psychological disorder has really been resolved and exorcized,
with Paul having passed through a very satisfying learning experience.

The first part of the opera that Erich worked on was a song which was to become probably his most famous composition, Marietta's Lute Song ('Glück, das mir verblieb' – 'Joy sent from above'). In the first act, Paul, overwhelmed by her resemblance to Marie, drapes Marietta in Marie's shawl, gives her a lute and asks her to sing. The glorious melody returns to close the entire opera, as Paul, drawing curtains across Marie's portrait, reframes the song with new words, transforming the fear of parting into a final acceptance of loss: 'Joy sent from above, fare thee well, my faithful love. Life and death must part – heart is torn from heart. Wait for me in heaven's plain – on earth we shall not meet again.' The song encapsulates the central conflict of the story.

The melody of the lute song is probably the best example of Korngold's fondness for drawing out the rhythms of his melodies. The principle of rubato was a particularly important feature of musical performance tradition at this time. Instead of leaving musicians to work this out entirely for themselves, Korngold, as we have seen already, composed rubato into his music with very precise notation. The lute song is basically a slow waltz, but is written out with several alternations between three-four time and four-four (units of three and four beats), so that the singers' lingering on high notes and important stresses and phrase endings is an integral part of the song. The device prevents a memorable melody from becoming predictable or banal.

A portrait of Karl Aagaard Oestvig as the tortured, obsessive Paul in *Die tote Stadt*, Vienna, 1921

Julius, in true pessimistic mode, found the Lute Song depressing. He saw in it 'a swan song of people threatened by war'. This was a good point: the runaway success of the opera and of this song especially may have sprung largely from the widespread identification with its sentiments among the audience. Julius's presentiment was also uncannily accurate, not only for the current conflict. For while he and his close family were fortunate enough to escape the devastation of Vienna's Jewish population some fifteen years later, many, many more would not.

The Lute Song was instantly and phenomenally successful, but so was another aria, which lies at the heart of the whole opera. During the dream sequence, a member of Marietta's performing troupe, a Pierrot – himself in love with Marietta – entertains the group with a love song of longing for his home in the Rhineland. 'Mein Sehnen,

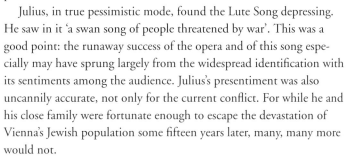

mein Wähnen, es träumt sich zurück' is another waltz and carries on the opera's background theme, that of longing for the past. The plot has a roughly symmetrical structure, and the 'Pierrot Tanzlied', as it became known, is the point about which the symmetry revolves, the structural point giving it more significance than the simple diversion it may seem. The beauty of the song and the heartfelt nostalgia of the words make this one of Korngold's most memorable and heart-rending creations; the words, 'Mein Sehnen, mein Wähnen, es träumt sich zurück' ('My yearning, my dreaming, returns to the past'), were only too close to Korngold's own developing sentiments as the years went by.

Why should Erich Korngold have been prey to nostalgia at the age of barely twenty? His father constantly wanted to look back, rather than forward, and to induce his son to do likewise in his music; he may have influenced the libretto, but not the heartfelt tenderness of the music itself. However much the Korngolds seemed to detach themselves from political events and even take the war for granted, its effect must have made a very profound impact on the sensitive and sheltered composer, who may have been mourning, with his contemporaries, the passing of an era; or on a more personal level, in the throes of maintaining his fame amid inevitable controversy, Erich might well have longed for the comparative ease of his childhood. How he had come to be east of Eden is not clear; perhaps he had indeed suffered some intense, unchronicled personal loss by this time. Ironically, his life ended in exile, longing for a homeland which no longer existed. Whether it was his musically backward-looking tonal method of composition, or later looking sadly back to his lost paradise, Vienna, or an unconscious idealization of his childhood, he seems always to have been longing for the past.

And once more we find Korngold dealing with the conflict of the body and the spirit. Paul is torn between the dead but ideal Marie, to whom he wants to stay faithful, and the sensual and vivid Marietta who is very much alive. Given the repressive nature of Korngold's own upbringing, it is scarcely surprising that he should deal with this conflict so successfully and personally.

That quality also makes the opera a producer's dream: recent productions have found Paul interpreted as a possible serial killer with suggestions of sado-masochism (Götz Friedrich in Berlin) and in one

recent American production, Marie and Marietta resembled respectively the film stars Kim Basinger and Marilyn Monroe. The heady
chromaticism of the music and its lush orchestration, the highly
charged atmosphere, the hysterical quality of Paul's responses, all lend
themselves marvellously to interpretations which plumb the depths
of Paul's psyche.

   Around the moving tale, Korngold weaves a score which is rich
in Wagnerian Leitmotiv (symbolic melodic fragments) and key symbolism (the association of a musical key with a character or emotion).
Marietta's key is B major, a favourite of Korngold's, bright and happy
with five sharps – the key of his Cheerful Heart motif and the
Sinfonietta. Marie's key is the mirror image of it, D flat major, which
has five flats. And when Paul kills Marietta he kills her bright key as
well and leaves her dead in B minor. There are Leitmotiv themes for
Bruges, Marie, at least two for Marietta, Love, Death – ideas that bind
together the continuous web of orchestral sound against which the
action takes place. Paul has no Leitmotiv of his own, being so wound

Maria Jeritza as the
fascinating, sensual Marietta,
heroine of *Die tote Stadt*

up in his lost love that the Love and Marie motifs stand for him as well.

The Death motif is particularly significant. It is a descending chromatic scale, deep in the bass range of the orchestra in an uncomfortable, syncopated rhythm; and in Korngold's ensuing works, including his films, there is scarcely an intimation of death which does not employ this motif.

Whether the ideas behind *Die tote Stadt* have personal significance to Korngold or not, one thing is certain: Korngold was a master craftsman. He knew how to produce a memorable song, how to paint atmospheres and emotions, how to provide dramatic flow and sympathetic characters, how, in all, to write a successful stage piece with mass appeal. *Die tote Stadt* is his most successful opera, and the most performed; in the first half of the twentieth century it was one of the most frequently staged of all contemporary operas, appearing on more than seventy stages in Europe and America. The Lute Song was so popular that it became a ubiquitous encore for numerous sopranos in recital. Julius Korngold attributed the opera's success to the fact that the hero's predicament was a universal issue with which everybody could identify; Erich Korngold himself later felt that the eroticism of the work had a lot to do with its popularity. Both were right.

The inspiration of Maria Jeritza, who would take the leading role of Marietta, was also important. The role is incredibly demanding – as is that of Paul. The singers have to be able to sustain the emotional intensity throughout the opera, the complex vocal lines have to project constantly over the enormous orchestra and the singing has for much of the time to be very high and very loud. Jeritza was delighted with the role that Korngold wrote for her, which involved her not only having to sing wonderfully but to take on a vivid and rounded-out character, and to dance. The build-up to Marietta's first entrance is one of the most stunning that any soprano can undergo: a wild sense of anticipation, followed by a passionate, glowing and rhapsodic outburst in the orchestra as Paul cries 'Wunderbar!' at the sight of her.

And Jeritza was a fitting figure to inspire and carry through such an entry. Here is one description of her as Marietta in *Die tote Stadt*'s first New York performance in 1921:

*tall as a grenadier … Under the mass of white-gold hair the features are piquant. She is a wonderful frame for clothes – for snowy silks and velvets of deep rose or jade. She is an actress and with all her length, almost an acrobat. She can leap cleanly on a table or jump upright on to the seat of a chair. She can twist and twirl in all the many movements of the dance. She is of a volcanic energy, she strikes out with the punch of a kicking pony, she has more than a slap or two for the clumsy male.*

It was Marietta's first entrance that held things up, however. Erich could not find a successful solution. He was continuing his army duties at the time he was working on the opera, and according to Julius Korngold the entrance of Marietta had him striving for about a year to find the right tone.

Early in 1917, Luzi von Sonnenthal was invited by another composer friend to a dinner party at which Korngold would be present. Under the watchful eye of a chaperone, her friend's elderly aunt, a lively evening ensued. Korngold, who certainly cut a figure, young and handsome in his army uniform, had arrived with a young woman whom Luzi refers to as 'Trude K', probably Gertrude Kolisch, Mitzi's little sister and the future second Mrs Schoenberg, to whom at about this time Korngold gave the manuscript of the fourth of his *Einfache Lieder*, Op. 9, *Liebesbriefschen* ('Little Love Letter'). Korngold – truly a legend in his own teens – was the sun around which the dinner party's planetary guests revolved. All the talk centred on him and performances of his music; his contemporaries regarded him with a certain reverence. And this was not an isolated occasion but one of many such evenings in which Korngold was required to light up the company with his music and his wittiness. Luzi felt herself something of an outsider, but when Korngold was pressed to play from his new opera she listened in great admiration. She was already aware of a certain affinity she felt for the *wunderkind*.

Luzi was slightly younger than Erich, a talented, cultured girl with blonde hair and golden-brown eyes and an excellent soprano singing voice. She was a good pianist and had studied musical analysis; she idolized Mozart; and she mixed in artistic and theatrical circles, thanks to her family, her grandfather having been director of the Burgtheater. One sister, Helene, became an actress and worked with Max Reinhardt, the other, Susi, became an artist. Luzi was bright and witty and was also interested in writing. Like Korngold, she was Jewish,

A portrait of Luzi von Sonnenthal: a bright, witty, musically gifted young woman, she was nevertheless subject to the inevitable disapproval of Julius Korngold.

*Following page*, Vienna's Burgtheater around 1925: the heart of Viennese dramatic theatre, it reached its peak under the directorship of Adolf von Sonnenthal, Luzi's grandfather.

WIEN, BURGTHEATER

An engraving of the actor
Adolf von Sonnenthal,
Luzi's grandfather

though this background at the time would probably have seemed
irrelevant. There could have been no better person to have drawn
Erich's romantic attention. They next met at a chamber music soirée,
during which they could not talk while the musicians were playing
and therefore wrote notes to one another commenting wryly on the
performance. Erich saw her home at the end of the evening.

Luzi began to be invited to more Korngold-centred dinner parties,
at which the young man would play his own music on the piano for
an hour after the meal. Each guest wanted to hear something different
and often a passage of *Die tote Stadt* would have its airing. Erich
displayed a talent for playing certain types of other music as well –
especially the waltzes of Johann Strauss. Listening to him playing
Strauss, Luzi found that 'I heard for the first time, with delight,
Johann Strauss not as mere dances but as ingeniously inspired music'.
Erich's gift for Strauss interpretation would later have considerable
significance for both their lives.

Korngold began to visit the Sonnenthal household regularly, and

pressed Luzi to sing for him. He accompanied her as she sang from
Schubert's *Schwanengesang* and afterwards encouraged her to the
extent of telling her that her voice in some ways resembled Maria
Ivögun's. One thing that especially appealed to Luzi was his unaffect-
edness; he was intelligent and humorous without ever being pompous.

When Luzi had occasion to visit her actress sister, who was working
in Berlin under Reinhardt, her new friend gave her tickets to hear a
concert of his music conducted by Nikisch, and a rendering at the
Opera House on Unter den Linden of his two one-act operas. Hearing
*Violanta* must have been a startling, even shocking, experience for a
teenaged girl already half in love with its composer – to observe
his fierce expression of power and sensuality. 'I left the opera house
stunned and overwhelmed,' she remembered.

As 1918 went by, the young people became as inseparable as they
were allowed to be. That summer machinations were necessary for
them to spend any time together, as the von Sonnenthals were to
spend the vacation at Alt-Aussee and Korngold was still with his
regiment. The occasion of a fire in the village that year gave them the
idea of arranging a charity concert to raise money for the injured
locals; in that instance, Erich would be given leave from his regiment.
'When Erich arrived, I got to know his considerable pedantic
precision,' wrote Luzi. 'Not only did he inspect the platform and the
piano, but he helped to arrange the audience's chairs himself, corrected the programme and examined the final receipts.'

Luzi and Erich began to call one another by the familiar 'Du'. Her
mother disapproved, so they had to keep their intimacy strictly secret.
But still Erich accompanied Luzi's singing lessons at the New Vienna
Conservatory, and it was not long before the Viennese at large began
to talk about young Korngold and the 'little Sonnenthal girl'. Though
if they were indiscreet enough to walk arm-in-arm in the street, that
was hardly surprising. Finally Frau von Sonnenthal took her daughter
in hand, announced that Luzi was compromising herself and decreed
that the young people either had to be formally betrothed or stop
seeing each other for a decent length of time.

Korngold's savings had been eaten up by runaway inflation during
the war and he had no position which could provide a regular income.
Marriage was therefore impossible. A separation would ensue. Now
for the first time Korngold began to express his own emotions directly

in the pieces he chose to write, and even to employ a sort of musical coded message to Luzi, a motif which he used again and again as a greeting to her, both in composition and improvisation. He aimed to catch the timbre of her voice as she said 'Wenn ich's erlaub' ('When I'm allowed'). Some of his film music displays how well Korngold could capture and transform into music the impression of a particular spoken phrase (*Between Two Worlds* contains a particularly good example of this).

He began to compose four tender and mournful songs, the *Abschiedlieder*, Op. 14 ('Songs of Farewell'), set first for soprano and piano; later he orchestrated the accompaniment. The poets he chose were Christina Rossetti (her *Requiem* in translation), Edith Ronsperger ('Dies eine kann mein Sehnen nimmer fassen' – 'The one thing my longing can never grasp') and the brother of Hans Müller, Ernst Lothar, from whom he commissioned two poems, 'Mond, so gehst du wieder auf' ('Moon, you rise again') and 'Gefasster Abschied' ('Calm farewell'). Each song deals with a different type of sorrowful farewell. The first suggestion of such a cycle came from the *Österreichischer Soldatenabschied*, a single song on the same theme. The operatic yet wistful quality of the songs even foreshadows Richard Strauss's *Four Last Songs*, while echoing aspects of Korngold's own *Die tote Stadt* – which also dealt, though in a very different way, with separation from the beloved. The composer's Cheerful Heart was no longer untroubled, although his 'pedantic' tendency is still evident – only two bars out of about 200 contain no verbal instruction to the performers.

The first song's melody is especially touching, with its downward plunge enhancing the purity and wistful simplicity of the mood. The third song, the first of the Lothar poems, features the 'Luzi' theme and formed the basis of one movement of the Piano Quintet which Korngold wrote in 1922. The message to Luzi is purely coded; the actual written dedication is to the conductor Franz Schalk. The songs received their first performance in piano arrangement on 5 November 1921 in Vienna and the orchestration had its first airing on 14 January 1923.

A new commission restored hope and gave Korngold an excellent excuse to contact his *ferne Geliebte* once more. A new production of Shakespeare's *Much Ado About Nothing* (in German, *Viel Lärm um nichts*) was in preparation at the Burgtheater; Korngold was asked to compose incidental music for it. Among the numbers would be a song for the page boy Balthazar. A singer was needed to take this role, so he telephoned Luzi, an obvious choice for the part, and she was able to obtain permission to see him – for professional purposes only.

Unfortunately, Direktor Heine of the Burgtheater had a major objection to Luzi's casting in the role of Balthazar. Without hearing her sing, he declared that the part had to be given to a man because he was afraid of actresses' 'bad legs' on stage. Korngold assured him that Luzi's legs were fine (how did he know?), but the scheme was brought to an untimely end. However, Korngold's music for *Much Ado About Nothing* became one of his most popular and often performed works. Korngold loved Shakespeare, and his affection shines through the light touch in the music. The concert suite, which he published later, abounds in dancing, sparkling rhythms, evoking the sparring of Beatrice and Benedict; the delicacy of Hero preparing for her wedding with a playful but earnest and appealing melody; and there is a spoof funeral march for the doltish antics of the night watchmen. The Garden Scene's triple metre employs a tender, sighing ostinato (a distinctive figure repeated again and again, usually in accompaniment), and the jolly good humour of the final Hornpipe, with a spirited, rhythmic 'hook' phrase, made it ideal and inevitable encore material.

The concert première of the orchestral suite took place alongside that of a very different work: Korngold's first-ever flop. He had written the ambitious overture *Sursum Corda* during the summer of 1919. Its nature was that of a symphonic poem modelled after Richard Strauss's works such as *Also sprach Zarathustra* and *Tod und Verklärung*, which offer a psycho-philosophical progression of emotion portrayed through musical episodes woven together into one long, unbroken musical span. *Sursum Corda* portrayed the struggle against despair – the effort, basically, to cheer up; it was an ambitious piece with grand gestures and serious demeanour. Over the summer he abandoned Vienna and took a room at Gmunden am Traunsee so that he could work in peace. As it happened, Luzi and her family were conveniently holidaying in a neighbouring resort, and each evening, after finishing his day's work, Korngold boarded a train to visit her.

The ambitious *Sursum Corda*, bearing an appropriate dedication to Richard Strauss, had its première on 24 January 1920, conducted by its composer. Perhaps the resounding flop that the surprised young composer found himself faced with was the result of disappointed expectations among the audience. Korngold was trying to be Strauss, and not succeeding. Instead of the lush, romantic, tuneful music the public had come to expect from him, they found themselves faced with a lofty, not instantly accessible, musico-philosophical statement which was not only untypical of the familiar Korngold but even untypical of Richard Strauss. Korngold was not too upset by the failure of his new work, however – Luzi reported that he simply appeared 'amazed – like a child who believes himself unjustly punished'.

The piece did not meet with any happier fortune on its other airings, whether in Italy or the USA, where in December 1922 it received the following review from one M. H. Flint:

> *The composer says his aim was to suggest a mood of struggle and aspiration, a joyous deliverance out of stress and storm. Young Korngold is clever in his understanding use of the resources of a modern orchestra, but the paucity of his original ideas was even more marked in this composition than in his opera* Die tote Stadt … *In the opera Korngold seemed to have imbibed ideas from many old masters of the art of composition; in the* Sursum Corda *he has apparently been content to limit himself to imitating Richard Strauss. Strauss, be it said, is not great enough to be imitated …*

Believing his overture a hopeless case, Korngold put it away until, some years later in Hollywood, he found an expedient slot for some of the music in his score for *The Adventures of Robin Hood*. Hollywood's taste and Vienna's were not always parallel. He duly won an Oscar.

The première of the complete *Much Ado* music with the Shakespeare play was given in the Schönbrunner Schlosstheater on 6 May 1920 under Korngold's own direction. Luzi was able to go to a rehearsal and told her friend that she thought he had written a mini-masterpiece. 'Eine kleine Bühnenmusik ('A little stage music')', he modestly replied. 'I am not so experienced in this, so nobody can take offence at me for having written it.'

Korngold had to make a major alteration to the music for the stage presentation, however. Indeed, he had to make an entirely new arrangement, as the run was extended; the original orchestra was no longer available and the replacement band was not up to the job. Quickly he rewrote the entire score for piano and violin and performed it himself with the violinist Rudolf Kolisch. The last piece, the Hornpipe, needed the additional rich sound of a horn, so Erich bribed the first horn player of the Vienna Philharmonic with a cigar. He came along to play the piece on his free evening. 'This powerful musician,' wrote Luzi, 'used to the dimensions of great opera houses, nearly blew the little baroque theatre away.' Happily, Erich and Luzi's friendship had not been blown away but resumed where it had left off, the feelings of both surviving unharmed.

The Vienna Opera was about to celebrate its fiftieth anniversary, and as part of the celebrations Korngold was to conduct his own two one-act operas, with a particularly excellent cast. In *Polykrates* the exquisitely lyrical Lotte Lehmann starred as Laura. Maria Jeritza once again took the lead in *Violanta*. The counterpoint of Lehmann in one opera and Jeritza in the other provided an interesting and significant contrast: Jeritza, who excelled in Richard Strauss and as Carmen, dramatic, sexual and charismatic; Lehmann, who excelled in the Lieder of Schumann and Schubert, pure, tender and poised. Jeritza, of course, stole the show; Lehmann was furious. Jeritza was Korngold's inspiration; and yet it would be Lehmann who sang the lead in his *Heliane*, taking on a role conceived for the other singer.

For the time being, however, Korngold was still working on the orchestration of *Die tote Stadt*. He had set a date in August 1920 as his deadline to have the score finished. He liked, his father tells us, to give himself such deadlines, stick rigidly to them, and then celebrate. But with *Die tote Stadt*, he allegedly kept putting off writing the last notes – the percussion part of the last sixteen pages. On the appointed day he had toothache, about which he was philosophical. After all, Polykrates had to sacrifice his ring to pacify the gods, so it seemed just that he should pay for his joy at the opera's completion with some small discomfort. 'At 9pm he put the finishing touches to it, looked through it in bed and then went happily to sleep,' wrote Julius. Schott's accepted the work as soon as Erich played it to them, and the event was celebrated with a rumbustious evening in Mainz wine cellars underneath the Rhine.

Vienna, after the war and with the end of the empire, was itself a very sick city. Austria, now termed the 'German-Austrian Republic',

was 'the state nobody wanted'; it was run, for the first time, by Social
Democrats, not emperors. There was a strong feeling among the state
leaders that to unite with the new German democracy would be a
good thing; they and the Christian Social moderate right felt that this
state of just six million people could not survive on its own. George
Clare describes its capital city thus:

> … *the once glittering Imperial City of Vienna was destitute. It was
> reduced to chaos and misery. The city's chief medical officer reported that
> at least 20,000 children were close to starvation. 130,000 men, a high
> percentage of the working population, were unemployed. Every day money
> bought less and less. Every day, even with money, there was less and less to
> buy. One violent demonstration followed another. People died in the
> streets, either of bullets or of hunger. Ill-clad, they shuffled through the
> town, past rubbish heaped in its parks, through streets littered with refuse,
> looking for work, for scraps of food, for hope.*

That was the winter of 1919, just a year prior to the first performance of Korngold's new opera.

On 4 December 1920 *Die tote Stadt* received the unusual distinc-
tion of a simultaneous double première, in Cologne and Hamburg.
Korngold evidently could not be present at both, and chose to go to
'his' town, Hamburg, where Maria Jeritza was to sing Marietta. Here
the role of Paul was taken by the tenor Aagaard Oestvig and Egon
Pollack was the conductor. Luzi too was present for the dress rehearsal
– and, maybe because her expectations had been raised too high,
found that what she saw was not a little disappointing. 'Bad dress
rehearsal, good performance,' finally held sway and, at the exhorta-
tion of Richard Strauss who had sent a gently prompting note to
Korngold's box, Erich Korngold took his bow with Jeritza and Oestvig
at the end of the first act.

The Pierrot waltz song was the most successful moment of all on
this occasion. Watching the bass-baritone Richard Mayr accepting the
ovation with bowed head, Luzi remembered watching her grandfather
accepting the love of the Burgtheater audience when she was four
years old. Julius Korngold, of course, was absent. On this occasion, he
had almost been persuaded to come to the performance, but apparently caught a cold at the last minute.

The conductor Otto
Klemperer was not initially
enthusiastic about
Korngold's music, but their
acquaintance strengthened
during exile in later years.
This portrait of Klemperer
dates from 1929.

In Cologne, Otto Klemperer was the conductor of *Die tote Stadt*
and Marietta was sung by his wife, Johanna. Despite the reasonably
universal success of the opera's 'hit numbers', the fervent atmosphere,
high emotion and excessively lush musical language of Korngold was
by no means to everyone's liking. It seems that in Cologne Klemperer
refused to take his curtain call. He was not always dismissive of
Korngold, however. One remark the composer later made to him
regarding Beethoven's Fifth Symphony made a deep impression – 'The
start of the first movement cannot come twice!' This was an idealistic
and romantic remark typical of Korngold, but Klemperer heeded
the idea and for many years would not play the first movement's
exposition repeat (i.e., the first long section of the movement). He and

Korngold renewed and strengthened their acquaintance as refugees in California some years later.

Public opinion did not share Klemperer's alleged disdain of *Die tote Stadt*; the opera opened to much acclaim in Vienna in March 1921 with Korngold himself conducting. At a celebratory dinner after the première, with the Strecker brothers from Schott's and Franz Schalk, Korngold admitted that he had been confident about the première because a good authority at the opera house had assured him it would be a success. Who was this friend? asked the distinguished guests. It was the fireman on evening duty. At one rehearsal he had heard Marietta's Lute Song and said, 'Herr Korngold, that is splendid.' Erich and the fireman remained good friends for years – and it was not to be only in Vienna that Korngold found his most trustworthy friends were not of the 'establishment' but of more modest, unbiased backgrounds.

A signed portrait of Richard Tauber who became one of Korngold's favourite tenors

Korngold's conducting activities were increasing and he had received, that February, an offer of a conducting post from the director of the Hamburg opera. This position – sadly short-lived due to the death of Dr Löwenfeld, the director in question (though Korngold did conduct a couple of performances there after Löwenfeld died) – was, however, the only opportunity Korngold ever had in an official post to conduct serious opera.

But performances of *Die tote Stadt* were in the meantime spreading like wildfire. Having made his way to Dresden for the first performance there, Korngold found himself listening to an enchanting young tenor in the role of Paul. This singer's name was Richard Tauber. In subsequent years he was to become one of the best-known and best-loved of all lyrical tenors in the Viennese repertoire, especially on the lighter side – Lehár, Johann Strauss and other composers of operetta. Korngold described him as having a 'devilish musicality' and it was not long before he would appear in Vienna in the leading role of Korngold's opera. When Tauber turned his attention in the direction of operetta, Korngold and Luzi were distressed that he seemed to be losing interest in serious works, although one of his first operetta performances was under the baton of Korngold himself, who by that time had begun to move in a similar direction.

*Die tote Stadt* soon migrated with its leading lady, Jeritza, to the Metropolitan Opera in New York where, because she had chosen it as the vehicle for her New York début, it became the first opera to be performed in German after the end of the war. One review that appeared in New York a couple of years after the opera's première is quite illuminating on the impression it created in conjunction with its leading lady, and on popular prejudices about child-prodigy facility.

> *For a boy of twenty it is certainly a remarkable composition, but its remarkable qualities are principally disclosed by his knowledge of* how to do it *and not by what he has done. His erudition is boundless. He shows an intimate acquaintance with the great masters of composition … but originality on his part is not the result. A master of orchestration, he has twined and intertwined phrases and ideas of one composer after another in a marvellous way, with no clear indication of Korngold himself left on one's mind … The role of Marietta was so well sung and acted by Mlle Marie Jeritza … that one must acknowledge the success of the new singer to be far greater than that of the opera itself.*

Korngold (above, aged about nineteen) cut a debonair figure as a young man.

The accusation that Korngold knew how to compose but had no ideas of his own crops up in a number of reviews and actually has little foundation. Certainly he was influenced by Richard Strauss, Puccini, Wagner, Brahms, Johann Strauss and his teacher Zemlinsky, not to mention his father – an eclectic enough list – but his musical idiom is wholly personal and can be rapidly recognized, not only from his 'signature' motif but from the textures, lines, colour and mood that form his personal voice. The 'clear indication of Korngold himself' is very much present in *Die tote Stadt*; in the dancing elation of Marietta's scenes; the sorrow, hysteria and tragic nostalgia of Paul; the dramatic involvement and pictorial strength of the scene painting in Bruges and in the religious procession of the third act; the glistening orchestration, full of keyboards and bells and percussion; the rich Viennese swing and original flexibility of the melodies; and the virtuosity and mutability of the harmonic progressions. All this comes from Korngold himself, partly synthesized out of those influences, partly reaching him alone from some rationally-inexplicable source of inspiration, and absorbed into his own idiosyncratic language.

Korngold next turned, as he habitually did after writing an opera, to chamber music. He had been working on his First String Quartet, which he dedicated to the Rosé Quartet, and the Piano Quintet in E major, with its interweaving of what Julius called 'the Luzi Sonnenthal

The Rosé String Quartet,
dedicatee of Korngold's
First String Quartet

theme' to bait his son. The Quintet was a far happier experience than
*Sursum Corda*; with just three movements, smaller in scale than the
hefty works for the medium by Brahms, Schumann and Dvořák, the
quintet is full of Korngoldian melody and good nature. It was first
performed in 1923 in Hamburg, but, despite its charm and the
relative scarcity of piano quintets, it has had pitifully few airings in
recent years.

   The first movement opens in unmistakably Korngoldian mode
with a melody that leaps upward in intervals of fifths and sevenths and
proceeds with airy, dancing rhythms and rich, decorated textures in
the piano and inner strings. Rubatos and mood painting are precisely
instructed by the composer. He stretches the musicians – especially
the poor pianist! – to their limits, striving as ever for the richness
of an orchestra: glissandos, vast chords, trills and decorative figures
all abound and the entire range of the piano's pitch, volume and
expressive ability is demanded within the concentrated span of this
short movement. The Adagio, shifting the key down by a tone to D
major, presents a tender, peaceful, wide-ranging melody (the 'Luzi
Sonnenthal' theme) on viola and cello, filled out by the piano with

dense chords in the bass register; gradually the music rises to fill the full span of the Quintet, again brimful with expressive instructions and the richest of textures demanding delicate performance. Korngold indicates no fewer than fifty-four changes of time signature within this movement's thirteen-page full score, and the opening eight-eight signature never returns. The final movement uses several favourite devices of Korngold's – the marking *pathetisch* (or *patetico* as he sometimes called it – lofty, solemn, expressive), the strong, march-like flourishing rhythms (accent on the down beat, quickly passed across) and again an abundance of time-signature changes and precise and plentiful instructions on expression and rubato.

Earlier in the same month as the Quintet's première came the performance of another Müller–Korngold collaboration. Korngold had written incidental music to Müller's play *Der Vampyr*; this music unfortunately was never published and has completely vanished from any performance spaces.

In 1922 Erich Korngold travelled to Italy for the first time to direct an orchestra in Rome, where he cleverly paired *Sursum Corda* again with the suite from *Much Ado*. The displeasure at the first was expressed in unmistakable terms – 'Basta! Basta!' – but after *Much Ado* Korngold had to wait patiently on the platform while the audience shouted amongst itself in debate as to which movement should be encored. The trip to Italy was not his only journey that year; he also went to Brussels and London with his father, which, of course, made communication with Luzi none too easy. Parents on both sides were still violently opposed to their relationship. 'Every attempt was made to end our friendship,' Luzi recalled. And so scared were the young couple of having their letters intercepted that they invented a more than usually complicated musical code in which to correspond, with notes standing for letters, but using awkward clefs such as the alto and the tenor to confuse potential readers.

Luzi was busy herself, studying singing at the Staatsakademie and also acting in silent films. But she had an unusual plan in motion to celebrate her friend's approaching twenty-fifth birthday. She organized a private orchestra, invited a number of friends, relations and the whole Korngold family, and then appeared in a dinner suit and conducted the *Much Ado About Nothing* suite herself. Julius Korngold was in a good mood; for once she found him quite charming. But the

gesture was modern and daring, not only in its emotional demon-
strativeness but also because women simply did not put on men's garb
and conduct orchestras. Such actions did not appeal to
the conventional Julius Korngold; he often objected to 'modern'
behaviour on Luzi's part.

The first biography of Korngold was published in 1922, written by
Rudolf Stefan Hoffmann. The composer was all of twenty-five – quite
a youthful age to have your biography written. But about this time,
Korngold was invited by Hubert Marischka to direct a Johann Strauss
operetta, *Eine Nacht in Venedig*, at the Theater an der Wien. From
then onwards the number of serious works he produced went into a
definite decline.

4

Erich and Luzi Korngold
walking in the Tyrol at Alt-
Aussee a few months after
their marriage in 1924

*My musical creed may be called the inspired
idea. With what displeasure one hears this
concept nowadays! And nevertheless: how
could the artificial construction, the most exact
musical mathematics, triumph over the moving
principle of the inspired idea!*

Erich Wolfgang Korngold,
interviewed in May 1926

## Playing at Marriage 1922-7

Vienna in the 1920s: '... a city still pretending to be a world metrop-
olis of cosmopolitan elegance. But behind the imposing façade of
former imperial splendour lurked defeat, poverty and fear. Behind the
baroque masonry of superb elegance lay dark, dank corridors filled
with the stale smell of over-boiled cabbage and human sweat and the
indefinable but clearly discernible odour of hatred and envy.'
(George Clare)

The condition of what was now the Vienna Staatsoper somewhat
mirrored the condition of the city as a whole. Of course the opera
house was as affected as any other organization by the galloping
inflation and social upheaval, but even so its management by Richard
Strauss and Franz Schalk was coming in for a good deal of criticism.
The critic Paul Becker, for instance, wrote scathing reports for the
English journal *The Musical Times*. In the February 1922 edition the
following appeared, making the nature of the complaint quite clear:

*This house – which since the 1918 revolution has been under the
management of Dr Richard Strauss in conjunction with Franz Schalk – is
gradually assuming the character of a place of merely superficial
amusement for the wealthy classes, and for those* nouveaux riches *whose
taste is all too often heeded by the management. The once perfect ensemble
of the theatre has become practically disorganised owing to a strong
preference on the part of the directors for 'guest' singers whose mission is
sensationalism, while some of the finest artists of the theatre are enjoying
involuntary leave. The consequent enormous outlay constantly increases
the deficit of the Staatsoper, which now amounts to well over a hundred
million crowns annually ... repertoire is now arranged according to the
whims of visiting stars. [Apart from Strauss] other contemporary
composers receive scant attention from the directorate with the possible
exception of Puccini's all too pleasing operas and the works of Erich
Wolfgang Korngold, which though doubtless effective thrills, cannot
possibly be said to represent present-day operatic tendencies.*

One important Viennese critic also wrote consistently against the
regime: Julius Korngold. To him the opera house had never been the
same since the days of Mahler. While he had consistently applauded
one great composer's approach to opera directorship, he had scarcely a
good word to say for Strauss, feeling that the composer did not possess
the necessary skills for the position and should rather be devoting
himself to writing music. Not that Julius liked Strauss's operas so
much. He had panned *Salome* on its première, but when *Elektra* was
first performed he began his review: 'How fair was the princess
Salome!' – using the opening line from the earlier opera to condemn
the later by comparison. This opposition put Erich Korngold in a
difficult position: not only was Julius's newspaper the formative
influence upon much Viennese opinion, but also he was the only
critic who had a son who frequently conducted his own operas in the
very theatre that his father was constantly condemning.

Accusations flew on all sides. 'Dr Korngold does not ask, "How
does this or that artist conduct, composer, play or sing?"' wrote Paul
Becker in *The Musical Times* (August 1922). 'His question is, "What
attitude does he or she take towards Erich Wolfgang Korngold?"
Composers and artists, even new books on musical subjects, are being
viewed by Dr Korngold solely from this angle.' He cited instances
when intended performances of *Die tote Stadt* were threatened by
Erich's alleged attempts to influence the casting ('a procedure which
was entirely beyond the privilege generally granted by the Vienna
State Opera even to more successful composers') and of singers and
a conductor dropping out of the opera because they were simply
afraid of what the composer's father would write about them, should
they fail to capture exactly Korngold's ideas on interpretation.

Julius Korngold was especially vitriolic about the way holidays and
guest appearances at the opera house were being scheduled. As a result
of such bungles, one tenor had been allowed to make certain cuts
in the leading role of *Die tote Stadt* so that his voice would be in good
enough shape to sing Tannhäuser the following night (no realistic
schedule should have put a singer in such a position), and Erich – or
Julius in Erich's guise, most likely – had written a letter complaining
about the way his opera's success was being affected by holidays and
the unannounced appearance of substitute singers. These complaints
also appeared constantly in Julius's reviews of other operas, notably of
Meyerbeer's *Les Huguenots* in early 1922.

Richard Strauss summoned Erich to his office and the young composer returned home highly upset. The two directors, Strauss and Schalk, had levelled exceptionally nasty remarks at Erich about the connection of Julius's reviews in the *Neue Freie Presse* to performances of his works. They had (according to Julius) announced that singers only took roles in *Die tote Stadt* because they were afraid of Julius's newspaper; they were angry that Julius had recommended that a Jew – Bruno Walter, in fact, and a very good suggestion – should have become director instead of Strauss (Strauss later became head of Hitler's Reichsmusikkammer in Germany for a while); and last, but not least, that because of his father's stance against the opera house it would no longer be possible for Erich to appear – even unpaid, as he always was – as conductor of his own operas.

Richard Strauss around 1919: joint director of the Vienna State Opera with Franz Schalk, he was frequently the subject of Julius Korngold's caustic criticism.

Erich was deeply hurt by the affair and wrote to the management requesting that his opera should be withdrawn. He took care to thank Franz Schalk for his excellent performance at the same time. Strauss told him not to be childish and refused to withdraw the popular *Die tote Stadt*. Julius too was distressed, of course – but that did not stop him from continuing to sling poisoned arrows at the opera directors at every possible opportunity. So Erich, who loved to control his own music, was forced into the ignominious position of watching it being less well conducted by others, through no fault of his own.

Things came to a head for the first time during a rehearsal in which a new conductor had been assigned to the opera. Erich, who was allowed into rehearsals although forbidden to touch the baton, quickly realized that the man did not know what he was doing. The singers, secure in their own roles, became impatient and one or two called out, 'Why isn't Korngold conducting?' Erich finally lost his temper. 'Why am I not conducting?' he yelled back to them. 'Because my father writes bad reviews of the opera's directors!' And he did not stop at that. 'Let's make a revolution!' he demanded of the singers and musicians. 'Korngold shall conduct!'

Korngold possessed a fierce temper, although he did not lose it this way frequently; basically a peaceful man, he rather regretted his outburst. Called to Strauss to explain himself, he simply told the truth: how he had suffered at the appalling rehearsal and how he felt that he would rather not have his work presented at all. He cleverly quoted Strauss at himself: 'Lieber ins Feuer!' ('Rather throw it into the fire!'), a line from the maestro's own opera *Ariadne auf Naxos*. In this work, a very young and talented composer is distraught to learn that his serious and beloved opera is to be performed in a context and manner that he feels will ruin it; 'Lieber ins feuer!' is his protesting reaction. The parallel with Korngold's situation was obvious. The line brought Strauss round; young Korngold would be reinstated.

Funnily enough, the 'Pierrot Tanzlied' of *Die tote Stadt* also echoes *Ariadne* – in the second act of which a *commedia dell'arte* player sings a wistful serenade with wordless interjections from a soprano. And Korngold's later opera *Das Wunder der Heliane* ends, just like *Ariadne*, with a massive love duet beyond the bounds of the world, two souls approaching heaven together. Just how much did Korngold identify with Strauss's opera?

Even if the personal difficulty had been resolved (for the time being), that did not stop factions in the audience from delighting in a row. Gossip had spread through the city about the conflict between Strauss and his one-time protégé, and the pros and cons divided accordingly. As always, it was the standing room – the *Stehparterre* section at the back of the stalls and the 'fourth gallery' at the top of the house – that accommodated the most passionate enthusiasts and the loudest detractors. Korngold was to make his return to conduct his one-acters and he was warned by a supporter that the *Stehparterre* was planning a demonstration. The minute he walked onto the platform the noise broke out – stamping, shouting, whistling from the *Stehparterre*, 'Hoch Strauss, pfui Korngold!' ('Up with Strauss, down with Korngold!'). The young composer's supporters returned from the gallery, 'Up with Korngold!' While the rumpus raged, Erich stood on his podium, in the footsteps of Mahler, and waited, baton raised. It was some ten minutes before the noise was brought to an unexpected end. From a box in the stalls came one loud, clear woman's voice uttering a none too polite word: 'Kusch!' The entire opera house, even the opposition, burst out laughing and when silence finally prevailed Erich began the performance. Afterwards he told Luzi: 'I am proud of one thing: I held up the baton through the entire demonstration without trembling at all.'

It must have been a great relief for Erich to set to work on lighter matters, arranging the music of Johann Strauss's operetta *Eine Nacht in Venedig*. This brought him into a world wholly different from that of the grand opera of Richard Strauss: that of the Waltz King himself, not related in any way but name to the opera house director. The original version of this operetta as passed to Korngold was dramatically weak, despite its melodiousness, and Korngold, who adored Johann Strauss, was only too happy to do some structural repointing to strengthen the show, switching round scenes or reorchestrating, and bringing in two extra numbers from other Strauss works for the star – Richard Tauber – to sing. The delighted reception at the first performance was unanimous and Erich became, overnight, a reputed Strauss expert. The revival of interest in Johann Strauss's music during the 1920s and 30s was largely inspired by Korngold's work in this field.

Luzi recalled in her book one particularly touching episode which demonstrated the keen personal connection Erich felt for this composer. Strauss's widow, Adele, with whom Erich had exchanged genial notes as a little boy, came at his invitation to witness a rehearsal of a duet scene of which he was particularly fond. When he told Frau Strauss that it was his favourite number, she replied: 'Remarkable – it was also his favourite number. Each time he reached this place he used to look up at me in my box.'

Erich genuinely loved his operetta work, but there was another reason too for his eagerness to pursue it. If Marischka would give him a long-term contract at the Theater an der Wien, he would have a regular income, in which case he and Luzi could finally marry. The argument worried Luzi; she did not feel it would be good for Erich as a composer to be contracted into operetta in this way. He had, of course, made up his mind already and took no notice of her objections, stating that, apart from being 'great fun', it would be no shame to stand in for Johann Strauss.

In any case, he had no intention of abandoning serious music. On 8 January 1924 his First String Quartet, in A minor, Op. 16, was given its world première by its dedicatees, the Rosé Quartet; he had begun this work in 1922 and finished it in the spring of 1923. In this piece Korngold combines his own idiosyncratic harmonic language with a traditional form which pays homage to the great string quartets of the nineteenth century: the *quasi fantasia* heading of the slow movement harks back to Beethoven (especially the 'Moonlight' Sonata) and the

The pianist Paul Wittgenstein lost his right arm in the First World War but commissioned a number of superb works for left hand alone, including Korngold's concerto.

choice of an Intermezzo for the third movement (as in the String Sextet) again recalls Brahms's fondness for this format. On a larger scale, in 1923 Korngold began to compose a concerto for the pianist Paul Wittgenstein.

Wittgenstein (whose brother Ludwig became the famous philosopher) had lost his right arm in World War I and, thanks to the family's moneyed status, had the funds to commission new concertos for left hand alone from a number of leading composers. The receipt of such a commission was regarded as a great honour. The most famous of Wittgenstein's left-hand concertos is probably Ravel's, but there are other fine pieces composed by Prokofiev (his fourth concerto), Benjamin Britten, Richard Strauss and Franz Schmidt. Korngold's Piano Concerto is a major work in one long movement (it lasts some thirty-five minutes), employing a sizeable orchestra including harp, celesta, glockenspiel and xylophone, and calling on extreme virtuoso ability on the part of the pianist's active hand, though it is written most idiomatically for the piano. The pianist Gary Graffman, who discovered the piece after hurting his right hand in the mid-1980s, compared it to 'a keyboard *Salome*' and also noticed in its 'big tune' a remarkable similarity to one by Rachmaninov which appears in the latter's *Paganini Rhapsody* (Korngold beat the Russian to it by a full ten years).

The Piano Concerto is the one piece, perhaps the only piece, of Korngold's early years which looks ahead to the bitter, dramatic terseness of his late Symphony in F sharp (and its key, C sharp, is even more unusual and complex for the orchestra to tackle). One programme note writer described it as 'one of the most peculiar instrumental works to have been written during the twentieth century'. Its extended form bridges a gap between symphonic structure and pure soundworld impressionism. The first theme, *Heldisch mit Kraft und Feuer* (heroically, with fire and power), is based on the composer's favourite upward-surging interlocked intervals of a fourth and a fifth and suggests the opening of a dramatic tone poem; the second theme, *Ruhig, weich und gesangvoll* (peacefully, softly and songful), turns round some of the motivic patterns of the first theme and hints at a 'slow movement' while the third, *Ziemlich rasch, burlesque und lustig* (considerably rapid, burlesque and humorous), suggests a scherzo. Korngold then plunges us into a world of the most extraordinary aural colours, marked *geheimnisvoll, nebelhaft* (full of mystery, nebulous); although it serves as a 'development' section, this part of the concerto makes its impression almost entirely through its phenomenal atmosphere. Korngold's ability to invent pictorial, even mystical soundworlds was one reason he was so gifted at producing cinema scores, but those invisible worlds he had invented for himself, as here, are perhaps even more effective. The first three themes return and are further developed before the opening Motif of the Cheerful Heart fragment surges the piece to its end.

Wittgenstein was another difficult personality for Korngold to deal with, possessed of artistic temperament in the extreme, with a proclivity for causing some offence and then being lavishly generous to make amends. Several years later, Wittgenstein spoke out against Erich's arrangement of Mendelssohn's music for *A Midsummer Night's*

In 1924 Korngold visited London and made some Duo-Art piano rolls for the Aeolian Recording Company. Here he is shown in a recording session, with an assistant at a console on the left noting down impressions of the tempos and dynamics.

*Dream* (for Max Reinhardt's film), but then made up for it by sending Korngold an original Mendelssohn manuscript two weeks later. He was not known for his politeness to composers generally, complaining to Ravel, 'If I had wanted a solo piece I would not have commissioned a concerto!' He gave Korngold's concerto its first performance in Vienna on 22 September 1924.

At the Theater an der Wien, Hubert Marischka came up with Korngold's longed-for contract. Erich duly invited Luzi and her mother to a performance of his arrangement of Strauss's operetta, went to their house for a light supper afterwards, and formally proposed marriage. The Korngold parents ignored the engagement (which was to remain private anyway for a time). 'The sole sign that his parents knew of our engagement,' wrote Luzi, 'was in an indescribably woeful expression in the eyes of "the old Korngold".' (Erich's close friend, the Count and composer Julius Bittner, used to describe Julius as the 'pater dolorosus'!) Even when Luzi made her official visit to the Korngold house to be introduced as Erich's bride-to-be, Julius delivered what she termed his 'Weltschmerz' look, and even Josephine would not give her a kiss. While Luzi was trailing about Vienna being introduced to Erich's friends – and being far more warmly received by them, notably Julius and Emilie Bittner – his parents still appear to have longed to impose a loveless regime on their famous son, whether because of their own possessiveness or a falsely idealistic artistic outlook. Julius avoided recording that hostility in his memoirs, rather boasting of his daughter-in-law's many accomplishments, though in a manuscript appropriately entitled *Conflikte*, which he worked on in Hollywood in the last year of his life, he dumps all the blame for the family's quarrels neatly upon her. For her part, she later recorded the statement by Erich that his father was 'straight away in love with her'. But nobody could ever, in Julius's eyes, have been good enough for his son.

Maria Hussa in the title role of *Das Wunder der Heliane* at its Hamburg première, 7 October 1927

But was that all there was to it? Of whom was Julius jealous? On several occasions descriptions of his behaviour, when disapproving of Luzi's actions in some way, sound more appropriate to a jealous husband than to a father-in-law. His endeavours to keep them apart even after their marriage go well beyond the bounds of rationality. Was he indeed 'straight away in love with her'? Were his psychological boundaries with his son so indistinct for him that he could have been attracted to Erich's chosen wife? Was his possessiveness directed consciously or unconsciously at Luzi as well as Erich? If so, tensions in the already tense father-and-son relationship, professionally over-involved more than ever, would have been quite intolerable.

One day Erich telephoned Luzi in some excitement and requested that she should meet him in a little café in the Wiedner Hauptstrasse as he had something important to say. Puzzled, she obliged. He pulled a manuscript out of his pocket and said, 'Read this!' The manuscript's title was *Die Heilige*; the author one Hans Kaltneker, a gifted Expressionist poet and dramatist who had died at the age of twenty-four. Nobody to this day has any idea where Korngold found it; perhaps it came to light in one of his beloved second-hand book shops, although it was not even printed. Korngold was drawn to Kaltneker's writing: wordy, turgid, complicated and with a proclivity for *risqué* and intense subject matter. And Kaltneker during his short life had been drawn to Korngold. The two never met, but

Kaltneker had apparently seen *Violanta*; the extraordinary fact emerged later, via a mutual friend, that Kaltneker had written *Die Heilige* with the express intention that it should be set to music by Erich Wolfgang Korngold. This makes it all the more extraordinary that the composer should have stumbled upon it and decided instantly that this would be his next opera. He had called Luzi out to ask her opinion of its suitablity – but he had already made up his mind. The opera became *Das Wunder der Heliane*.

The writing of the libretto was once more entrusted to Hans Müller, who seized upon the bizarre psychological drama with enthusiasm. Kaltneker's original play was never published, but Müller's libretto apparently retains much of the inordinate loftiness of the poet's style, which Korngold so enjoyed. These qualities in Müller's own writing were, coincidentally, what Erich and Julius had both objected to in his original attempts at a libretto for *Die tote Stadt*; however, his style was undoubtedly more suitable for Heliane's highly serious erotico-spiritual experience than for the more human scale of the earlier work.

What was it that attracted Korngold to *Die Heilige*? The hallmarks of his enthusiasms are present without a doubt: the quasi-mystical religious element, the conflict of body and soul, of spirit and sexuality – the feelings of which are heightened by that conflict – and now the power of love to conquer all.

Lotte Lehmann and Jan Kiepura starred in the Viennese première of *Heliane*, 29 October 1927

The story is convoluted and complex. It presents us with a triangle: a holy stranger preaching love, who has captivated the people of an unspecified timeless and mythical land; a tyrannical ruler who has banished love from his realm; and his wife, Queen Heliane, who is so holy and pure that the tyrant has never been able to consummate his marriage with her. This has led to his total condemnation of love. The Ruler has sentenced the Stranger to death, but agrees to save him if he can make Heliane requite his love; the Stranger, however, himself falls in love with Heliane, who has taken pity on him and visits him in prison. She is drawn to him and complies with his requests to see first her golden hair released, then her white feet, then her naked body. Discovering them, the Ruler – who punishes all love with death – has her dragged away.

The second act deals with Heliane's trial, in which it has to be determined whether or not she and the Stranger have enjoyed actual sexual contact – and the central conflict of the tale is Heliane's own. She has not physically given herself to him; but in her mind, she has. In spirit she has loved as richly as anybody can love. In the great aria with which Korngold provides her, 'Ich ging zu ihm', she defends herself, yet gives away her feelings with the ardour of her pronouncements. The Stranger, denied her love, stabs himself and dies. The Ruler declares that since Heliane is pure, she can work miracles; he orders her to bring the Stranger back to life. She falters in the undertaking, breaking down and exclaiming that she has, after all, loved him. To her, the fact that she had wanted to is equivalent to having done so, although no sexual act had taken place. But back to life he comes, achieving a Christ-like power and mobilizing the people of the land with him; and now the Ruler is so incensed that he stabs Heliane. Life and death become confused; Heliane, with the aid of the resurrected Stranger, apparently returns to life. But the opera ends as she and the Stranger – now united in pure spirit – walk together up to the gates of Heaven, singing an ecstatic, transcendental love duet.

'I shall not forget how Erich, entranced, with blazing eyes and breathing heavily, played and sang it for us as it had just occurred to him,' wrote Julius Korngold, referring to the last duet of *Heliane*. 'He felt that nothing had to be changed … He said that this music should disarm all enemies; he had the feeling of having created a great work.'

*Die Heilige* sprang from a Catholic background suggestive of virgin worship, sexual guilt, a messiah redeeming through love, struggles with the devil. Korngold was not, however, a Catholic and *Heliane* even caused extra controversy by offending certain Catholic sensibilities which felt the work was blasphemous, daring to mix these elements with eroticism. Brendan Carroll, in his notes to the first complete recording of *Heliane*, suggests that Heliane's aria 'Ich ging zu ihm', 'like Tristan – attempts a musical expression of the sexual act'. And there are strong resemblances in this aria and in the beyond-the-grave love duet at the opera's end respectively to those other great operatic spiritual-sexual sublimations, the Liebestod of Wagner's *Tristan und Isolde* and the transcendental love duet at the end of Richard Strauss's *Ariadne auf Naxos*. Korngold, making this element his own, like his forebears is suggesting not only the sexual act but also a mystical experience of spiritual unity which transcends the physical.

Korngold undoubtedly had a religious leaning, but it was of a mystical and unspecific variety. As an assimilated Jew in a basically Catholic society, he was surrounded, especially in Vienna, by churches and the vast Cathedral of St Stephen – which dominates its small neighbouring buildings and the little, narrow streets of the old city. The influence of Catholicism, with its glorious art and architecture and enticing incense, must have been impossible to ignore – especially as the Korngolds, though Jewish by race, seem to have had no religious convictions of their own. Erich was left to make his own decisions about his spiritual life and he never practised his native religion, nor converted to Christianity (unlike Mendelssohn and Mahler, two of the composers most akin to him, and Schoenberg, who became a Lutheran but later converted back to Judaism). Like his burgeoning sexuality as an adolescent, this non-specific spiritual leaning was best explored for Korngold through his music. He did not apparently believe in God or an afterlife; but his own life certainly bears out his moral convictions and his idealism about love as a redeeming force. Luzi described her life, in her book about her husband, as 'one long love story'; and it is clear that Erich put his love for her and their children first.

What is especially striking and even disturbing about *Heliane* in relation to its composer's life is that he discovered it at a time when he himself was fighting for his right to love Luzi against a father who could almost have been trying to banish love from his realm – a possessiveness from which marriage to Luzi would save him. His identification is clearly with Heliane – the only named character – rather than the Stranger; it is always her story and it is she who experiences the great conflict of inclination and action, the metaphysical transmutation of the leanings of the soul into a higher, spiritual reality.

To this singularly peculiar libretto Korngold composed a massive score requiring an orchestra with a vast array of percussion instruments, no fewer than five keyboards (including harmonium, celesta and piano), off-stage ensembles and excessively demanding roles for the singers. He takes expressive and colouristic chromaticism to its limits, often uses polytonality – several different keys superimposed in the same music – and employs harmonic manipulations that are really virtuoso. While there are again Leitmotivs, as he used in *Die tote*

*Stadt*, the musical structure is more fluid, with fewer 'set-piece' episodes and less evident key symbolism – though the key in which the opera opens (F sharp) is Korngold's perennial favourite and is contrasted throughout the opera with D minor, symbolizing respectively the eternal power of love and the gloom of the Ruler and his land without love.

The Leitmotivs themselves are associated frequently with concepts, as well as particular characters. Resurrection and the power of love (a sudden and blazing F sharp major) opens the opera; and the Stranger's despair (represented by a descending, whole-tone theme) can be heard just after the curtain rises for the first time. (Whole-tones produce a mysterious effect: an ordinary scale consists of a combination of whole tones and semitones, so the absence of the expected smaller divisions creates interesting musical colour.) The opera begins with the off-stage chorus, angelic in its effect, singing the theme from which both musical and dramatic action springs: 'Blessed are they that love. Those who have loved shall not die. And those who have died for love shall rise again.' Melodically, it takes as its basis a simple musical motif of a falling third which then returns stepwise up to its first note. This melody follows the first statement of the Resurrection motif (a distinctive rising progression of massive chords) which returns at key moments in the action – for instance, when Heliane reveals herself to the Stranger, when she 'resurrects' him and, of course, in the final apotheosis of love. The melodic line of Heliane's aria 'Ich ging zu ihm', the very heart of the opera, is based on a development and extension of the chorus's melodic motif, like Isolde's Liebestod in Wagner's *Tristan und Isolde*, building ecstatically ever upward towards a massively anticipated climax. And it can be found in innumerable guises throughout the rest of the score.

The Motif of the Cheerful Heart puts in an appearance as well, when the character of the Messenger (the alto 'supporting' role of a woman who has been the Ruler's loveless mistress) announces in Act II the uprising of the people against the Ruler. Character motifs are plentiful too. The friendly Porter, the jailer who is sympathetic to the imprisoned Stranger, has his own motif of a rising modal scale, while the Ruler's bitter and twisted personality is portrayed in his Leitmotiv by a rigid rhythm, swinging between major and minor chords.

Structurally, *Heliane* is through-composed (i.e., continuous, without recurring chunks of music) in the Wagnerian tradition, the score woven out of its Leitmotivs and serving as both accompaniment to and commentary upon the action on stage. But the music itself ranges enormously across the musical spectrum – from the bitonal (i.e., two conflicting keys used at the same time) violence of the dramatic moments to the gloriously lyrical arias – of which there are only two, one for the Stranger early in the first act when he anticipates and longs for freedom, and Heliane's aria in Act II – in which the undulating melody owes almost as much to Johann as to Richard Strauss. Korngold seems to be using every device he can lay his hands on to create a condition of total aural ecstasy.

Korngold outlined the musical philosophy he had espoused for *Heliane* to the *Neues Wiener Tagblatt* (23 May 1926):

The Rathaus (Town Hall) on Vienna's Ringstrasse, where Erich and Luzi were married in April 1924

*Harmonically speaking,* Heliane *is rather more radical than* Violanta *and* Die tote Stadt. *By no means do I isolate myself against the harmonic enrichments which we owe to, say, Schoenberg. But I will not give up*

The riverside centre of
Salzburg, Mozart's
birthplace, which was the
location of a brief but
blissful honeymoon for the
newly wed Korngolds

16. SALZBURG, Staatsbrücke

*claim to eminent possibilities offered by 'old music'. In my Kaltneker songs*
*there are places which one might designate as truly atonal. I do not*
*subscribe to any one doctrine. My musical creed may be called the inspired*
*idea. With what displeasure one hears this concept nowadays! And*
*nevertheless: how could the artificial construction, the most exact musical*
*mathematics, triumph over the moving principle of the inspired idea!*

The ecstasy of the *Heliane* score can hardly be coincidental, for
most of it was composed during the first two years of its composer's
marriage. On 30 April 1924 Erich Wolfgang Korngold and Luzi von
Sonnenthal were married at last in a civil ceremony at the Vienna
Town Hall. They had successfully survived their family tensions and
by six o'clock on the day of their wedding they were sitting safely on
the train to Salzburg for a short honeymoon alone. They were bliss-
fully happy. Korngold sent his new mother-in-law a postcard. 'Dear
mother! We are playing "Married". A lovely game! Luzi is always
winning.' This light-hearted attitude was, in Luzi's opinion, the key
to the continued happiness of the marriage. 'Yes, we played at being
married – all our lives.'

The brief idyll in Salzburg came to an abrupt halt when the pair
embarked on their official honeymoon travels which took them to
Paris, London, Hamburg and Berlin. With them embarked a violinist
called Robert Pollack, appointed by Julius as official escort. Seeing
the three off at the station in Vienna, Julius took Pollack aside. 'Don't
leave the children alone together!' he instructed him. Pollack unfortunately obeyed.

It is often said that after the wedding one can wake up and find
oneself married to somebody quite different. Despite their seven-year
friendship, Luzi quickly discovered that there was more to her
husband than the witty, easy-going young man she thought she had
married. 'His cheerfulness, his clear, healthy and realistic outlook
could gently obscure his true personality … I could only suspect
the private oscillations of his soul, all the more as he was a reserved
man who did not disclose himself easily.'

The immediate problem revealed itself in Paris, where the
Korngolds were guided about by the poet Paul Geraldy and met the
composer Maurice Ravel and also the son of Georges Rodenbach
(author of *Bruges-la-Morte*). Naturally this social life demanded their

Egon Pollack, director of the
Hamburg Opera, pictured
here in 1926: he conducted
the première of *Das Wunder
der Heliane*.

presence at formal dinner parties. About an hour before they were
due to leave for one, the young composer suddenly became panic-
stricken and wanted to call off the visit or go only for the dessert. At
Geraldy's house he excused himself with a headache when he saw the
many types of cutlery on the table, though when his host went to
beg him to leave the sofa in the salon on which he was lying, he found
the composer perfectly well. Soon Luzi discovered that it was only
possible for Erich to attend the theatre or a concert if he could
sit in a corner seat or in a secluded box. Apparently he was suffering
from agoraphobia.

Following page, Luzi and
Erich Korngold at their
farmhouse retreat at Alt-
Aussee, summer of 1924

Having left Robert Pollack behind at last in England, Erich and
Luzi made friends in Hamburg with another Pollack – Egon, the
conductor, who was director of the opera there. Egon Pollack and
Korngold became very close; and in 1927 it was Pollack who took on

the massive task of giving *Das Wunder der Heliane* its first performance. Berlin too had new friendships to offer – in this case the tenor Richard Tauber and the young conductor George Szell, who terrified the newly-weds with their fast driving.

Next the Korngolds went to Alt-Aussee for their summer break where two weeks alone in a farmhouse lulled them into a false sense of optimism regarding Erich's parents. Luzi was still expecting Julius and Josephine to soften towards her once they knew her better. But when the elder Korngolds arrived to join them in the Tyrol, her illusions began to splinter. To begin with, Julius did indeed seem won over, but he became increasingly critical and distrustful of his daughter-in-law. First of all, he disliked her 'dark origin' – a family of actors, albeit from one of the most distinguished theatrical figures of the country (though von Sonnenthal was rumoured to have met a blissful death, *in flagrante* in his dressing room); and he disliked her modern, cheerful and casual ways in mixed company. At a gathering at the holiday house of Friedrich Buchman, the Rosé Quartet cellist, she danced several times with a young baritone from the Vienna Opera, which induced Julius to leave the party instantly (an example of that inappropriate 'jealous husband' behaviour). And the parents had completely taken over, planning their days, taking them on unwelcome social calls and carping criticism at the young wife. As it became clear that she was pregnant the fights became worse and worse.

There was at the time a critical housing shortage in Vienna. It was only through personal string-pulling that the young couple were able to have a flat reserved. Until it was ready they had to move in with Julius and Josephine, where a room had been prepared for them – with two separate and immovable beds. The miseries of this time reinforced their resolution to make sure their marriage was happy and undisturbed by quarrels in future. In due course they were able to move out into their own apartment.

But the Korngold generations continued to fight amongst each other. It was not unusual for them to fail to speak to one another for months on end – notably once when Julius apparently wrote to his son demanding that he and Josephine should be provided for in Erich's will, which provoked an understandably angry response and a six-month break in family relations.

The Korngolds' first son was born in March 1925, while his father was absent at a performance of *Die tote Stadt*. Newspaper sniping was carrying on as ever and one paper carried the jibe that Erich Wolfgang's son would be named Johann Sebastian (not knowing that the baby's birth had originally been predicted for the great Bach's own birthday). But Ernst Werner was the chosen name, preserving his father's initials. The boy's earliest memories would be the sound of his father at the piano, composing *Das Wunder der Heliane*, in the study next to the nursery.

At around this time Korngold also wrote a set of three songs (his Op. 18, referred to in the *NWT* interview) to poems by Kaltneker. These settings have much in common with the musical as well as the poetic language of *Heliane*, rich in bitonal and, as the composer said, even atonal writing that can produce the effect of dissonant tone 'clusters', sometimes dark and tortured, sometimes almost violently ecstatic. 'In meine innige nacht' ('Into my deep night') is the darkest of the three, while the dense and virtuoso piano writing in 'Tu ab den Schmerz' ('Away with pain') and 'Versuchung' ('Temptation') mirrors the colours of *Heliane*'s huge orchestra. In these songs Korngold offers not so much a midway point between Mahler and Johann Strauss as between Mahler and Messiaen.

That autumn Korngold had further 'Strauss-expert' duties to perform, conducting *Eine Nacht in Venedig* in Berlin, with Richard Tauber as lead tenor, and then being invited to Copenhagen for the first time, where he would conduct Johann Strauss's *Die Fledermaus*. Stopping in Berlin on the way to Copenhagen, Korngold was approached by Richard Strauss's publisher, Otto Fürstner, who was prepared to offer him a massive sum of money for his new opera. Korngold turned the offer down. Repeated entreaties, well oiled with champagne, made no difference. Since his father's fight with Universal Edition many years earlier, Korngold had been contracted to the Mainz-based firm Schott's, which offered him a small honorarium in contrast to the large fee proposed by Fürstner, and he felt it would be ungrateful behaviour to abandon his publisher.

After a summer 'holiday' in Semmering, where Korngold worked intensively on *Heliane*, Erich and Luzi stopped on their way to Mainz in Salzburg, where they visited the conductor Bruno Walter, by now a seasoned interpreter of Korngold's music. He was then the director

A sketch of the conductor Franz Schalk, who became sole director of the Vienna State Opera after Strauss's resignation

of the Charlottenburg Opera in Berlin and responded positively to Erich's hope that he might give the new opera its first airing. The Korngolds went on to visit a number of towns in Germany to discuss possible productions. In Nuremburg a huge rally of the National Socialist Party was taking place. Luzi, left alone in the hotel while her husband visited the opera director in the evening, looked out of the window to see a torchlit procession of Nazis stamping by and was filled with a vague sense of horror. Preoccupied with their family and artistic lives, the Korngolds were still apolitical and relatively unaware of the rising tide of the far right.

In one ongoing feud, Julius Korngold had finally won: in 1924 Richard Strauss resigned from the Vienna Opera, prompted in no small measure by Julius's continuous criticism. Franz Schalk – the one-time fellow student of Julius and the ally who had first conducted *Der Schneemann* – was left as sole director. Thus it was possible for the Vienna Staatsoper to be the only opera house not to announce a performance of a work that had achieved major success on its pre-mière in Leipzig in February 1927: *Jonny spielt auf*, by a young composer named Ernst Krenek. The opera was sensationalistic, used unlikely stage effects and committed the heinous crime of being inspired by the new music that was rampaging through Europe from black America: jazz. (Despite the popular craze for jazz, the Nazis condemned it because of the origins that they despised.) Despite *Jonny*'s popularity everywhere else, Franz Schalk stuck by the incensed opinion of his old friend Julius Korngold and refused to stage it. It seems extraordinary that any critic could come to have this degree of control over an opera house's artistic policy.

Was Julius Korngold's opinion of *Jonny spielt auf* really an objective one? Certainly he would have hated the work, himself having an intense dislike of jazz. And the irreverent attitude of the opera to what Julius, with nineteenth-century pomposity, considered his lofty 'sacred art', cannot have helped. The story shows Jonny, a jazz-band leader, stealing the fiddle of his concert violinist friend Daniello and making the entire world dance the Charleston. The focus of the tale is the old order giving way to the new (i.e., black American jazz), provocative to Julius and Hitler alike. All the same, it seems unlikely that the fervour with which Julius opposed it at this particular time could have been purely coincidental. For, although his son had finished the piano score of *Heliane* in Semmering in summer 1925, signed the publishing contract with Schott's on Christmas Eve that year and finished orches-trating the opera the following spring, it took a very long time for Schott's to produce the score and parts – small wonder, given their complexity. Korngold hoped for a double première in spring 1927, in Hamburg and Vienna, though that was soon proved impossible. A rival new opera, of such contrasted and essentially populist character, staged at the same time as *Heliane*, was certainly a threat to the mystical and complicated new opera by Julius's son.

Franz Schalk did not have the final say in the matter: the general manager of Austrian state theatres, Franz Schneiderhan, saw *Jonny*'s

Ernst Krenek around 1929: his opera *Jonny spielt auf* was the antithesis of Korngold's *Heliane*.

potential for box-office draw and insisted that it be staged at the
Vienna Opera. That gave Julius another opportunity to air his views
in favour of artistic autonomy for the opera's director and to speak up
against Krenek and his publisher, Universal Edition – the same
publisher that seventeen years earlier had allowed the staging of *Der
Schneemann* without Julius Korngold's consent.

Schalk and Korngold *père* soon found some surprising allies in
their campaign against the jazz opera. Schalk had German friends who
were allied to the National Socialist Party, the musical policies of
which were violently opposed to jazz, modernism, the twelve-note
serialist school and anything remotely negro or Jewish. Schalk's friends
mobilized the appropriate forces to the conductor's aid. It may seem
astonishing that Nazi propaganda should have spoken up on the same
side as a Jewish music critic – and how surprising to find similar
diatribes in the *Neue Freie Presse* (run by a Jew, Moritz Benedikt), in
Nazi newspapers and in such journals as the *Zeitschrift für Musik*,
founded by the idealistic Schumann, but by then in the forefront of
the campaign against the jazz-influenced composers Krenek and
Kurt Weill. But the Nazis were not actually speaking up in favour of
Korngold – only against Krenek and his 'degenerate' (*entartete*) music.
Julius Korngold was being used while his reactionary opinions and
influential position were expedient.

While Julius Korngold was waging his ideological war, Erich
Korngold was trying to solve the more practical problem of who
would sing the leading role in *Heliane* for the Viennese première.
Maria Jeritza was not available to perform the phenomenally
demanding part that he had composed for her. Korngold did all he
could to rearrange the schedules to accommodate her, but Jeritza
had been invited to appear in the USA, where she had made a great
success with her first appearance, as Marietta in *Die tote Stadt*, and
given the problems which already surrounded the new opera, she
declined the role. She may also have been deterred not only by the
technical difficulty of the role of *Heliane*, but also by its character,
which though composed for her was very different from those roles
for which she had become so celebrated (although Jeritza was
astonishingly versatile both as actress and singer). Salome, Carmen
and Marietta have in common a powerful sexuality and strength of
will. Heliane, however, had a Madonna-like purity; her struggle is

Lotte Lehmann, the 'elemental and womanly' soprano who first sang the role of Heliane in Vienna

inward and, although she has at one point to appear 'naked', her conflicts bypass the physical aspect of sexuality in favour of the spiritual, which is altogether more difficult to portray charismatically on stage. So the première was put off again until October. Ironically, Jeritza never did sing in *Heliane*.

A possible leading lady of a very different nature was the classically lyrical Lotte Lehmann. She was dubious when offered the role. Korngold won her agreement by playing the whole score to her at his home (using only his own piano and voice!). He in turn was delighted by her qualities and is even quoted as saying: 'One half of Vienna is for the fascinating Jeritza, the other for the sweet Lotte Lehmann. Who wins? I am more for heart and head, for the elemental and womanly and therefore: Lehmann is my motto!' Lehmann did bear some grudge against Jeritza, who had thoroughly upstaged her in Korngold's double bill in which Lehmann sang Laura in *Polykrates* and Jeritza was Violanta; Jeritza's refusal of *Heliane* may have spurred

At the dress rehearsal of
*Das Wunder der Heliane*:
left to right, Hamburg
Stadttheater intendant
Leopold Sachse, conductor
Egon Pollack, a nervous
Korngold and the enigmatic
librettist Hans Müller

Lehmann on to prove her wrong. Although Lehmann enjoyed the role of Heliane, she did claim later that it had perhaps not been well suited to her.

The role of the Stranger was to be taken in Vienna by a young Polish tenor named Jan Kiepura, who had stunned the city when he arrived for the first time to sing Calaf in the Viennese première of Puccini's *Turandot*. With lashings of charisma, good looks and a high, penetrating voice which could sustain its power across the vast orchestra Korngold had set out, he seemed the perfect choice for the part. Lehmann hated him.

The Hamburg première was set for 7 October 1927, the Viennese première for 29 October and anticipation in the press was growing. Now not only were there diatribes against *Jonny* but also articles in favour of the new Korngold opera, by such eminent critics as Richard Specht, Hans Liebestockl and Ferdinand Pfohl – although common sense and experience should perhaps have dictated that it is always a mistake to build up a new work before its public has had a chance to make up its own mind, especially in a critical city like Vienna.

Jan Kiepura, the Polish tenor, was a tremendous success in Vienna when he first appeared there in Puccini's *Turandot*; but even he could not sing the role of the Stranger two nights running.

Egon Pollack took the baton for the first performance of *Das Wunder der Heliane* at the Hamburg Stadttheater. Maria Hussa sang the leading role with Carl Günther as the Stranger and Rudolf Bockelmann as the Ruler; the production was directed by Leopold Sachse. Hamburg, being 'Korngold's town', was perhaps the most naturally receptive place for the opera's launch and its opening promised well. But in Vienna, where Schalk conducted a spectacular production led by Lehmann and Kiepura, *Heliane* got off to a bad start that was more accidental than artistic. A second cast had been announced for the second night, which increased the city's expectations since consecutive performances were not common. In the second cast, Alfred Piccaver, a lyrical tenor who had starred in *Der Ring des Polykrates*, had been assigned the role of the Stranger. Thanks to a personal feud between Piccaver and Schalk, the tenor at the last moment refused to learn the part. A press release quickly made the excuse that the role would have made excessive demands on the qualities of his voice. No other singer knew the part and even Kiepura could not sing that role on consecutive nights, so the performance was cancelled and Schalk put on *Die tote Stadt* in its place. The immediate general assumption was that Korngold's new opera was a failure.

The Viennese première of *Jonny* was to take place on New Year's Eve. Fired up by the press campaigns, it sold out well in advance. Nazi exhortations to keep it out continued: the broadsheet *Deutsch-Österreichische Tageszeitung*, or '*Dötz*' as it was known, gave its front page over to an outcry against 'Jewish desecration' and the 'pornographic plot', and on the evening Nazi youth attempted to picket out the public. And, more surprisingly, *Dötz* reprinted Julius Korngold's twelve-column review of the opera in an attempt to prove its lack of musical worth. Naturally, everybody wanted to see this infamous composition! 'The box office exceeded my direst expectations,' commented the dismayed Schalk. 'We have a success without an opera!'

A marvellous irony: Warner Brothers' *The Jazz Singer*, the first 'talkie', received its première the day after *Das Wunder der Heliane*, in October 1927. Korngold later wrote film music almost exclusively for Warners.

In fact, *Heliane* was not such a flop. Despite the controversies surrounding it, reviews had been reasonable and it had drawn good box office figures. And when the Austrian Tobacco Company cashed in on the furore and produced two new cigarettes named Jonny and Heliane, the latter boasted lilac paper and a golden mouthpiece which resembled a rose petal and sold at an inflated price, while Jonny was

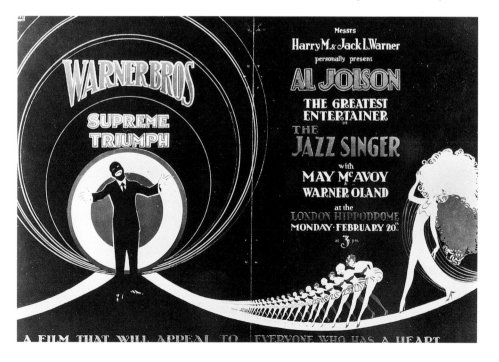

just a 'cheap smoke'. (However, Jonny is still available years later, while Heliane was discontinued!) The sensationalization of *Jonny spielt auf* cast *Heliane* into shadow and led to fewer performances being scheduled; outside Vienna, other cities which planned to produce it were put off by the rumpus and by the sheer difficulty of staging the opera – six of an original eighteen other towns cancelled their productions.

It was Berlin, now a major centre for experimental music and home to modernist composers including Schoenberg, Hindemith, Weill and Krenek himself, which finally dealt the death-blow to *Heliane* – with the help of its composer's father. In 1928 a lavish and surreal production by a renowned director, Oscar Strnad, was planned for the Berlin première, to be conducted by Bruno Walter. All might have been well had Julius Korngold been able to let sleeping dogs lie. But he could not. To every German theatre that had planned to stage *Jonny spielt auf,* he sent a copy of his article against it, exhorting them not to proceed with their productions. Universal Edition, at the head of the Krenek faction, printed advertisements in every newspaper denouncing Julius Korngold's action and quoting the opera's rave reviews beside Korngold's article. This was timed to hit the build-up to *Heliane*'s first performance dead in the centre. Naturally it mobilized feeling against Julius Korngold and against his son's opera which necessarily flopped, through no fault of its own.

The fight between Krenek and Julius Korngold did not end there. In 1932 Krenek and Willi Reich, a musicologist and pupil of Alban Berg, launched a magazine called *23* – the number of a press regulation which permitted anyone to demand a printed rectification of an error in a newspaper. The first edition spent much bile over the critic they named 'Onkel Julius' and reprinted a twenty-year-old comment about the way he had pushed his son's career. True to form, Julius sued – drawing much greater attention to the new magazine than it would otherwise have received.

*Das Wunder der Heliane* had its world première on 7 October 1927. On 8 October another première took place on the other side of the Atlantic: *The Jazz Singer,* the first motion picture with sound. The irony of this timing could not have been stronger.

*5*

A sketch of Julius Korngold by
B. F. Dolbin for *The Musical
Courier*. The critic is shown
listening to Erich conducting
the incidental music to *Much
Ado About Nothing*.

*… the stream of rhythm on which he launched
his orchestra flowed freely, melodies rippled
with laughter and surged with passion, while
harmonies were pure and deep as an alpine
lake. Not one rubato, crescendo or diminuendo
was calculated or 'voulu'. In obedience to some
inner law of his, they were simply right and
unassailable.*

Gottfried Reinhardt describes Korngold's
conducting

# Opera and Operetta 1927–34

In the early 1930s a popular poll by the *Neues Wiener Tagblatt* named
Arnold Schoenberg and Erich Wolfgang Korngold as the two greatest
living Austrian composers. But by that time, Korngold was writing
less and less music of his own and concentrating more on the
arrangement of operetta. It was not only financial necessity which had
driven him to it. Korngold was deeply demoralized by the fiascos
which surrounded what he knew to be his greatest work, *Heliane*. His
father's description, in his memoirs, of the havoc in his son's soul, and
Julius's own admission of responsibility, verges on the tragic:

> *The Berlin experience had a disastrous psychological effect on Erich.
> Being wronged, persecuted by an active musical party, boycotted in its
> German sphere of influence, he awakened from the naïve dream of
> creation and lost his joy in it. These were hard times for me also, since
> I had to admit to myself that my convictions as a critic had contributed
> to reprisals against my son.*

Korngold's involvement with operetta arrangement provided him
with a welcome contrast from the in-fighting and scandals of the
world of grand opera. In 1927, alongside preparing *Heliane*, he had
worked on the arrangement of a Johann Strauss operetta, *Cagliostro
in Wien*. In 1929 he not only arranged but also completed an unfin-
ished operetta by Leo Fall entitled *Rosen aus Florida*. 'I am looking for
an opera libretto. However, I can't find one,' Korngold told the
*Hamburger Zeitung*. 'Therefore I've kept to operetta, to Strauss and
Fall. I need a regular outlet for the reservoir of good humour which
underlies this working "adultery".'

His enthusiasm for these pieces is evident: the Leo Fall work,
which in its final form offers a fair number of Korngold original
songs and arias, is a light, fluffy operetta in which there is some very
beautiful music, notably an aria for the Russian princess Irina in the
second act. In the third act, Korngold provided 'variation' numbers

for the contestants in a 'Miss World'-type beauty contest: each entrant appears to her own national style of music. Miss Austria enters with a Viennese waltz tune of Korngold's creation. Later in Hollywood, reworked into march tempo and fitted to the background of Robin Hood and his band of merry men, that tune helped to win Korngold an Oscar. The operetta was a great success and played for more than 200 performances. It does seem extraordinary that the composer of *Die tote Stadt* and *Das Wunder der Heliane* should also have excelled in operetta. Opera and operetta were slowly becoming, for Korngold, virtually the musical equivalents of his own Marie and Marietta.

In 1926 Korngold had been approached by an exceptional artist whom he had encountered briefly during his child prodigy days: the renowned Max Reinhardt, who, at his Salzburg Festival, was presenting for the first time Schiller's drama *Turandot*. Korngold refused to accept the task of writing incidental music for it. Puccini's

Max Reinhardt, photographed in 1934 during his stay in Hollywood to direct *A Midsummer Night's Dream* – a portrait full of light, shade and dramatic depth, much in the style of Reinhardt's own approach to drama

opera of the same title was being given its première that same year and that was deterrent enough.

Max Reinhardt, born in Baden in 1873, started out as an actor at the Deutsches Theater in Berlin, where he went on to be appointed director. In the first three decades of the twentieth century he staged 455 plays, drawn most frequently to the great dramatic works of Shakespeare, Molière, Goethe, Strindberg, Wedekind, Ibsen and Shaw, but not above turning his attention to musical comedy. When he approached the Austro–Hungarian Emperor Charles in 1917 with the idea of making Salzburg the home of a cultural festival his idealism was clear, not only for the theatre but all art; in 1919, a year after approval was granted for the Salzburg Festival, the credo he published with Hugo von Hofmannsthal ran: 'Theatre and opera shall be developed to the highest degree and Salzburg will become a cultural beacon to the entire world'. Reinhardt's postscript stated: 'We want to bring to the world a spiritual renaissance with our dramatic presentations and beauty and joy with Mozart's music.' To this day the Salzburg Festival continues to offer that cultural beacon of high standards.

Dramatically, Reinhardt's productions emphasized experiment and intensity, playing with light and colour, drawing out the depths of the dramatists' mood and the psychology behind the action. Acting was to him 'the truest form of life'; he believed 'the true actor does not dissemble but unveils'. True to this powerful spirit of idealism, he formed not only a Reinhardt Theatre in Vienna but a Reinhardt Seminar in 1929 to train young actors, where he and his wife Helene Thimig placed emphasis on 'learning through doing': 'Jump into the water and swim!' And Reinhardt influenced everyone who came into contact with him. His productions revolutionized theatre – for if other directors were not trying to emulate him, they would deliberately be doing precisely the opposite.

Reinhardt became Korngold's most regular stage collaborator. And the great director and his wife also became close friends of Erich and Luzi Korngold, a friendship that lasted all their lives and saw them through the trauma of escaping Europe and moving to the USA. It was an interesting pairing. Korngold was warm and generous, Reinhardt imperious, charismatic and with a tendency, as some people felt, to view those who worked under him simply as a vehicle with

which to realize his own artistic vision, although he would make a
point of asking opinions and discussing aspects of the work in hand
and listening to the opinions of those he worked with, as Korngold
was to find. Many years later, in Hollywood, Korngold's son Ernst
became a student of Reinhardt. He recalled the way Reinhardt would
rehearse his actors, summoning them with a 'You!' – never by name
(perhaps learning names was a distraction from the purpose of theatre)
– and then demanding of them something which at first seemed
impossible. 'It was impossible – but they would do it, for him.'

Reinhardt may have been a demanding taskmaster, but his satellites
were devoted to him, recognizing his genius. Luzi Korngold found
herself blushing desperately when introduced to the great man,
although subsequently in the fifteen years that the Korngolds knew
him he called her by name on one occasion only. When she met
him in New York shortly before his death and he referred to her
husband by his first name, Luzi was more moved by this than by all
the complimentary things Reinhardt had to say about Korngold's
achievements. 'Who would ever have left a wish of Reinhardt
unfulfilled?' wrote Luzi. '… When Reinhardt turned away with
disappointed or resigned grey eyes, one felt guilty, as if one had taken
a favourite toy from a child.' He 'possessed the unique ability to …
keep people at a distance and at the same time to get the best and
the last of everything out of them.'

Korngold stood by his refusal to write the incidental music for
*Turandot*. His next encounter with Reinhardt, however, turned out
very differently. In 1929 Reinhardt invited him to arrange and
conduct Offenbach's operetta *La Vie parisienne* for a new production
at the Deutsches Theater in Berlin, which needed something light
and popular to fill its auditorium over the summer months. Korngold
went into the meeting with severe doubts about the project – and
came out with a contract to arrange Johann Strauss's *Die Fledermaus*
instead. When he told Reinhardt his reservations towards the
quality of the Offenbach work, the director asked him to suggest for
something else and Korngold made the inspired exclamation, 'Why
don't you do *Die Fledermaus*?' By the end of the meeting Reinhardt
had not only accepted the idea as if nothing else had ever been
considered but also called his secretary to book immediately a young
singer named Maria Rajdl whom Korngold had recommended to
sing the leading role of Rosalinde.

Reinhardt intended to give the operetta a total rewrite, as far as the story was concerned. According to his son Gottfried's memoirs, the director hated triteness and had a 'deep aversion to the sham Vienna depicted by coy and sentimental operetta kitsch'. And the 'cute slapstick' of *Die Fledermaus* would also have 'offended him'. Even managerial considerations would not have overcome his resistance to it, 'had Korngold not played the score on the piano for him and shed such radiance on the familiar airs that he was bewitched by the interpreter.'

Korngold's house at 35 Sternwartestrasse, Vienna, as it looks in the 1990s

Korngold's continued involvement with operetta was as important to the family financially as it was 'fun' for the composer. The imminent arrival of a second child in 1928 had made it necessary for them to move to a new home, 35 Sternwartestrasse, a large and pleasant semi-detached house on a leafy hill in the suburbs a short way northwest from the centre of Vienna. Georg, nicknamed 'Schurli', was born on 17 December 1928.

The new Reinhardt–Korngold *Fledermaus* came into being over a matter of weeks in Berlin. Korngold did not so much alter the score as expand it with delightful extra pieces numbered as, for instance, 'No 2½' or 'No 6¼', lifted and adapted from Strauss's wonderful repertoire of waltzes, polkas and the like. They were provided with words by Reinhardt, who let his sharp theatrical wit loose on the dramatic contexts of the farce and gave the work a tauter and slightly more credible story. The difficult singing parts of Rosalinde, Adele and Eisenstein were allocated to professional singers; the rest of the cast were mostly actors.

The plot, in its best-known form, concerns the revenge of Dr Falke on one Eisenstein following a practical joke on Falke who was at the time clothed for a fancy-dress ball as a bat (*Fledermaus*). Eisenstein is in debt and is supposed to be escorted to jail. Eisenstein's wife Rosalinde is being heavily courted by the singer Alfred; the maid Adele is trying to make excuses to get the evening off to go to Prince Orlofsky's ball. A crazy evening at Orlofsky's ball ensues with all the characters present, mostly in disguise, which results in a number of hilarious situations. In the final act the confusion is somehow resolved in the jail, with the effect of champagne blamed for the whole thing.

It is hardly a credible sort of plot, but in musical glory it is nevertheless Johann Strauss's masterpiece. And the Korngold–Reinhardt

A programme from
Berlin's Deutches Theater; the
performance celebrated
Reinhardt's twenty-fifth
anniversary as its director.

arrangement quite astonishingly makes a masterpiece into an even greater masterpiece. The characters come to life. Eisenstein is obsessed with gourmet food; Rosalinde really is having an affair with Alfred and Adele blackmails her in order to get her night out, threatening to go and make the bed; Prince Orlofsky is played by a man in place of the usual 'trouser-role' female alto. The second act party at Prince Orlofsky's palace includes a superb 'Septettino' where characters overhear themselves being talked about and interject at a fantastic pace on individual notes of the waltz melody. The additional numbers culminate in an extra waltz and a toast proposed in waltz rhythm by Orlofsky which leads straight into the Champagne Song – after which the audience is bombarded with Strauss's glorious numbers one after another until they are, as Luzi put it, in a state resembling 'blissful drunkeness'. The dramas as set up in Act I lend some measure of sense to the zany resolutions of Act III. And the whole operetta begins not with Alfred's serenade but with Falke, dressed in his Bat costume, dancing around the stage alone to the melody of *Geschichten aus dem Wienerwald* ('Tales from the Vienna Woods') – for he alone is in control of the action to follow. The Reinhardt–Korngold *Fledermaus* was first performed on 8 June 1929 and played, mostly to sold-out houses, for no fewer than eighty-six performances at the Deutsches Theater that season. A young violinist named Yehudi Menuhin, for one, was left 'walking on air for three days afterwards'.

Korngold conducted the work himself. His style of conducting was quintessentially Viennese – spacious, yet with exceptional rhythmic precision, unexaggerated but full of humanity, tenderness and warmth. The sound was velvety and luscious, the tempos excellently judged with a real feeling for theatrical pace. (Fortunately for us, the film musical he wrote for Paramount Pictures, *Give Us This Night*, can still provide an impression of how a Viennese operetta would have sounded as conducted by Korngold.) Gottfried Reinhardt described the style:

> … *the stream of rhythm on which he launched his orchestra flowed freely, melodies rippled with laughter and surged with passion, while harmonies were pure and deep as an alpine lake. Not one rubato, crescendo or diminuendo was calculated or 'voulu'. In obedience to some inner law of his, they were simply right and unassailable. (When I*

*did* La Belle Hélène *with him on Broadway fifteen years later, Arturo Toscanini sat in the audience at least once a week, hypnotised by Korngold, his counterpole.)*

Korngold accompanied his inserted scenes himself on the piano. Gottfried Reinhardt wrote: 'Of those crash-smashing hands the greatest pianist of his time, Artur Schnabel, once said to me, "With those two fat puddings of his, Erich Korngold plays the piano better than all the stiletto-fingered virtuosos I have ever heard."'

Gottfried Reinhardt also casts an interesting light on the relationship between his father and Korngold. Here is part of his account of the première of the new *Die Fledermaus* – exaggerated on all counts, but as vivid a personal recollection as one could hope to find:

*… a pasty-faced, round shouldered, jelly-bellied young man wheezing under the weight of an old man's fat stepped up to the conductor's stand in the pit … I saw my father smiling encouragement back at him and applauding (taboo of all theatrical taboos before an opening!). With this boost, Korngold pinwheeled toward the proscenium box and collapsed reverently before Frau Strauss; then … sprang up again and connected his pudgy paw to a slim baton. Extending both arms to the orchestra, he gestured that he was drowning and begging for help.*

*It puzzled me to see my father, to whom human ugliness was an unforgiveable sin, glowing with pleasure at the sight of this flailing bulk, the more so since he had always been opposed to the spotlighted presence of a conductor distracting from the performance. That this musical seal must distract from the performance was obvious to me. Until he flapped his fins for the overture to begin and, with the first whiplash of chords and cascading strings, I and everyone else in the audience were spellbound. I had heard the piece countless times before, performed by greater virtuosos, but never before with such drama, gaiety, elegance and mischievousness. It was then that the first magic transformation of the evening took place. Before my eyes, Korngold grew beautiful …*

*My father adored transformations. One quick glance at him was enough for me to detect how deeply he had fallen in love.*

Korngold's involvement with operetta took precedence over his own compositions for several years after the stagings of *Heliane*. The downfall of the opera was for the composer the bursting of a bubble of musical adventure: never again did he attempt a work with such esoteric subject matter or such complicated musical content. Even his late Symphony, in which there are echoes from time to time of the colourful bitonal writing, the attempt feels a little half-hearted. From now on, Korngold wanted to be more assured of popular success.

Popular success also enabled him, through his operetta work, to help a friend in need. Julius Bittner was fighting a losing battle against untreatable diabetes, which in due course led to the amputation of both his legs. Korngold, in a typically generous gesture, decided to help him (though Bittner was a successful lawyer and was probably financially solvent) by including his works in concerts which he conducted and by signing over to him proceeds from his work on his next Strauss operetta, an intimate piece based on the story of the Strauss family itself and entitled *Walzer aus Wien* ('Waltzes from Vienna'). This work was later transformed into a musical called *The Great Waltz* (of which, in turn, nothing was left by the time Hollywood created a film of the same title).

The seven original works Korngold composed between his operas *Das Wunder der Heliane* (Op. 20) and *Die Kathrin* (Op. 28) are strung out in time between 1927 and 1935, which represents a serious slowing down of creative activity. According to Luzi, who was worried by her husband's preoccupation with light theatrical arrangements, he would sit down punctually at his desk every morning to compose. Among these works are his fiery and virtuoso Third Piano Sonata in C major (Op. 25), a series of three songs – his opus 22 dedicated to his mother – his Second String Quartet, the song cycle *Unvergänglichkeit* (the published English title is 'The Eternal') and an unusual Suite written for two violins, cello and piano left-hand, at the request of Wittgenstein. The songs were first performed as a set on New Year's Day 1930 in Vienna, the Suite on 21 October 1930, the Piano Sonata on 3 March 1932, the String Quartet not until 16 March 1934 and the song cycle on 27 October 1937.

The Piano Sonata, bearing the inscription 'Dedicated to Julius Bittner in friendship', is less weighty than his second sonata, but is full of Korngoldian upswing and exuberance. The first movement contrasts a fanfare-like first theme with a lyrical, upwardly yearning second subject that could easily have formed a tenor love song in *Die Kathrin*. The short *andante religioso* is more redolent of *Heliane*, using the full range of the piano's pitch and dynamic abilities to create another glowing Korngold dream-world in which major and minor chords change places eerily. The third movement, Tempo di Menuetto, harks back to the graceful, neo-classical world of *Polykrates*: a simple melody is increasingly decorated with counterthemes and chromatic underlay. And the Rondo's closest relative is the hornpipe from *Much Ado*: strong, cheerful rhythmic motion, upward surges in both line and dynamics, terrifically energetic and demanding – certainly an outlet from that Korngold reservoir of good humour.

To celebrate the birth of his second son, Georg, in 1928, Korngold wrote a suite called *Babyserenade*, Op. 24, scored for fourteen brass instruments, banjo, piano, harp, percussion and string orchestra. Its five movements portray scenes in Baby's young life, including a jazz number and finishing with a lullaby. That was the first appearance of a 'jazz' movement in Korngold's music. He was as good at jazz pastiche

Korngold with his younger son, Georg (later known as George), in California during the mid-1930s. Georg was the dedicatee of his father's *Babyserenade*.

as he was at Strauss, although the style is so far removed from
his big operatic works that it feels as if he is simply surrendering to
commercial pressure in using it. Sweet, melodic and spirited, this
piece had its première on 5 December 1932, by which time Baby
Georg was just short of four years old.

Although these works contain much beautiful music, it is clear that
Korngold is not attempting anything like the scale of serious form
and content that he might have been expected to aspire to after
creating a work the size of *Heliane*. None of the works from opus 21
(piano arrangements of Strauss) to opus 27 (*Unvergänglichkeit*) is truly
substantial. Korngold was either too busy, too disheartened or both
to give his musical powers their full freedom.

A further distraction from composition came with Korngold's
appointment in 1930 to run an opera class at the Vienna State
Academy, in collaboration with the producer Lothar Wallenstein.
But the job was short-lived. The Academy's bureaucratic inflexibility
soon came into conflict with Korngold's enthusiasm and high
standards. He would put on, and play the piano for, public performances of operatic extracts in the Academy's theatre. Rules demanded
that no encores be given, but on one occasion the audience response
was so enthusiastic that he took it upon himself to repeat a number.
This was frowned on. Not long afterwards he took an orchestral
rehearsal of d'Albert's *Tiefland*, which called for a high standard of
cor anglais playing. When dying duck sounds from the wind section
proved that this young musician had been learning his instrument for
just one week, Korngold complained to the academy president; on
hearing the unsympathetic refusal of his objections, Korngold walked
out of the Academy and never went back.

Korngold's next collaboration with Max Reinhardt was on
Offenbach's operetta *La Belle Hélène* (*Die Schöne Helena*). They
worked on the text with the writers Egon Friedell and Hans
Sassmann. Friedell, a real Renaissance man who was also fond of
practical jokes, became a close friend of the Korngolds. As with
*Fledermaus*, Korngold and Reinhardt expanded on the original
Offenbach music with extracts arranged from the composer's other
works. But once again Korngold's gift for pastiche came in useful.
Time grew short and Reinhardt was uncomfortable with his results,
despite the talented cast (including the soprano Jarmila Novotna in

the title role). Reinhardt, who according to his son was 'prone to these desperate situations' and 'life or death decisions', demanded that Korngold provide an epilogue for the lovely young actress Friedl Schuster who played the small part of Orest. Reinhardt saw in Schuster a 'secret weapon' – and he was right – but by this time there were only fourteen hours left until curtain up. Rather than plundering Offenbach's entire output looking for a suitable tune, not to mention words, Korngold put to good use his gift for pastiche composition and wrote, overnight, a new piece for Schuster to sing in front of the curtain as if in 'intimate dialogue with the audience'. Sassmann hurriedly produced some lyrics, Schuster learned the piece in two hours and later the same evening, 15 June 1931, Gottfried Reinhardt found himself in the audience at the Theater am Kurfurstendam, 'watching Berlin lie at Friedl Schuster's enchanting feet'.

While *Schöne Helena* was undoubtedly good for Berlin, Berlin was less good for its musical director's health. Korngold was staying on the Kurfürstendam opposite the theatre, in the same building as a famous cake shop, Rumpelmeyer. He loved sweet food and, as Luzi recalled, 'during the whole rehearsal period our meals consisted of chocolate ice cream and cake'. Reinhardt and Korngold would often sit up the whole night talking, ending only with breakfast of chocolate ice cream and cake at Rumpelmeyer's and snatching a few hours' sleep before the next rehearsal began. Their wives despaired. 'When he worked,' wrote Luzi, 'he had no concept of time and it happened more than once that he assured me something would take ten minutes at the most and then left me for a full two hours standing in the street or sitting in the car.'

Luzi Korngold went back to Austria to take the children to the countryside for a holiday at Aschau bei Ischl, but Erich Korngold went to a sanatorium in Loschwitz, near Dresden, for a serious diet. If Gottfried Reinhardt's account of his appearance while conducting is remotely accurate, it was certainly needed. But he gave it up in misery after barely two weeks, having lost some, but not much, of his weight.

He did, however, manage to lose all the savings from the money he earned on *Schöne Helena*. Luzi had brought warning from a Viennese friend that there were bad rumours about the state of the Darmstadter Bank. Her husband's reaction was 'Ridiculous!' He went straight to that very bank with his savings from his fee, to find that it was slightly past closing time. A clerk was still working inside and Korngold knocked until the door was opened, after which he spent some time persuading the reluctant fellow to accept the sizeable deposit, telling him that he had heard the bank was in trouble and wanted to prove his confidence in it. The very next day the bank went into liquidation. This, wrote Luzi, was typical of her husband's character. 'He, who was not at all careless or foolish in matters of money, stubbornly risked and lost his hard-won fee just to be true to his conviction. His sense of humour saved him from feeling any regret about this self-induced loss.'

Luzi was herself gifted with a ready wit and sense of humour. During the infuriating period of the *Schöne Helena* preparation, she wrote and drew a book of verses and caricatures called *Max und Erich*, based on the very popular German children's books *Max und Moritz* by Wilhelm Busch. 'Luzhelm Buschgold' portrayed the exploits of her own two characters, who like their prototypes were naughty but lovable, and the choice was more than appropriate since in the original *Max und Moritz* there is even a character named Schöne Helena.

Back in Vienna, having abandoned his 'cure', Korngold began once again to look for a new subject for an opera. He was drawn to a story by Franc-Nohain, the author of Ravel's *L'Heure espagnol*, called *The Chinese Hat*. Delighted by the fairy-tale, he composed the better part of a one-act opera in a matter of days, only to be told that the Society of Authors demanded an impossibly high fee for the rights to the story. Sadly he abandoned the idea. But something else soon caught his attention: a novella by Heinrich Edward Jacob entitled *The Maid of Aachen*. This project was to become Korngold's *Die Kathrin* and its history shows us not only the troubled times in which Vienna was now increasingly immersed but also the composer's continued idealism – or naïvety – in the face of impending political disaster.

The story was heart-warming and inspiring: a love affair between a German maidservant and a French soldier, implying the alliance of opposing nations through good, loving human beings. Korngold was attracted to it for its lyrical qualities and its sense of humanity and ethics. Julius Korngold suggested as librettist the music writer Ernst Decsey, a Vienna correspondent for the *Berliner Tagblatt* and a frequent and friendly critic of Korngold's works. Composer and writer both set to work with excitement. As the work progressed into 1932, Korngold wanted to send his publisher Schott's a report on the new opera and arranged a meeting in Passau. Korngold described the story and was horrified when he found himself facing his first disagreement with a publisher since 1910. His old friend Willy Strecker said to him: 'You can't do that.' Strecker insisted that the story would not be taken in good part, that there was still too much bitterness in Germany to accept the sight on stage of an alliance with France. To the composer's bewildered arguments he replied: 'I don't think you know what's happening, Erich.'

What was happening? After the Wall Street Crash of 1929, Germany went into a period of economic decline. Musical life was affected in a number of ways – in reduced subsidies for the arts, shortened performance seasons and high unemployment, made more severe by the simultaneous catching-on of the sound cinema which

A German newspaper shot of hectic trading on the New York Stock Exchange. European (and especially German) economies were severely affected by the Wall Street Crash – it almost certainly contributed to the financial necessity of Korngold's commercial work in operetta.

put thousands of musicians from cinema orchestras out of work. Music and politics were growing increasingly entwined; the right-wing music press was a powerful voice and conservative feeling ran strongly against anything that its sympathizers felt was directed against the 'purity' and 'spiritual regeneration' of Germanic musical tradition. At the same time, anti-Semitism against musicians was being expressed in weighty tomes by such German authors as Hans Joachim Moser in his three-volume *Geschichte der deutschen Musik* ('History of German Music') (1924) which was crucial in shaping Nazi musical ideology, and Richard Eichenauer's *Musik und Rasse* ('Music and Race') (1932), arguing vitriolically against the prevalence of Jews in influential musical positions, dismissing Mendelssohn and Mahler as superficial, and gaining full endorsement under the Hitler regime.

In such a climate, a Jewish composer dramatizing a work by a Jewish novelist on the subject of a German girl's relationship with a foreign soldier would seem to have found the worst possible moment to come forward in the guise of an exciting new project. Why should Korngold have tried it? Was he that ignorant of current events? Or was he, as ever, an idealist? His musical outlook was so traditional, compared to the figures of Schoenberg, Stravinsky, Krenek and Weill whom the Nazis abhorred, and his racial position was so utterly assimilated, that it probably would never have occurred to him that his music too could fall under the right-wing axe. And he was an optimist as well as an idealist. He still believed that humanity would hold its own, despite the upheavals taking place around him. In any case, no rational mind can really believe in the possibility of a holocaust until it is plunged into the heart of it, where rational thought has no further relevance.

Jacob himself became an early victim of the witch-hunt later the same year, dismissed from his post as newspaper correspondent in November. Under the Nazi regime in 1938 his books were banned and he was deported to concentration camps at Dachau and Buchenwald. Amazingly, he managed to escape and emigrated to New York.

Disappointed over a beloved project for a second time, Erich packed up his sketches for *Die Kathrin* and disregarded his wife's suggestions that the setting of the story could be changed. They set off to spent the summer travelling and house-hunting. Having no intimation that before long they would be forced into exile, they had decided to buy a country house where Erich could work in peace over the summer. They had no success at first and the family instead spent a miserable spell overheating on the Venice Lido, finally escaping to the Dolomites. On holiday as in work, Korngold was something of a pedant. Before departure he worked out a complete itinerary in which he planned out every overnight stay, every mealtime and every snack break.

It was winter before the Korngolds heard of a summer retreat that interested them. Erich was fond of Gmunden and when they heard that a castle near there was up for sale they decided to take a look. They visited the 'Schloss Hüselberg' one snowy night, to discover that it was not a castle so much as a spacious and sprawling old farmhouse around a courtyard, with a small tower to one side. No sooner had they set foot inside the building than they knew they wanted it. Luzi's description of it makes it sound like something out of *Die tote Stadt* – which may account for its attractiveness to Korngold: 'When we stood in front of the oak door carved with the year 1769 and entered the low hall with Gothic arches above, we were at home. A strange, musty smell of old walls and old wood came towards us.' While Erich went to Berlin to conduct two Strauss reworkings, *Das Spitzentuch der Königin* ('The Queen's Piece of Lace') and *Das Lied der Liebe* ('Song of Love'), Luzi – always in charge of practical matters (other than financial affairs) – went back to check the farmhouse with an architect and gained full approval for the purchase. The Korngolds furnished their new country home with antiques and donations of old furniture from friends and relations. One prize possession was a Biedermeier billiards table; like his namesake, Mozart, Korngold was passionate about billiards.

Korngold's operetta arrangements, though all the rage at home, did not always export well. There had already been something of a fiasco in London, when a production of *Schöne Helena* had been staged in Baroque costume ostensibly to conceal the lumpish build of the leading lady. Reinhardt had been working on a plan to take their version of *Die Fledermaus* to Paris and in the autumn Korngold set off for France. The cast included some excellent singers – two Rosalindes were Jarmila Novotna and Maria Rajdl – and Lotte Schöne was to sing Adele. But without Reinhardt's presence, the choosing of the chorus was entirely up to Korngold and he selected singers of excellent voice. Reinhardt took one look, however, and declared that his music

Richard Tauber and Anny
Ahlers, pictured c. 1932, in
*Das Lied der Liebe*, one of
Korngold's masterly Johann
Strauss arrangements

director had hired 'tree trunks', forcing Korngold to seek out prettier
replacements. The composer soon found himself going up to any
attractive young woman he saw around the town and asking, 'Excuse
me, mademoiselle, can you sing?'

The Paris results were well received, but the next tour of the show,
to Italy in February 1934, was an unqualified disaster. Everything went
wrong, from the Korngolds' car getting stuck in the snow and having
to be towed by a bus, to the complete lack of any repetiteur, stage
manager or rehearsal facilities for the dancers in the Casino Theatre in
San Remo. Luzi took over both the former jobs herself and sang the
music for the dancers to practise to in the theatre foyer; but she could
do nothing to help the appalling choreography, a hopeless leading
lady or the fact that the orchestra pit was too small and that the
conductor could not be seen at the same time by orchestra and stage.
Replacement choreographer and Rosalinde arrived scarcely before the
première and finally, 'an hour before the performance Erich was lying
in bed trembling and with a cold, clammy forehead'. Sure enough,
the show flopped miserably and for the second time in Italy Korngold
was met by calls of 'Basta!'

Max Reinhardt left Milan for New York, where he was to produce
the Austrian playwright Franz Werfel's *Eternal Road*. The Korngolds

thought little of their friend's departure for America, other than that they might not see him for a long time. The fact was that his career in German theatre was finished. The Nazi regime had been 'purging' German culture of its Jewish influences, replacing leading figures, from critics to conductors, with those who displayed the right political affinities. The conductor Wilhelm Furtwängler, who was highly sympathetic to the cultural ideals of the Nazis but wished to judge his colleagues only by their artistic qualities and not by race, took it upon himself to write in protest to Joseph Goebbels, head of the cultural wing of the NSP: '… men like [Bruno] Walter, Klemperer and Reinhardt must be enabled to have their say in Germany in the future … let our fight be concentrated against the reckless, disintegrating and shallow spirit.' But Goebbels twisted Furtwängler's words to imply, in his response, that these three were indeed not 'true German artists'. Reinhardt would not be coming back.

Korngold went to Barcelona for a guest appearance with Pablo Casals's orchestra; *en route* from Spain to Austria, they stopped over in Aix-en-Provence where watching students in the streets gave Luzi an idea. Her husband was still sulking quietly over the loss of *Die Kathrin*, despite looking at other possible subjects such as Charles Dickens's novel *Little Dorrit*. If the problem (i.e., the politics) could be removed from *Die Kathrin*, then the story might be acceptable after all. She put it to Erich that the tale could be set instead in a French university town; that Kathrin herself could be not German but Swiss – safely neutral – and she could then meet her François, the soldier, who is stationed in that town; the conflict of civilians against military occupation would be exchanged for the lighter animosity between students and garrison. Korngold at once began to dream again.

By 1934 Schreker and Schoenberg had lost their teaching posts in Berlin, and Klemperer and Walter their conductorships. The Berlin Staatsoper and Philharmonic had been taken over by the Reich. German Jews had been banned from teaching music. Richard Strauss himself was president of the Reichsmusikkammer, with Paul Graener and Furtwängler as his deputies, and composers such as Zemlinsky, Hindemith and Bartók were falling prey to banning orders and controversies while the likes of Pfitzner – less gifted but politically correct – were receiving official honours. Although the Reich as yet had no direct control over events in Austria, tensions between the

In Austria's increasingly pro-Nazi atmosphere during the 1930s, Korngold's planned opera *Die Kathrin* had little chance of acceptance.

countries were uncomfortable. Austrian factions took up positions for and against unity with the Reich next door – the pros consisting largely of young people captured by Hitler's oratorical skills and high-worded aims and promises.

Such political and racial tensions and Korngold's own evident lack of fresh musical outlets can perhaps seem warning enough that *Die Kathrin* was bound to be ill-starred. And if that was not clear enough, one might have expected Korngold, with his superb dramatic sense, to have realized that in annulling the political conflict and resetting the story in this way, he would be removing from it a level of seriousness and real motivation that would immediately weaken its impact and hence its chances of long-term survival. But certainly it could not have progressed in its original format; and Korngold was longing to write an opera of his own once again. He had a burgeoning tenor lead that would admirably suit his favourite Richard Tauber and a heroine who had captured his imagination and sympathy. Back in Vienna he set to work with his librettist, Decsey, at once.

The story of *Die Kathrin* is basically boy-meets-girl, boy-wins-girl, boy-loses-girl, girl-has-baby, boy-finds-girl-again. Kathrin is a Swiss maidservant in a small French university town where François, a French cabaret singer, has been drafted into the army. He invites her into the cinema with him and a romance ensues.

François is little interested in being a soldier: he loves to sing his ballads and exasperates his captain with his romantic, happy-go-lucky nature (his bright, lyrical aria in Korngold's favourite key of F sharp major, 'Es ist ja wahr: in meinem Herzen bin ich nur ein Sänger', translates as 'It is true, in my heart I am just a singer'). Margaret, Kathrin's room-mate, urges her to give up the romance as it can only lead to disaster when François is finally sent away: Kathrin could be left all alone, maybe with a child. Kathrin sings a tender and poignant letter song, 'Ich soll dich nicht mehr wiedersehn' ('I shall not see you again'), as she tries to write to him to break off their relationship. The letter song has something of the quality of Marietta's Lute Song in *Die tote Stadt*: the same genuine, tender, regretful emotion and the same kind of alternation between duple and triple time, the written-out form of rubato which in this case beautifully suggests Kathrin's own hesitancy at writing her letter.

Kathrin is interrupted by François himself; there is an ecstatic love duet and the inevitable happens as the curtain falls. Margaret's prediction is proved correct: Kathrin falls pregnant and François leaves with the army. She goes to look for him, wandering half-mad to the border and begging the soldiers to let her across to look for her lover although she has no passport or papers. The second act follows François to a nightclub in Marseilles where a white slave trader, Malignac, exhorts him to serenade a beautiful woman on his behalf; unknown to François, this is Kathrin herself. He sings a catchy and charming song for the occasion. Ultimately, in Act III, the pair meet again by accident, five years later in an idyllic scene outside Kathrin's house at the foot of a snowy Swiss mountain; there is a touching, sentimental scene where François and his little son converse without knowing one another's identity. Finally the lovers are reunited with one another and with their child in a tender, content C major.

*Die Kathrin*, when it was finally completed many years later, was a complete contrast to *Das Wunder der Heliane*. Korngold's ideal of love as a supreme force is still in place, but this time he has his feet firmly, maybe too firmly, on the ground. The opera's opening, in place of an ethereal chorus singing of eternal love, shows – ironically for Korngold – young people going into a cinema. And in place of two transfigured souls entering the gates of heaven, it closes with two ordinary adult human beings entering the house where their little son is asleep.

The nature of the story reflects both a different point in the composer's life – he had settled down and assumed the same adult responsibilities as his characters – and a different attitude on his part towards the composition of opera. For *Die Kathrin* is straightfor-wardly melodic, the plot and characters are simple, down-to-earth and realistic. It presents a much simplified and more accessible Leitmotiv system – for example, a pair of falling thirds for François and a tender melody based on Korngold's Cheerful Heart motif for Kathrin. The musical structures too are simpler and more 'old-fashioned', including more set-piece arias, duets and dramatic scenes. The roles of Kathrin and François are demanding but do not call for the impossible heights of Heliane and the Stranger, or of Marietta and Paul. The orchestra is unconventional in a different way from that used in *Heliane*: as well Korngold's favourite hefty percussion and keyboard section it includes saxophones, guitar and accordion, indeed a whole jazz band.

In short, Korngold was consciously setting out to write an opera which he thought would be accessible and appealing. He desperately wanted to write something which would be a sure success, after the fiasco which had surrounded his beloved *Heliane*. Now that his father had retired, one obstacle – at least on the public front – was removed.

So absorbed was Korngold in his work on his new opera that Luzi felt glad Max Reinhardt was not there to distract him. 'It's not such a bad thing that this restless mind has gone away for a while,' she said one evening. Instantly there was a ring at the doorbell. It was a lengthy telegram from Reinhardt requesting Erich's urgent presence in Hollywood to arrange Mendelssohn's music for a film of the Shakespeare play *A Midsummer Night's Dream*. Reinhardt, as usual, was more than persuasive – and the project, he said, would not take more than about eight weeks to complete.

Had he known the actual scale of the work he was undertaking, Korngold might well have declined the invitation. Fortunately, he did not.

6

Jack L. Warner in April 1938.
In a radio broadcast many
years later, George Korngold
publicly thanked Warner for
saving the lives of his family.

'When there are sequences when the eye,
and not the ear, is the primary object, then the
composer has his fling in the writing of
incidental background music. In this branch
of musical writing there have been some of the
finest examples of orchestral music which our
age has produced.'

Erich Wolfgang Korngold commenting
on the composition of film music, 1936

# The Dream 1934-8

Max Reinhardt's *A Midsummer Night's Dream* started life as a stage production in the massive Hollywood Bowl. It attracted such public popularity that Jack Warner, head of the Warner Brothers film studio, was drawn to the idea of putting it on screen; and it finally metamorphosed into the most lavish and expensive movie yet made in Hollywood.

Calling for the presence of Korngold was a typically extravagant gesture on the part of the director. After Reinhardt signed his contract with Warner Brothers, he began to think wistfully of his Viennese friends. 'We should have someone here like Werfel or Korngold,' he remarked to Helene Thimig. Then he realized that Korngold was a superb idea as he could arrange Mendelssohn's music for the film.

Erich and Luzi Korngold set sail on the *Majestic* for New York. From there they travelled by train to Los Angeles. After arriving in the USA they were chaperoned at every stage by Warner Brothers officials and fêted by journalists. For to Hollywood, Korngold was a catch. With his child prodigy credentials, his operatic fame, his heavy Viennese accent which he never lost (at this time he scarcely understood English), he was, to distant America, the archetypal figure of a Great Composer. Everyone wanted to know what he thought of the USA and what he thought about Hitler. Luzi, perplexed at being called 'honey' and 'sugar' by these strange people, translated for him and finally her husband offered the journalists the opinion: 'I think that Mendelssohn will survive Hitler.' Overnighting in New York, the couple were presented by their new Warner Brothers associates with tickets for *The Great Waltz* on Broadway. The show no longer had anything to do with Korngold's arrangements of Strauss and, unimpressed with what they saw and heard, the exhausted Viennese couple fell quietly asleep in their seats.

The Los Angeles in which the Korngolds found themselves in 1934 was not the violent, smog-ridden city we know today. The air was scented with orange blossom from the groves which lined the rolling hills, the sun beat down on the Pacific Ocean and the most legendary film stars – Charlie Chaplin, the Marx Brothers, Bette Davis – held parties and played tennis. The possibilities of film were still unlimited; the studios had seemingly endless space to sprawl out and create their fantasy worlds. Money was plentiful, as was talent, and indeed the ready quantities of both often led to considerable waste as writers and musicians were signed up with pomp and circumstance and then left stranded, either without actual work or working on projects that never saw the light of day. Film composers led a tough life, working to stringent deadlines and often ordered around by executives whose musical ideas could often be more than a little misguided.

All this was yet to reach its apex, for in 1934 the Hollywood star was still very much in the ascendant. And Korngold and Reinhardt did not regard themselves as part of this world. Korngold certainly had no intention of becoming a film composer; it would be a combination of dogged persistence on the part of Warners and

An aerial view of the Warner Brothers studios in Hollywood

political and financial necessity on his own part that eventually pushed him into it.

The Korngolds were uncomfortable in Hollywood. Everything seemed larger and brighter than life and somewhat artificial; and they were astonished by wearing summer clothes in October. But once they met their old friends Max Reinhardt and Helene Thimig, who lived not far from the house they were renting, they immediately began to feel at home. 'Max und Erich' again sat making their plans until dawn.

Korngold's first visit to the Warner Brothers Studio has become something of a legend in the film music world. Henry Blanke, the assistant producer, was assigned to him as guide and he was introduced to Jack Warner and to Leo Forbstein who was overall head of the studio's musical activity. On the 'sound stage', where an orchestral recording was in process, Korngold asked, 'How long is a foot of film?' 'Twelve inches,' replied the mystified Blanke. 'I mean, how long does a foot last in music?' clarified the composer. Nobody had asked this question before and it took a little time to find someone who could answer it. The answer, once found, was exactly two-thirds of a second. 'Exactly the first two measures of the Mendelssohn scherzo,' commented Korngold. (He must have been thinking of a very fast performance!)

One of Erich Korngold's most unusual abilities thus became obvious: an unerring instinctual understanding of the relationship between music and time. This had already produced some interesting effects in Vienna. Once Korngold sat in a box at the Opera listening to Franz Schalk conducting an exceptionally leisurely *Die tote Stadt*, beating time for himself quietly under the ledge. Ten minutes before the end of Act I he turned to his companion, the critic Josef Reitler, and sighed, 'I've finished.'

The same instinct for timing enabled him to work on his film scores in a most unconventional way. Most composers in Hollywood used a 'cue sheet' on which a technician would have written the exact timing for a scene to which music would be fitted; Korngold never did. For the recording sessions in which the composer conducted his own music and fitted it to the film, he never used a 'click track' – the standard device of headphones providing clicks with the exact tempo that was required for the music to fit the film. Korngold refused mechanical aids of all types, finding them more confusing than helpful.

The famous Hollywood wit and musician Oscar Levant provides another tale of Korngold's musico-visual instinct. On being introduced to James Cagney, who played Bottom in *A Midsummer's Night Dream*, Korngold asked the actor to 'hold still a minute'. Then he 'rubbed his chin reflectively and began to hum a little. Walking around to the other side, he continued the inspection and the humming, meanwhile whistling contentedly under his breath. Finally, when the image of Cagney had been securely captured in musical terms, he thanked his subject and departed'. That story may well be apocryphal, since there was no need for Korngold to tailor-make a tune for Cagney – he was simply arranging Mendelssohn on this occasion. But time and again the films he scored himself prove how exactly he could find the right melodies and rhythms to enhance and illustrate both a character and a mood.

*A Midsummer Night's Dream* was a starry affair. Korngold was not the only international luminary summoned to be part of it: the dances were arranged by Bronislava Nijinska, sister of the legendary Nijinsky

Korngold (second from right) with members of the *Midsummer Night's Dream* cast. In front, Mickey Rooney and Olivia de Havilland; at the back, left to right, Dick Powell, James Cagney, Joe E. Brown and, far right, Hugh Herbert

and herself a leading choreographer, counting among her creations *Les Noces*, to Stravinsky's music. And the cast included, with Cagney, Victor Jory as Oberon and Anita Louise as Titania, with Dick Powell as Lysander wearing pink tights, a youthful Mickey Rooney in his first movie, playing Puck, and an unknown eighteen-year-old girl, who had been originally spotted in a school production by a talent scout, as Hermia. She had toured with Reinhardt's stage version but expressed anxiety about playing Hermia on film. Reinhardt and Korngold, along with their Warner Brothers colleagues, helped to persuade her to stay and be part of the film. Her name was Olivia de Havilland.

The making of *A Midsummer Night's Dream* took about six months against the expected matter of weeks. Reinhardt, unused to the different practices employed in the film industry, continued to work exactly as if he were directing a theatre production. He expected a long rehearsal period and was shocked at the idea of filming without it (Warners relented and gave him a rehearsal stage); moreover, he was not used to being expected at work promptly in the morning. William Dieterle, who looked after the actual filming of the *Dream* (Reinhardt knowing nothing about camerawork) had to explain to the great man that in a commercial enterprise one could not afford to wait until two o'clock in the afternoon for the director to arrive. Dieterle himself was another European émigré, who had acted in Reinhardt's own production of *Jedermann* in the Salzburg Festival.

There were other setbacks too. Mickey Rooney broke a leg; a bear, which appeared in a dream-sequence, died and was replaced by a less tractable animal; and the technical requirements for sets, costumes and props were incredible. Reinhardt's vision called for, as one account describes, 'huge leaves to become violins, a moonbeam for 103 girls to dance on, jewelled cobwebs, lilies to become trumpets' – all of which had to be made. 'WHAT FOOLS THESE MORTALS BE', quoted the programme in large letters.

Korngold, for his part, drew not only on Mendelssohn's incidental music to *A Midsummer Night's Dream* but on other works too, such as the *Lieder ohne Worte* ('Songs without Words'), the 'Scottish' Symphony and the 'Italian' Symphony, weaving the themes into a pattern of recurrent Leitmotivs as he would for an opera.

'For this production,' wrote Korngold, 'I had to make preliminary recordings, the so-called playbacks, of Mendelssohn's Scherzo and

Nocturne, which were relayed over huge loudspeakers during the actual filming [this related to the ballet episodes]. Further, I conducted an orchestra on stage for complicated, simultaneous "takes", and lastly, after the film was cut, I conducted a number of music pieces which were inserted in the completed picture as background music. In addition, however, I had to invent a new method, which was a combination of all three techniques, for the music that accompanied the spoken word. I wrote the music in advance, conducted – without orchestra – the actor on the stage in order to make him speak his lines in the required rhythm, and then, sometimes weeks later, guided by earphones, I recorded the orchestral part.'

The biggest alteration to Mendelssohn's music that Korngold made was to transpose the Nocturne down a semitone from E major to E flat major, which he felt was a 'darker' key. 'Here I have taken the moon out of the night, so that it is all darkness.' This was a better match, in his opinion, for Reinhardt's mysterious Oberon. Otherwise, as was usual in his arrangements, he left Mendelssohn unchanged, but for a few cuts where necessary.

The St Luke's Choristers were taking part in the musical performances and the choir's founder, William Ripley Dorr, remembered how Korngold rehearsed them. 'During the preliminary rehearsals … Mr Korngold used a small studio upright with the top removed, which he lambasted mercilessly, not paying too much attention to what notes he struck as long as he secured the desired results from the boys. After the rehearsal, a little soprano asked me, "Mr Dorr, do you suppose they will ever be able to use that piano again?"' Warners claimed later that Korngold ruined eight pianos during his years at the studio.

Most Hollywood filming relied solely on playbacks of the music, but, apart from the ballet sequences of the Scherzo and Nocturne, Korngold insisted on direct recordings on the stage. This led to some extraordinary moments, such as one when Korngold had to lie on his stomach under an artificial bush to conduct a musical scene with Oberon without getting in the way of the camera. Warners, who must have wondered what had hit them, agreed to everything Reinhardt and Korngold requested and soon the pair of them had 'turned the film factory into a real theatre'.

In 1935 A Midsummer Night's Dream premièred to great acclaim in twenty different countries. Above, a programme from the Adelphi Theatre, London; plus two stills from the film itself, showing (centre) Anita Louise as Titania and (right) James Cagney as Bottom

*A Midsummer Night's Dream* was two-and-a-half hours long and cost Warner Brothers $1.5 million – the most expensive picture yet made by the studio. It 'burst upon the world simultaneously in the large cities of twenty different countries, October 9, in the finest theatre each city can provide,' as one newspaper put it. The stars went to the première in New York and needed a week to get back to the West Coast, so it did not open in Los Angeles until 16 October. The film was termed 'an enchanting blend of broad comedy and exquisite fantasy with a background of fine music and photography that leaves one at a loss for words in which to praise its beauty, its ingenuity and its almost magical power of interpretation'.

Korngold's imagination was also fired. He was passionate about Shakespeare, whose works had inspired him (*Schauspiel Overtüre*) and led him to write some of his best-loved music (*Much Ado About Nothing*). The potential of film also excited him and one newspaper reported him as eagerly advocating a whole series of Shakespeare films, especially *Twelfth Night* and *Hamlet*. 'I was surprised how easily Shakespeare lends himself to the movies,' the article quoted him. 'They left the original Shakespeare and they left the original Mendelssohn. It's a miracle. It's artistic.'

Beyond the studio the Korngolds were leading an active life in Hollywood. They were out almost every night at a party or going to the Trocadero (then the 'in' spot for night life) with Max Reinhardt and Helene Thimig. They met Greta Garbo, Bette Davis (Korngold's favourite) and plenty of other film stars and were reunited with another old friend and refugee from the Third Reich, Otto Klemperer, who was now music director of the Los Angeles Philharmonic. Klemperer invited Korngold to conduct a concert with his orchestra. On Sunday afternoon, 17 February 1935, Korngold took the podium at the Philharmonic Auditorium and performed the *Babyserenade*, the *Schauspiel Overtüre*, two songs from *Die tote Stadt* and some music by Johann Strauss. Glancing across at Max Reinhardt as Korngold struck up the Radetzky March, Luzi saw that the director was in tears.

Another acquaintanceship was renewed, at one of the interminable but financially crucial teas laid on by the Los Angeles ladies in support of artistic events in the city. This time the Korngolds ran into the Schoenbergs. Thanks to the intransigent attitudes of Julius Korngold, the two composers had never been friends. By now Julius had retired,

and was safely at home in Vienna, and Schoenberg had married
Gertrude Kolisch, Korngold's childhood friend the 'Fratz' and former
youthful romance. Strangely, Schoenberg himself was now friendlier
to the Korngolds than his wife, who addressed Erich persistently with
the formal 'Sie'. In exile, differences were forgotten; Schoenberg and
Korngold were both Viennese composers in a strange land and were
soon to become good friends, especially later after the Korngolds
moved permanently to Hollywood, when their respective children
Nuria and Georg became close companions.

Warner Brothers offered Korngold a contract for a year, which he
turned down straight away. Next, however, he had an approach from
another studio, Paramount, whose director Ernst Lubitsch asked
him to write a musical. Oscar Hammerstein would be the lyricist and
the lead singers were the lovely soprano Gladys Swarthout and the
tenor Jan Kiepura, the Polish heart-throb who had created the role of
the Stranger in *Das Wunder der Heliane*. Korngold refused at first, as it
was high time that he and Luzi returned to Vienna and their children,
but he agreed to think it over and took the unsigned contract with
him on the *Majestic*.

The Austria they returned to was a rapidly changing country. The
Austrian Chancellor Engelbert Dollfuss, a popular man committed
to keeping Austria independent of Germany, had been murdered in
a Nazi *putsch* in July 1934. He was replaced by Kurt von Schuschnigg,
a Catholic and conservative lawyer. Although the *putsch* was put
down, it demonstrated the growing influence of the Nazis and the fact
that the threat was growing ever nearer. Now the general tension
was partly covert, partly expressed in open hostility (Luzi provides no
exact details in her book) which they encountered on the journey
between Vienna and the Hüselberg. Although deeply immersed in his
work on *Die Kathrin*, Korngold saw the dangers of remaining in
Austria and sensibly decided that it would not be clever to cut off a
possible escape route to the USA. He signed the Paramount contract
and, just four months after their last voyage, the Korngolds, this
time with Ernst and 'Schurli', were on their way back to Hollywood,
leaving behind Julius and Josephine Korngold who were upset by
the removal of their grandchildren.

The musical that was to become *Give Us This Night* had great
potential in its gifted cast and creators. Unfortunately, the results as a

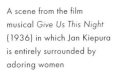
A scene from the film musical *Give Us This Night* (1936) in which Jan Kiepura is entirely surrounded by adoring women

whole did not match up to that potential. Korngold and Hammerstein met in New York before the Korngolds headed for Hollywood and the composer was pleased with what Hammerstein showed him. The story, however, was not strong to begin with and after several different writers had worked further on it, as was customary in Hollywood, Korngold declared to his wife, 'The book is getting worse every week. By the time we start shooting it will be unusable.'

The tale was of an Italian fisherman whose exceptional singing gifts are discovered; he is 'tamed' and taught to act, and falls in love with a beautiful soprano. For this light romance Korngold wrote some exquisitely lovely music, heavily under the influence of Strauss operetta. There was a miniature opera for Kiepura and Swarthout (excerpts from *Romeo and Juliet*, without any suggestion of tragedy), a spirited and typically Korngoldian ditty for Kiepura the fisherman, a romantic and lyrical fishermen's chorus, a Viennese-style waltz, 'Music in the Night', and three love songs, 'Sweet Melody of Night', 'I Mean to Say I Love You' and 'My Love and I', which, had the film been made twenty years later and starred Mario Lanza, would now be being sung all over the world by popular tenors. Conducted by Korngold, the score overflows with Viennese lilt, a wonderful spaciousness, warmth and beauty. But sadly the film has disappeared.

Kiepura was partly to blame. He in no way foreshadowed the screen idol Mario Lanza, for while his looks had brought him success on the operatic stage, he was not photogenic and his limited acting ability comes across as distinctly unsuitable for the intimacy of close-up cameras. His Polish accent sat incongruously in the film's Italian setting. And despite the tenderness of Korngold's accompaniment, Kiepura seemed only able to sing hard and loud. He held high notes with a manic gleam in his eye, while Hollywood papers ghoulishly reported the strange Pole's eccentricities and neuroses: 'Jan Kiepura is a gifted, temperamental egotist … Jan is an enigma, his screwy deeds legion … snubs luxury; lunches on dry bread, apples, doughnuts, sandwiches, herring, onions on set … always vocalising. Wears old clothes. Cuts wood à la Kaiser for exercise. Skips as he walks.'

But additionally, Korngold's score was overambitious for the purpose it would be made to serve: it was too operatic for the numbers to become popular hits. As one account in *Variety* put it: 'Music and lyrics are exceptionally good, but of a type too classy to appeal generally … A dozen numbers have been incorporated … mainly to eliminate Kiepura's acting … Writers can't take the blame for the weakness of the story due to the overabundance of music crammed into the seventy minutes.' Musical overabundance was to be a problem in a few of Korngold's films in which the movie itself was just not strong enough in itself to support the score.

Paramount press releases had ambitiously announced: 'This is the first picture to encourage serious, modern composers toward regarding the screen as a new art form,' and quoted comments by Korngold at some length.

*The reason the modern composers of serious music do not complain about working for the movies is that they are given an even chance to be as original as they want. It is only in vocal music that they have to keep within the bounds of popular demand, but there is already an indication that movie audiences will soon accept novelty and innovation in this line. At the present time we would scare people out of theaters if a star like Jan Kiepura, for instance, were to appear in close-up singing in modern tonalities which have heretofore not been heard by the popular ear ... When there are sequences when the eye, and not the ear, is the primary object, then the composer has his fling in the writing of incidental background music. In this branch of musical writing there have been some of the finest examples of orchestral music which our age has produced. There have been some ordinary, program pictures which are forgotten after three months but which will be long remembered by musicians as containing some rare musical writing.*

Unfortunately, Korngold was here prophesying the fate of many of his own films. He was ambitious not only for his own music but for Hollywood as a whole.

*I feel certain that this picture starts the transition period. We no longer have to lean on Puccini, Verdi or Mascagni. Producers have realised that public taste in music has risen, and we are now conducting a test which will eventually lead to the writing of entire modern operas for the screen. When that day comes, composers will accept the motion picture as a musical form equal to the opera or the symphony.*

What a wonderful idea. And how sad that, as yet, that day has not come.

While Korngold was busy with orchestral recordings for *Give Us This Night*, he was contacted once more by Warner Brothers, who were eager for him to provide them with music for a newly completed movie based on Rafael Sabatini's novel *Captain Blood*. This film represented considerable risk for Warners, for their original choice of lead actor, Robert Donat, had dropped out and they had been forced to replace him in the title role with a complete unknown by the unpromising name of Errol Flynn. As if that was not enough, the leading lady was a newcomer too: Olivia de Havilland. A Korngold score could perhaps help them to boost this dodgy movie.

Korngold refused, too busy with the project already in hand and having no plans to write any further music for films. While working

*Captain Blood* (1935)
rocketed Errol Flynn and
Olivia de Havilland to fame
as film stars and Korngold to
fame as a composer of
original film music.

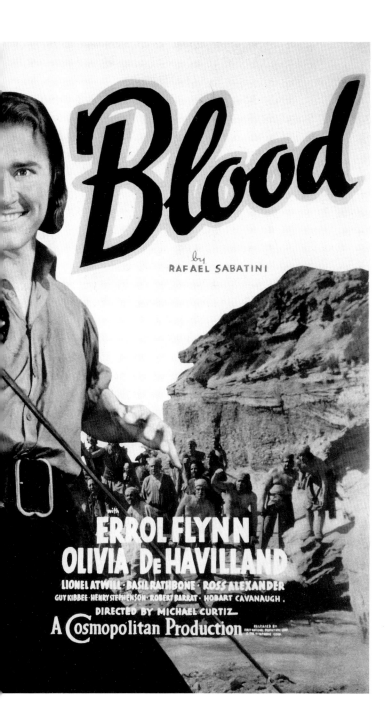

on *Give Us This Night* he had written one song for another Paramount picture starring Swarthout, *Rose of the Rancho*, but that was all.

A project to film *The Life of Ludwig van Beethoven*, rumoured in the papers and claiming to have Korngold arranging the subject's music, never materialized. Nevertheless, he and Luzi watched the new film, a patriotic and humanitarian adventure story set in the sixteenth century, little knowing that it would be the first of a distinguished line of Flynn 'swashbucklers'. 'I can't do it, you have to go and refuse for me,' said Korngold to his wife. Anxiety and initial refusal would be the pattern with which he responded to almost every further film request. But Jack Warner persisted and eventually Korngold capitulated, with less than three weeks to complete the score.

All day he conducted for the Paramount film and then by night he went to Warner Brothers, watched extracts of the film and com-posed music to them. At Warners he was given a private screening room where portions of the film in hand could be run and rerun; he would improvise to them and compose thus through his beloved 'inspiration'. He would always write his film music in this way and he was the only Hollywood composer with the privilege of doing so.

Even working flat out with the help of his young orchestrator, Hugo Friedhofer, Korngold could not quite manage to write the entire score himself in such a short time. In a duel scene between Flynn and Basil Rathbone towards the end of the film, he added a short extract from one of Liszt's 'Transcendental Studies'. The extract lasted only moments, but because of this Korngold insisted that his credit in the titles ran 'Musical arrangements by Erich Wolfgang Korngold', despite the fact that he had composed every other note in the score. On the last day he spent the entire night, after a full day's conducting, in the dub room fitting music to film and then invited the technical staff out for breakfast at Sardi's at 5.30 a.m. Such gestures quickly made him a popular figure at the studio.

*Captain Blood* was a tremendous popular success and launched the careers of its beautiful young stars as new screen idols. It was also Korngold's first original film score. He never compromised his own compositional style, but wrote in his inimitable, rhythmically intricate, harmonically lush and idiosyncratic way as if composing an opera. Gone was his operatic *alter ego*: now he wrote in his natural manner under the influences of the great romantic symphonic poems by Mahler, Liszt and Richard Strauss, fashioned precisely to the tone of the story. He used Leitmotiv technique, challenged the players in his excellent orchestra – the rhythm of the opening fanfare is fiendishly complex – and caught and enhanced to perfection the atmosphere of tension and romantic thrill that the audience would respond to with such enthusiasm.

Working to this time schedule would not have been possible had Korngold been orchestrating the music himself. But in Hugo Friedhofer, with whom he always worked after that, he had found a thoroughly sympathetic friend. Friedhofer spoke German, so they could communicate; above all, Korngold could trust him absolutely with his music. Friedhofer went on to become a distinguished film composer in his own right.

'We would sit together at the piano with the sequences to be orchestrated, and he would play them through, with me filling in the occasional notes that were outside the capacities of ten fingers,' recounted Friedhofer. 'He had, incidentally, the most extraordinary way of making a piano sound like an orchestra that I have ever encountered. After the run-through at the keyboard there would be a detailed discussion of colour in the orchestra. This was a give and take sort of affair, with me telling him what I heard, and he giving me his conception of what the colour should be. Then I would make careful inquiry as to those places in his sketch which were capable of being set as they stood … When I had all these points more or less straight I would go home and start scoring. When I had completed the sections he had given me, he and I would go through the full score together and in detail. As time went on he came to rely more and more on my discretion in the matter of colour, voicing etc., and in many instances would discuss with me the orchestration of sections which were to be farmed out to other orchestrators. I was extremely fortunate in having a fairly comprehensive knowledge of the Wagner–Strauss–Mahler–Puccini orchestral idiom, certain features of which he had absorbed into his own style. Because of this knowledge I was perhaps a little better suited to orchestrating for Korngold than were those of my colleagues whose tendencies lay in other directions.'

No sooner was *Captain Blood* finished than Warner Brothers asked Korngold to write a score which was to prove decisively his new status as one of Hollywood's most important and influential composers.

A poster for the vast epic movie *Anthony Adverse* (1936). Korngold's score won him his first Oscar.

*Anthony Adverse* by Hervey Allen was a great tome of a romantic, historical novel and copies sold like hot cakes. Crossing the Atlantic, one of the Warner executives saw innumerable passengers reading it on the boat and he wired Jack Warner: 'PLEASE READ ANTHONY ADVERSE. WOULD MAKE GREAT PICTURE FOR US.' Warner wired back: 'READ IT? I CAN'T EVEN LIFT IT.'

The movie was a true epic. Frederic March starred as the illegitimate hero who develops from abandoned infant to innocent youth to cynical slave-trader. He returns home after many years to find that his wife, whom he was forced to desert immediately after their marriage, has borne their child but is a famous opera singer and the mistress of none other than Napoleon. The film opens with the saga of Anthony's parents; his mother, Maria, is married to the cold and calculating nobleman played by Claude Rains who kills her lover (Anthony's father, Denis) and remains evil genius to Anthony throughout the story. Olivia de Havilland played Angela the opera singer, Anita Louise the unfortunate mother Maria. Korngold found it suitably operatic – and gave it appropriate treatment.

The scope of the plot was vast and demanded of Korngold his most ambitious score. The first twenty-five minutes of film, the story of the star-crossed lovers Maria and Denis, are accompanied by an unprecedented, unbroken stream of music; Korngold used a positively Wagnerian approach involving no fewer than forty-two Leitmotivs in the film as a whole; the film's first part really feels like an opera without singing. This music does more than simply enhance the mood: for instance, the use of Denis's Leitmotiv can tell the audience who Maria's furtive letter is from even before she opens it and the statement of Anthony's sombre, scalic motif as the lovers rendezvous under the branches tells us that the meeting will result in the conception of the child. But with the intensity of *Violanta* the music increases the tension and melodrama of the situation. One of the greatest impacts it makes is by stopping, for the very first time, at the moment Claude Rains catches the lovers trying to communicate and exclaims 'What does this mean?'

Korngold also began to experiment with a technique which he continued to use throughout his Hollywood career: pitching music just beneath that of the actor's voice so that it would not interfere with perception of the words; and his natural feel for counterpoint and dramatic flow ensured that the music interacted with the spoken lines as sensitively as in any of his own operas. Although the music becomes less prevalent as the film goes on, the invention and skill that went into the production of this score was extraordinary.

Hollywood acknowledged the achievement with an Oscar – not, unfortunately, for Korngold in person but for Warner's music department as a whole. Korngold was absent from the ceremony and Leo Forbstein, Warner's music chief, accepted the Academy Award. For some years Korngold refused to take the trophy, generously saying that as it was awarded for the excellence of the studio's department it should stay there, even if he was privately miffed. But that was the lot of a composer of film music: to be, as Oscar Levant and many after him succinctly put it, merely 'a cog in the wheel'.

As cogs went, Korngold was fortunate: he could name his terms. While composers such as Max Steiner, a favourite of Jack Warner, were being worn nearly into the ground scoring film after film, Korngold's contracts with Warner allowed him to do as little as two films a year with the right to refuse an assignment; he was allowed more time in which to create the score than was usual and, in another unprecedented move, he would have his own single credit card in the films' titles and his name would be included in any advertising that included the film's director. And, significantly, he could make use of his film music for any purpose he wished.

While being a 'cog', Korngold developed a reputation around Hollywood not only for being the most privileged composer in the 'wheel' but also for having one of the sharpest and readiest wits about. At Paramount, making *Give Us This Night*, his mail used to get mixed up with that of an arranger named Sigmund Krumgold. 'Siggy, are you getting any of my letters?' he asked his colleague one day. 'Well, I hope to God they're more interesting than yours!' On another occasion, Forbstein asked for his opinion on one of the outsized musical extravaganzas that the studio was producing. Korngold watched the film and then told the proud Forbstein, mocking typical Hollywood exaggeration, 'Leo, it's fantastic, colossal, stupendous ... ' then adding, 'but it isn't very good.' Such Korngold stories abounded and the project he undertook after *Anthony Adverse* provided one of the best – one which also demonstrates the composer's sense of justice.

At the same time as *Anthony Adverse*, in the spring of 1936, Warners were producing a film entitled *Green Pastures*, a beautiful, original and sentimental interpretation of biblical stories seen through the eyes of small negro children. The all-black cast was backed up by negro spirituals movingly sung by the Hall Johnson Choir from New York; but it required a few episodes of incidental music, such as for the creation and the great flood. Korngold was enchanted by the film and took up the assignment eagerly. He got on particularly well with the chorus master Johnson and repeatedly invited him to lunch in the Warner Brothers restaurant, the Green Room. He could not under-stand why Johnson repeatedly declined the invitation. One day, lunching there with producer Hal Wallis, Korngold learnt the truth: black people were banned from the restaurant. All of them, even Rex Ingram who played 'De Lawd', had to eat in the cafeteria on the lot. The moment Wallis told him this, Korngold got up to leave. 'Where are you going?' asked the puzzled producer. 'To the cafeteria, to eat with God,' replied Korngold.

Much to Jack Warner's surprise, Korngold, who had previously commanded the highest fee he had yet paid a composer and was

*Opposite, A scene from Green Pastures (1936). Korngold loved this film so much that he refused to accept a fee for his musical contributions.*

GP501

known to turn down films he was offered, refused any payment whatsoever for his contribution to *Green Pastures*. He adored the film, he argued, so to provide music for it was simply a pleasure. The money-oriented movie mogul was thunderstruck.

As the Korngolds were homesick for Austria, Korngold refused another contract from Warners and set off for Europe shortly after the completion of his latest film. Despite all the warning signs from Germany, from where reports of strange concentration camps at places called Oranienburg, Sachsenhausen and Dachau had already been reaching Austrian newspapers for some time, the Korngolds still believed that they had a homeland to return to. The immediate signs were indeed positive: a few months later, in July, Hitler's delegate, von Papen, secured with Schuschnigg a treaty of 'Normalization of Relations between Austria and Germany' which guaranteed the former country's independence from the latter. Mussolini, though encouraging the Chancellor to accept the treaty, also warned him about the value, or lack of it, in Nazi guarantees. But as for Austrian Jews, as Stefan Zweig commented, 'they still sit comfortably in their homes and drive around in their cars. And every one consoles himself with that foolish phrase: "Hitler cannot last long."'

Something rather resembling divine intervention in an unpleasant form conspired to send the Korngolds back to Hollywood that autumn, after a summer happily isolated on the Hüselberg discussing the somewhat neglected *Kathrin* with its librettist. The Korngolds' younger son Schurli fell ill and was diagnosed as suffering from a form of tuberculosis that affected not the lungs but the glands. Keeping him away from Vienna was crucial and their doctor declared 'the Californian sun' the best remedy. So when a telegram from Warner Brothers arrived offering Korngold a further contract, he did not hesitate in accepting. On 18 November 1936 he sent a telegram to Warner Brothers from New York informing them of the family's arrival and stating:

*I also desire to further advise you that I am at this time applying for my first citizenship papers to become a citizen of the United States of America.*

Korngold might have shown a certain naïvety at times, but he could not have been described as stupid.

The Korngold family arrives in New York on the SS *Ile de France*, 6 August 1935

During this visit Korngold scored two films. The first, entitled *Another Dawn*, starred Errol Flynn and Kay Francis and is significant not for its content (it too has vanished from the cinematic scene) but for its music. Korngold created for it an exceptionally beautiful melody based on his much-loved undulating and rising fourths and fifths of the Motif of the Cheerful Heart. This melody, haunting and aching with romanticism, he would later rework as the opening theme of his Violin Concerto.

In the first months of 1937, as Schurli's health improved, Korngold worked on the music for another period piece which starred Errol Flynn and a pair of utterly interchangeable twin brothers, Billy and Bobby Mauch: an adaptation of Mark Twain's novel *The Prince and the Pauper*. This was a timely production thanks to the detailed scene of an English coronation. 'Mr Korngold, who is a famous composer,' blustered a press release, 'says that never has he worked with such delight and spontaneity as in the writing of the music for this picture. Into the fairytale mood of the main thread, he has blended pomp and ceremony, heroics and swashbuckling, the innate dignity of the little prince.' Again Korngold, who always responded well when writing for children's scenes, provided a wealth of superb music, displaying his adeptness with variation technique and aptitude for capturing mood. The folksy, rustic main theme from *The Prince and the Pauper* was also to serve him well, later on, as the basis for the last movement of his Violin Concerto.

For the coronation scene the St Luke's Choristers sang medieval chants and music by Tallis and Farrant; Korngold also provided a new setting of the anthem *Zadok the Priest*. Handel's *Zadok* was sensibly ruled out as it would have been anachronistic in the year 1550, but no other original could be found. William Dorr explained the situation to Leo Forbstein, '… he called in Mr Korngold … told him what we needed and gave him the text. He said, "OK, Boss!", grabbed a piece of music paper, went over to the commissary, ordered two pieces of pie and five cups of coffee, and in half an hour came back with a fine setting of our text.'

Two further film projects failed to materialize, this time both ideas which Warners had hoped Reinhardt himself would produce. One was *Danton*, the other promisingly entitled *The Miracle*. Korngold got as far as writing some music for the former which did not go to waste: he apparently found it a home in a later score, *The Sea Hawk*.

In early summer the Korngolds once more took to the ocean, thinking that this time the farewell to Hollywood might be forever. The première of *Die Kathrin* was scheduled for the 1937–8 season at the Vienna State Opera, accepted officially by Korngold's old advocate Bruno Walter, who was now co-director of the Opera. Ernst was attending a *Gymnasium* (high school) in Vienna but his younger brother still needed to be kept out of the city, so the family spent their time at their country home where Korngold put the finishing touches to his new opera.

Preparations for the production of *Die Kathrin* were interrupted by the absence of a suitable tenor. Richard Tauber, who Korngold had had in mind for the role of the carefree François, was not available; Kiepura, who was offered the role, had to refuse the part because he was due to appear in the USA in January, when the première was scheduled. Jeritza, for whom Korngold was still hankering for the female lead, was also in America. Finally the first performance was postponed until March 1938, by which time Korngold hoped the right cast would have been found.

But there was an increasing sense of danger – friends were telling the Korngolds horrific tales of events in Germany. In Vienna itself Nazi activity was ever growing. George Clare described Vienna in the season of the Opera Ball, 1938: 'Petrol and smoke bombs landed in synagogues, creating panic among the congregations. Huge swastikas and Nazi slogans appeared on house walls overnight. Mobs of teenage boys and girls roamed the streets molesting anyone who looked the least bit Jewish in their eyes …'

When the Korngolds said goodbye to Max Reinhardt and Helene Thimig, who were heading back to the USA, it seemed that they might be saying goodbye to a whole way of life. Had it not been for a telegram from Hal Wallis and Henry Blanke at Warner Brothers, the Korngolds might have been saying goodbye to a great deal more than that.

*Can you be in Hollywood within ten to twelve days for scoring Robin Hood stop JackWarner okayed twelvethousand fivehundred for job but without paying travelling nor living expenses stop strongly advise acceptance cable answer regards Wallis Blanke*

Luzi received the telegram and took it with her to a concert where Erich was listening to a performance of one of his piano sonatas. Reading the telegram, he felt there was more significance in the offer than might be obvious and from the Konzerthaus telephoned the opera house's intendant Dr Eckmann to tell him about it. 'Herr Korngold, take it as an omen and go,' said Eckmann, promising him an October première of *Die Kathrin* under Bruno Walter, with Novotna and Tauber in the leading roles. Another condition was essential for the trip to the USA: Korngold would only agree to cross the Atlantic in winter on one of the larger ships. They went straight from the concert hall to find out which ship would be sailing. It was the *Normandie*, a sizeable liner, and they booked two cabins.

In one day the Korngolds and their younger son were ready to leave. Ernst, whose schooling they did not want to interrupt, would stay with Luzi's mother and sister – for although they had taken the call to Hollywood as an omen, it still did not occur to them that they and their entire family could be in mortal danger. They drove across snowy Europe in their American car and made an uneventful journey

Errol Flynn and Basil
Rathbone as hero and
villain in *The Adventures of
Robin Hood* (1938). This
film won Korngold a second
Oscar and rescued him and
his family from Austria just in
time.

back to Hollywood, where they rented a house by Toluca Lake, five minutes from the Warner Brothers studios.

Korngold went to the studio to watch the new film that he had been asked to score. Errol Flynn, Olivia de Havilland and Basil Rathbone were starring in *The Adventures of Robin Hood*, which unusually for the time was filmed in full colour. The film was jam-packed with adventure, action, sentiment and fighting and Korngold refused to score it. There was, he felt, too much action. He was far happier scoring slower-paced and more psychologically oriented stories like *Anthony Adverse*. (Korngold's objection to battle scenes was not motivated by any pacifist sentiments but by the fact that battle scenes demanded appropriate music – fast, busy, noisy and hard work to write – which then oftener than not could hardly be heard over the battle noises themselves.) Despite this last-minute withdrawal, the Korngolds planned to stay in Hollywood until the spring as the sunshine would do their little boy's health good.

On 12 February the Korngolds' telephone rang. 'Luzi,' said Helene Thimig, 'everything is over. Schuschnigg is in Berchtesgarten.' Chancellor Schuschnigg was meeting Adolf Hitler. On 4 February Hitler had dismissed conservative nationalist generals from his army and replaced them with extremist Nazis, effectively giving himself an absolute power that had been little anticipated by the rationally minded citizens. Schuschnigg himself had assumed that Hitler would abide by the rules of international diplomacy. But Hitler had forced Schuschnigg to appoint Hitler's own approved candidate, Dr Rudolf von Seyss-Inquart, as Austrian minister of the interior. This move crucially weakened Austria's ability to resist further aggression from Germany, and it was evident to the Reinhardts and to the Korngolds that the very fact that the Austrian premier was meeting Hitler meant that he, and therefore the country, was already in Hitler's power.

At almost the same moment as the ring of the telephone came a ring on the doorbell. Leo Forbstein, Warner's music chief, came in to plead with Korngold to compose the film he had just rejected. Deeply depressed by the news from Vienna, Korngold reluctantly agreed at least to try to write the music.

Over the last few weeks of Austria's independence, the Korngolds did nothing to call their families, even Ernst, out of Vienna. They, and many like them, continued to hope that the situation would calm

Hitler arrives in Vienna in 1938 to a warm welcome from the citizens.

down – and indeed there were indications in Austria itself that things were calmer and the mood more optimistic. Elections were announced: all Austrians over the age of twenty-four were to vote either for or against a 'Free, German, independent, social, Christian and united Austria'. As the vast proportion of Hitler's Austrian supporters were in fact younger than twenty-four, a successful vote against Hitler seemed virtually guaranteed. However, Korngold himself guessed what would happen. 'He has to march in,' he said to his wife. 'Don't you see that Hitler won't risk elections in Austria?'

On 11 March it was announced that the plebescite had been postponed. A few hours later the first Nazi lorries entered Vienna, packed with men brandishing swastika flags and armlets, yelling out in chorus, '*Ein Volk, ein Reich, ein Führer! Juda verrecke! Juda verrecke!*' Within minutes, Jews were being assaulted and within days many were rounded up and forced to scrub the streets. Himmler took control of the Austrian police files, Hitler himself arrived in Upper Austria and the long-standing Viennese anti-Semitic sentiments were released into a joyous welcome for the invaders.

The Korngolds' immediate worry was how to rescue Ernst. Fortunately Julius Korngold the pessimist had obtained a visitor's visa for the USA some time before, but when he and Josephine left Vienna to take their grandson to Switzerland they actually intended to return to Vienna once he was safely away. They caught what proved to be the last train. In Switzerland they spoke on the telephone to Erich, who told them not to return but to come straight out to Hollywood. They had packed little more than overnight bags.

Korngold's house in the Sternwartestrasse was rapidly taken over by Nazi soldiers and his property confiscated – 'for his many debts' was the excuse. His greatest worry was his manuscripts, which he had left behind in the house. He sent a wire to Weinbergers, the publisher of his Strauss arrangements and of *Die Kathrin*, which had been refused by Schott's.

In the small hours of a Viennese spring night, two employees of Weinbergers arrived at Korngold's house. A flight of stairs led up to the front door, on a well-raised ground floor level. The basement, where the manuscripts had been left by the occupying soldiers to be burned later, must have been relatively easy to break into. The Weinberger employees managed to salvage almost the whole collection of manuscripts without being noticed by the drunken Nazis upstairs. Among the manuscripts were most of his original autograph scores from his child prodigy days. Weinbergers smuggled the manuscripts out of the country and over to their composer in Hollywood by hiding them between the leaves of printed music that was being exported.

In Vienna the Korngolds' paediatrician killed himself with an overdose. The writer Egon Friedell, who had worked with Korngold and Reinhardt on *Schöne Helena*, threw himself out of a window. Mahler's niece, Arnold Rosé's daughter Alma Rosé, later died in Auschwitz where she had survived for a while by conducting a bizarre women prisoners' orchestra. Mass deportations of Jews to concentration camps began almost at once and the works of Jewish artists, writers and musicians – including Korngold – were swiftly banned. Those who had not yet escaped were desperate. Luzi's mother, sister and brother and his family were on their way to Hollywood, but daily there were calls and letters from relatives, friends and even total strangers begging for help. Korngold signed so many affidavits for would-be immigrants that eventually the authorities refused his name as guarantor. He had become, for the first time in his life, a gloomy, preoccupied pessimist.

7

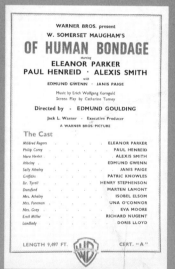

WARNER BROS. present

W. SOMERSET MAUGHAM'S

# OF HUMAN BONDAGE

*starring*

**ELEANOR PARKER**
**PAUL HENREID · ALEXIS SMITH**

*with*

EDMUND GWENN · JANIS PAIGE

Music by Erich Wolfgang Korngold
Screen Play by Catherine Turney

Directed by · **EDMUND GOULDING**

Jack L. Warner · Executive Producer

A WARNER BROS. PICTURE

**The Cast**

| | | |
|---|---|---|
| *Mildred Rogers* | . . . . . | ELEANOR PARKER |
| *Philip Carey* | . . . . | PAUL HENREID |
| *Nora Nesbit* | . . . . | ALEXIS SMITH |
| *Athelny* | . . . . | EDMUND GWENN |
| *Sally Athelny* | . . . . | JANIS PAIGE |
| *Griffiths* | . . . . | PATRIC KNOWLES |
| *Dr. Tyrell* | . . . . | HENRY STEPHENSON |
| *Dunsford* | . . . . | MARTEN LAMONT |
| *Mrs. Athelny* | . . . . | ISOBEL ELSOM |
| *Mrs. Foreman* | . . . . | UNA O'CONNOR |
| *Mrs. Grey* | . . . . | EVA MOORE |
| *Emil Miller* | . . . . | RICHARD NUGENT |
| *Landlady* | . . . . | DORIS LLOYD |

LENGTH 9,497 FT.          CERT. " A "

A programme for the film *Of
Human Bondage* (1946), the
least successful of Korngold's
movies despite its beautiful
score

*Music is music whether it is for the stage,
rostrum or cinema. Form may change, the
manner of writing may vary, but the composer
needs to make no concessions whatever to what
he conceives to be his own musical ideology …*

Erich Wolfgang Korngold,
interviewed in 1946

# Music is Music 1938–46

All hope of returning to Austria was lost for the foreseeable future.
Korngold bought a beautiful, 'old', Spanish-style house, 9936 Toluca
Lake Avenue; he was resigned to an indefinite stay in Hollywood and
to continuing life as a composer of film music. He was enthusiastic
and even idealistic about his duties. Interviewed in 1946 for *Overture*,
while he was working on the recording of music for *Deception*, he
expressed a succinct view of music for film, which continues a time-
honoured tradition of believing that music is music, regardless of
its purpose.

> *It is not true that the cinema places a restraint on musical expression.
> Music is music whether it is for the stage, rostrum or cinema. Form may
> change, the manner of writing may vary, but the composer needs to make
> no concessions whatever to what he conceives to be his own musical
> ideology … Fine symphonic scores for motion pictures cannot help but
> influence mass acceptance of finer music. The cinema is a direct avenue to
> the ears and hearts of the great public and all musicians should see the
> screen as a musical opportunity.*

The interviewer clearly enjoyed watching Korngold at work.

> *When he is composing at fever pitch … he sings atrociously, never
> words, but always raucous da-de-das and boom-de-booms, while he beats
> time with a flailing right arm. He is a sight to see at the studio eating
> lunch and mumbling his da-de-das. With lunch over, he rushes back to
> the battered small piano in his office-studio, plays out two or ten or a
> hundred unbroken bars of original melody. And it is usually timed to fit a
> scene down to the split second and final inch of the final foot of film.*

There can be no doubt that Korngold helped to revolutionize film
music. At the time Korngold arrived in Hollywood, film music was
just beginning to come out of the background doldrums into which it

had been pushed by the advent of the 'talkies'. Obviously, music had been far more prominent in the days when it accompanied silent films; the problem of finding a suitable technique for recording background music for the new films with speech had exacerbated the problem of how suitable music could be written. A firm compositional technique had not yet been developed. Although Steiner and Newman had made considerable inroads into this, their scores also took a turn for the better after Korngold's arrival in the mid-1930s. His use of large blocks of music, complex interweaving of Leitmotivs, and sensitivity to music's interaction with speech left an indelible impression on the future of the field.

One critic observed cruelly of his compositional style that Korngold had always written for Warner Brothers without knowing it – but, quite to the contrary, he was largely responsible for creating the archetype that is today called 'film music'. Instead of scribbling 'wall-to-wall' atmospheric accompaniment, Korngold showed how music could be woven integrally into the structure of a film; he not only raised the quality of the music but also its relevance to the movie as a whole. Friedhofer, his orchestrator, described the 'triumvirate of Korngold, Steiner and Newman' as 'progenitors of the genre' and Korngold himself as 'a giant'. Following Korngold can have been no easy task; and the film scores by other Hollywood composers that have been most enduring in their own rights all arrived alongside or after Korngold's. In this role, Korngold became one of the countless European immigrant Jews who helped to fabricate 'the American dream'. He was the first internationally famous composer of serious concert and operatic music to have been signed up in Hollywood, thus becoming, in the words of Bernd O. Rachold, 'a fixed star between Gustav Mahler and Errol Flynn' – and as such he commanded great respect from his employers and colleagues.

This gave him the freedom to compose his film scores in the way that he wished to and to the levels of which he was capable, which in turn enabled him to make an even greater impact on the industry. Most of his contemporaries – Max Steiner, Franz Waxman, Alfred Newman – came from backgrounds in light music, operetta, musical comedy or Broadway, and were controlled far more by their film producers than was the legendary Korngold. Steiner, for instance, another Viennese immigrant, a Warner favourite and the composer of the influential *King Kong* score and, later, *Gone with the Wind*, was instructed by Jack Warner to write 'wall-to-wall' music, while Korngold was allowed to select exactly which passages he wished to compose for.

Hugo Friedhofer told Elmer Bernstein in an interview in *Film Music Notebook*: 'Naturally there was tremendous respect for Korngold who really had *carte blanche*, and Korngold was one of the only men that I knew that had the chutzpah to go to Hal Wallis or his associate Henry Blanke, who were producing all these wonderful epics and say, "Look, would you give me a little more footage here," or he would say, "I would think this scene would be better transposed to this spot." And they would listen to him, and he was invariably right. This of course is based on his long experience in the theater in Vienna.'

Friedhofer said of Korngold in another interview, 'His contribution was enormous and he influenced everyone working at that time.

Korngold, right, at a session in which sound track is fitted to film. On the screen, Paul Muni as the eponymous hero of the film *Juarez* (1939).

He was the first to write film music in long lines, great flowing chunks that contained the ebb and flow of mood and action, and the feeling of the picture. Of course his assignments – those gorgeous spectacles – were pushovers for his kind of music. Some critics thought he lowered himself by writing for films, but he didn't think so. He was excited by the medium.'

In short, Korngold was the first to write film music of such sterling and unfailing quality – and of stupendous harmonic, melodic and coloristic beauty. In the shattered post-war world, serious concert works that were tonal, romantic, expressive and aesthetically beautiful went out of vogue. But this type of composition did not disappear. It went, complete with its inheritance from Wagner, Mahler and Strauss, with Korngold into the cinema, and there it stayed for at least four decades.

Korngold bridged all the gaps between the intense world of Germanic classical music, the lightness and sophistication of Johann Strauss operettas and the popularity of the movies – a most astonishing, and very unusual, versatility. He never 'wrote down' to his audience. 'Even if I wanted to, I could not write beneath my level,' he commented. Many others were not blessed with such a flexible outlook.

The experience of Arnold Schoenberg is a case in point. Schoenberg relied for his income on his teaching work at the University of California, Los Angeles. He was eager to write for film, since he had a family to support and could certainly have done with the sort of generous fees which Korngold commanded. But it seems he had no grasp of the processes involved. On one occasion he was asked to prepare a score for a picture called *The Good Earth*, which contained a dramatic scene in which a woman gave birth in the middle of a ferocious storm. 'With so much going on, what do you need music for?' was his response. After he announced that his terms would be that 'I will write music and then you will make a motion picture to correspond with it,' he was not approached again.

Similarly, when Igor Stravinsky, another immigrant to Los Angeles, was asked to write some film music, he left his meeting with the producer full of enthusiasm, went home and wrote the music. He called the studio ten days later to say that it was finished. Unfortunately, the film itself had not yet been made.

'I feel very happy as an artist here,' Korngold commented on his life in Hollywood.

*No one tells me what to do. I do not feel part of a factory. I take part in story conferences, suggest changes in the editing when it is dramatically necessary to coincide with a musical structure. It is entirely up to me to decide where in the picture to put music. But I always consult thoroughly with the music-chief [Forbstein] ... I also keep the producer well informed and always secure his consent for my musical intentions first. But in none of my pictures have I ever 'played' my music first to either the music-chief, the director or the producer. And the studio heads never make the acquaintance of my music until the day of the sneak preview. As for my working habits, I like the idea of perfection. If a thing is not right it is done over and over again.*

Korngold's particular brand of perfectionism was well appreciated by audiences. Korngold fan clubs sprang up around the USA: the composer often received letters from people who had gone to see films eight or ten times – one even sixty times – simply so they could hear the music again. He was asked to write suites that could be performed in concert and recorded. For one major problem with film music was that it disappeared along with the film. 'Isn't it great that one can have one's music played immediately by an excellent orchestra?' Korngold remarked. 'But then you have heard it for the last time.'

Because Korngold crossed from the world of Viennese opera into the world of American film music, he found, both musically and socially, that he fitted in precisely with neither. In their personal lives in Hollywood, the Korngolds became something of an island, not least because they were a great deal better off financially than the vast majority of their contemporaries among the immigrants. Financial inequalities produced jealousies and tensions within the community. Korngold was undoubtedly comfortably off – he must be 'unhappy making all that money,' commented his friend Artur Schnabel – and he may well have kept to his position simply because it was so comfortable. But in many respects Hollywood was not unlike Vienna itself – full of talented, famous, thinking people under a great deal of pressure of one type or another, and full of gossip, backbiting and scandal. If you could survive one, you could survive the other.

The immigrant community in Los Angeles included some of the most distinguished artistic talent of the time: *above*, the composer Arnold Schoenberg, and *left*, the writer Thomas Mann

The Korngolds' friends came from the old, German-speaking world: the Reinhardts, the Schoenbergs, occasionally the great writer Thomas Mann and especially Franz and Alma Mahler-Werfel were their preferred companions. They were not fond of Hollywood film-star parties and Korngold himself avoided the glitzy first-night receptions on the opening of a new film, preferring to go out to celebrate with the technical staff instead. He worked with one world and socialized with the other; something was missing from both.

One day Schoenberg dropped in to visit while Korngold was out. Ernst, by then in his late teens, opened the door and Schoenberg came inside to wait. After a short while he began to doodle a music stave and some notes on a piece of paper. When he had finished he pushed the paper over to Ernst and turned it around. The line of music read exactly the same upside down as it did the other way up. Schoenberg left the music and departed. Korngold came home, found his friend's peculiar calling card, smiled and put the piece of paper in his pocket. 'I never saw it again,' Ernst told me. 'I always wonder what happened to it!'

Thomas Mann was working on his massive novel *Doctor Faustus*, in which the central character is a strange, eccentric composer who devises a totally new system of composition. Although it was Schoenberg who eventually tried to sue him (over what he saw as the plagiarism of his twelve-note serial system), Mann was interested generally in composers' behaviour and several times attempted to quiz Luzi about her husband's working practices. She told him little, despite the clarity in her own biography of Erich that when he composed he walked around in something of a daze, as if in another world.

*The Adventures of Robin Hood* won Korngold his second Oscar – this time awarded to him personally. The technicolour movie instantly became a classic, with Flynn and de Havilland ideally cast as Robin and Marian and Basil Rathbone as their adversary, Sir Guy of Gisborne. The duel scenes were brilliantly shot; meanwhile, leaves in the California park that became 'Sherwood Forest' had to be painted green. Korngold's score was exciting, innocent and heroic, fitting the fairy-tale atmosphere to perfection while remaining unmistakably Korngoldian in style. One film critic called his score 'Robin Hood in the Vienna Woods'. 'Miss Austria', from Korngold's

Korngold is presented with his second Oscar, for *The Adventures of Robin Hood* (1938). Unlike the first, for *Anthony Adverse*, this award was made to Korngold personally, not merely the music department of Warner Brothers.

Leo Fall operetta completion *Rosen aus Florida*, found an inspired new home, reset in march tempo and orchestrated sumptuously; so did some music from the poorly-received overture *Sursum Corda*, which seemed more at home accompanying Robin's escape from Nottingham Castle than it had in the concert hall. And the original music moved critics to ecstatic commentary. Bruno David Ussher wrote: 'The orchestra sings with the inwardness of a musician who has himself been moved by the film … The double motiv of love for England and love for Lady Marian is inspirational … abundant in ideas, yet sufficiently persistent in melodic reiteration to allow the ear a certain rest, to create familiarity and impetus by renewed hearing.' Korngold created a suite from the music, which he conducted in concerts in San Francisco and San Diego.

Korngold's contract with Warner Brothers allowed him to be 'lent' to other studios. However, when RKO offered him the scoring of

*Gunga Din* in 1939 he turned it down – 'Too many battles'. It also appears that the journey from his home near the Warner studios across to RKO was too arduous. For Korngold was not, by this time, a particularly well man. His weight may have got the better of him, for he began to suffer from heart pains, no doubt exacerbated by stress and depression. His father, now living nearby, constantly remonstrated with him for abandoning concert composition and was deeply distressed by the picture that greeted him on arrival at 9936 Toluca Lake Avenue: the family gathered in the garden, Luzi playing cards with her friends and Erich lazing bulkily in a hammock. Julius's presence in his son's life was scarcely diminished. The old feuds continued – though Luzi would telephone her parents-in-law every day at 4 p.m., come what may. Julius, retired and exiled, settled down to write his memoirs – and long, mostly unsent, letters to his errant genius son. He sat in at all Erich's recording sessions at Warners, avidly following every note; but always hoped that his son would return to the world of serious music. As he wrote:

A portrait photograph of Julius Korngold dating from 1942

> *Erich Wolfgang Korngold, as an artist living in seclusion without manager or customary publicity, and especially as a 'European' musician exposed to the ever more pronounced national tendencies of American musical life, has entered into a period of stagnation. But will not a significant operatic renaissance – not for the least part in America – flower after the war? Erich Wolfgang Korngold can bide his time till this natural evolution will call forth his most vigorous powers: the powers of an inspired opera composer …*

But Korngold was not only stagnating; he was depressed. 'Whenever he had time,' wrote Luzi, 'he sat by the radio and listened gloomily to the news and talked about his fears for Europe and the world.' He began to spend long hours sitting around doing nothing except thinking. 'When I carefully tried to suggest that he wrote something for himself, he replied, as if irritated, "I wouldn't dream of it."' They had to miss the long-awaited première of *Die Kathrin*, which took place in Stockholm on 7 October 1939. Korngold's music, banned along with that of all Jewish composers, could not now be played in its spiritual home, Vienna. 'It was as if he had made a vow that he would write no more "absolute" music as long as the horror in Europe was weighing on the world,' Luzi wrote. And she also expressed the view that he would not have written for films either but for financial necessity. Korngold was effectively supporting three households: his own, his parents' and Luzi's mother and sister.

His next film score was closely related to his Viennese background: a movie entitled *Juarez*, based on his friend Franz Werfel's play *Juarez and Maximilian*. Directed by William Dieterle, it starred the superb character actor Paul Muni in the title role, with Bette Davis as Carlotta and Claude Rains as Napoleon. It was the third in a series of three 'bio-pics' starring Muni, the others having been *Pasteur* and *Zola*. Muni felt that the parallels in the current world situation would make the film timely 'and hopefully influence people against dictatorships, no matter how benevolent'. This underlying theme, combined with the Viennese connections, made *Juarez* a project close to Korngold's heart.

Bette Davis and Errol Flynn in *The Private Lives of Elizabeth and Essex* (1939)

*Motion Picture Herald* declared: 'An entirely original score by Erich Wolfgang Korngold accompanies the picture, in descriptive and interpretative tonal background, emerging at times to strike a dominant note in the furtherance of the action or to sound a diapason of otherwise inarticulate emotion. Like all of this music-master's scoring, the tonal content never obtrudes or overshadows the dramatic.' Korngold used existing melodies such as the Mexican national anthem, 'God Save Emperor Franz', 'The Battle Hymn of the Republic for Lincoln and the Civil War' and 'La Paloma' as an integral part of the score; however, he did not attempt to ape traditional Mexican music. As with the African scenes in *Anthony Adverse* and later the South American episodes in *The Sea Hawk*, he felt that his own inventions, inspired by the exotic settings, could better mirror the action and atmosphere than any pastiche of ethnic music.

This view held true for historical music as well, as Korngold explained for his next film, *The Private Lives of Elizabeth and Essex*. 'It is a play of eternally true principles and motives of love and ambition, as recurrent today as 300 years ago,' he said when questioned on why he had not used pseudo-Tudor music. 'The characters speak the English spoken today. Why then should the composer use "thou" and "thee" and "thine" if the dialogue doesn't?'

The film, adapted from the stage play *Elizabeth the Queen* by Maxwell Anderson, featured a *tour de force* by Bette Davis as Queen

A poster for *The Sea Hawk* (1940), one of the most successful of the Flynn swashbucklers and one of Korngold's most beautiful and memorable film scores

Elizabeth with Errol Flynn as the lover she forces herself to execute. The anguish of this doomed love later helped to add anguish to the slow movement of Korngold's Symphony in F sharp, for which he drew on this film's score. Korngold's sensitivity to the fine details of action on screen is obvious in the theme which exactly matches the pace of Davis's walk to her throne or the subtle combination of tenderness and tension which helps to underscore the psychological dilemmas that the characters face. Bette Davis was his favourite actress and helped, à la Jeritza, to inspire the music that he wrote for her films.

In 1940 Korngold wrote one of his best-loved film scores: *The Sea Hawk*, which was his last historical epic. Set, like so many of the others, in Elizabethan England, and based, like *Captain Blood*, on a Sabatini novel, it starred Errol Flynn in the title role, Brenda Marshall as the half-Spanish noblewoman he loves and Flora Robson as the Queen. The rousing and patriotic tale was in no way coincidental to the continuing horrors in Europe; because of the subject of enslaved men emerging in triumph, and the Queen's stirring closing speech, it was expected to have an important effect on the morale of the allied troops. On set, Flora Robson and Brenda Marshall were knitting woollen helmets for the soldiers at the front.

It was a story which Korngold would certainly have sympathized with and been inspired by, and it gave him every opportunity to write heroic, richly chromatic music in his finest style. It brought him another Oscar nomination. The score ranged from the Panamanian jungle (an opportunity to introduce the now much-used Death motif from *Die tote Stadt*) and chained galley slaves to the exquisite love theme which unifies the hero's love for his country and for Maria. Again, it is really an opera without words – and sometimes with them. The lute song for Maria (rehoused as the 'Old Spanish Song' of Korngold's opus 38 songs) and the triumphant chorus into which the freed sailors suddenly break as they sail for the shores of Dover, both feel entirely natural. One scene involves an escaped pet monkey at the court of Elizabeth; for this sequence Korngold provided an exquisite skittering and squeaking which blend to perfection with the animal's sounds. Although he wrote only a detailed four-stave piano score, his indications of orchestral colouring, which would be passed on to Friedhofer, were extremely precise. Many thousands of people have had their first introduction to Korngold's music through this film or through *Robin Hood*.

Ronald Reagan starred with Ann Sheridan in *King's Row* (1941), a tale of physical and mental health and sickness in small-town America.

In 1941 Korngold tackled another sea film, but of a very different nature. *The Sea Wolf*, loosely based on Jack London's novel, was a vehicle for Edward G. Robinson as a sadistic captain, Wolf Larsen, dying slowly of a brain tumour. The plot was virtually unrecognizable from the original book (justifying London's original ban on the filming of his books, which he feared would damage his reputation). But it stirred Korngold so much that he even considered for a short time writing an opera on the subject. The claustrophobia of this ship, the eerie sea mists, escaped convicts and increasing psychological tension are all intensified and focused by Korngold's score. *Pacific Coast Musician* produced this review:

> *Korngold's musical score is somewhat of a departure from what we have come to more or less expect from him … Here is searching music; music that enriches the emotional content of the ugly and horrifying story … San Francisco Bay fog, the cold deck of a ferry boat, the departure of Larsen's ship 'The Ghost' and many other scenes underscored by rather indeterminate melodic line but with harmonies suspended – more psychologically than musically – take on real dramatic significance.*

The same year, Korngold worked on the score of *King's Row* – a film that today is best known for Ronald Reagan's line: 'Where's the rest of me?' on discovering that both his legs have been amputated. Akin to today's soap operas, the film's theme is changing fortunes and mental disturbance in a small Midwest town at the turn of the nineteenth century, following the fates of a small group of friends from different backgrounds. Korngold's virtuoso variation technique proved a masterstroke, for the strong, fanfare-like theme which appears with the main title is the basis for the vast majority of what follows, along with characterful Leitmotivs for each role. *Film Music Notes* reported:

> *… after having seen the first film run, the composer had completely outlined in his mind the entire musical score … When each episode was concluded, Korngold too, had finished his theme and remarkable as it may sound, not one item had to be changed. Korngold stated that it is not the first time, however, that he has composed an entire sequence that matched the film perfectly, but this is the first score that he ever composed*

Rehearsing on the set of *The Constant Nymph* (1942); Korngold is at the piano, Charles Boyer in front of him and Joan Fontaine to his right. On the right, wearing blazer and slacks, is the director, Edmund Goulding.

*all the way through. As he says, 'I arrived in the projection room and the film was run through to the end at which time I was sure of my entire score, timing or measure for each sequence, each theme and action.'*

The film closes with an operatic-style chorus setting of Henley's *Invictus*, climaxing 'I am the master of my fate', celebrating the blending of fate with fortitude and courage. *The Constant Nymph* was a best-selling novel by Margaret Kennedy, centring on the family of an eccentric contemporary composer. The 'constant nymph' of the title is the sensitive, weak-hearted fourteen-year-old Tessa (played by Joan Fontaine, Olivia de Havilland's sister) who falls in love with a young composer named Lewis Dodd (Charles Boyer), only to be helplessly sent away to school while he marries an unsympathetic socialite. Eventually composer and schoolgirl declare their love and plan to run away together, but Tessa's bad heart gives out and she dies. The notorious Hayes Commission, responsible for censoring all Hollywood film plots, must have insisted on the mangling of the original story – a teenager could not possibly be shown running away with an older man, as Tessa actually does in the book just before her death – and some of the impact is lost. Instead, Tessa dies listening to the strains of a tone poem by her beloved Lewis on the wireless. The tone poem, provided by Korngold, is called *Tomorrow* and the film's score follows the development of its haunting theme through various guises – a piano trio in traditional, simple, romantic vein played at home by Tessa and family, a 'modernist', discordant crashing on two pianos as performed at a society party, and the tender, sentimental and briefly massive six-and-a-half minute tone poem for an orchestra of seventy musicians, a choir of thirty women's voices and a solo contralto.

Korngold gave *Tomorrow* an opus number – Op. 33 – the first time he had done so for any of his film music. Its text, by Margaret Kennedy herself, dealt with Korngold's perennial theme of love, death and renewal: 'When I am dead, another love will cheer thee ... the sun will rise as bright tomorrow morn.' The film was very much in tune with Korngold's own musical philosophy, emphasizing heart above head, beauty and emotion above cold and impersonal modernism; the influence of the composer's presence on the script is almost tangible. *The Constant Nymph* remained one of his own favourites among his films.

In 1941 Korngold also wrote his only non-film music of the war years – also his only religious music. He was approached by a local Rabbi for what became *A Passover Psalm*, Op. 30, and *Prayer*, Op. 32. Rabbi Jacob Sonderling seems to have been an artistically enlightened and imaginative individual, and supportive of Los Angeles' immigrant artistic population. He commissioned Jewish liturgical music not only from Korngold, but also from Schoenberg. As Korngold was one of that large number of Jews who would have declared themselves made Jewish only by Hitler, it is no surprise that he had not shown interest in writing religious works any earlier. But his motivation for writing these short pieces – the first for soloist, chorus and orchestra on texts from the Hagadah, the second for tenor, women's chorus, harp and organ on a text by Franz Werfel – was not purely religious. He was asked to write them; and he had not been formally commissioned to write anything other than film music for a very long time.

Max Reinhardt had started a new enterprise: a workshop for young actors based in Hollywood, modelled after the similar courses he had run in Berlin. In May 1939 Korngold put the music together from Rossini operas for the school's first production, Goldoni's *Servo di*

*Due Padrone* (as *At Your Service*). The immigrant community that
motivated the school had high hopes for its success and invited
leading Hollywood producers to the opening night – but only to be
disappointed. The European stage performance style advocated by
Reinhardt and the 'modern' acting required for film in close-up were
utterly incompatible; the former elicited only patronizing chortles
from the visiting VIPs. Times were changing; Reinhardt's approach
had dated and dimmed under the bright camera lights. The Goldoni
lasted one night only.

The school had to move to a new home where it had the use of a
small theatre and here Reinhardt mounted a Shakespeare evening
incorporating Korngold's song settings from *As You Like It* and
*Othello*, later published as his opus 31. The evening was produced
on a shoestring budget and Korngold himself rented the props from
Warner Brothers. When he was congratulated on his music after
the show, he replied: 'Yes, yes, but what do you think about
Desdemona's bed?'

The New Opera Company in New York had announced a new
staging of *Rosalinda* on Broadway in 1942 and Korngold was invited
to conduct. He missed working in live theatre and, although he
disliked the idea of working on *Rosalinda* without Max Reinhardt, he
agreed to go. On his arrival he found that this production was a little
too familiar for comfort. The director, Felix Brentano, had been a
former assistant of Reinhardt's and as Korngold watched a rehearsal
for the first time he realized that what he was seeing was a plagiarism
of Reinhardt's production, without the rights to the official, published
Reinhardt–Korngold version having been obtained. He put his foot
down. Either the New Opera Company must pay up for the rights
and engage Reinhardt officially as director or he would have nothing
to do with the show. In the end Reinhardt, dissuaded from full
involvement by his son, who was convinced the production would
flop, took credit as supervisor rather than director. But the production
did not flop – it was, in fact, a great success and established *Die
Fledermaus* as a firm favourite in the USA. It seemed for a while that
the 'good old days' of Berlin were back again.

This joy was short-lived. In 1943, shortly after some preliminary
meetings regarding a production of the Reinhardt–Korngold *Schöne
Helena* in New York, Max Reinhardt suffered two strokes. His death

was a great blow to Korngold. Homesick as ever for Vienna, the loss of his close friend and strongest link with his old life was deeply upsetting for the composer. He took part in a memorial concert, for which he prepared an arrangement of *Urlicht* from Mahler's Second Symphony and performed some works of his own. This death was the first of two which helped to propel Korngold back in the direction of serious composition.

He was by now taking less and less pleasure in writing film music. Perhaps his novelty value had worn off for Warner Brothers; perhaps it was simply bad luck that he was being offered second-rate films to score. His music had, if anything, become even stronger. His next score, *Devotion* – a bio-pic of sorts about the Brontë sisters with Olivia de Havilland as Charlotte and Ida Lupino as Emily – included an exquisite melody which he later turned into an art-song, *Glückwunsch* ('Congratulation'), one of his opus 38 songs; some wild and atmospheric music for the Yorkshire moors; and also a powerful, visionary episode reminiscent of some of the most turbulent passages of *Die tote Stadt* as Emily glimpses and is later swept away by a cloaked horseman representing death. Detail was rich and perceptive – Korngold's music exactly mirrors the drunken Branwell's unsteady steps with a typical sharpness of wit. The script, however, was stilted and uninspired; the character of Charlotte came across as distinctly unsympathetic; and the film was held back for three years before finally being released in 1946.

Devotion: the bio-pic of the Brontë family starred Ida Lupino and Paul Henreid. Korngold's score was composed in 1943 but the film was not shown until three years later.

*Between Two Worlds* was a very different type of film, and this score became Korngold's favourite of his entire screen output. Based on Sutton Vanes's play *Outward Bound*, the story concerns a group of people who find that they are travelling together on a boat to a destination that they believe to be America. They are forced during the course of the journey to face up to aspects of themselves and one another that prove deeply fateful – for, as they realize after a while, they are not on their way to the USA; they are in fact dead. The boat is their journey to the beyond; and each person is meted out his or her reward or punishment for all eternity by 'The Inspector' – unforgettably played by Sidney Greenstreet.

Obviously *Das Wunder der Heliane* bore the closest relation of Korngold's earlier works to this story; as that opera and this film were both favourites of his, he must have found visions of an afterlife attractive and inspiring. The Korngold scholar Brendan G. Carroll has even suggested that there are resemblances to the music of *Heliane* in the music of *Between Two Worlds*. Whether or not this was deliberate on the composer's part, he certainly produced a marvellous score – full of mystery as figures wander in and out of the mist, triumphant and loving as the central pair of lovers (Paul Henreid and Eleanor Parker) are reunited in life after a mercifully unsuccessful suicide pact. And it brilliantly captures the brittle, bitter and insecure journalist character played by John Garfield, ascerbically echoing his catch-phrase 'Take a card – go on, take a card' with a jagged, characteristic rhythm and a drawn-out tritone (an augmented fourth, dissonant in aural effect) in an instrumental Leitmotiv that actually sets the words, perfectly uniting script, portrayal and atmosphere.

Unfortunately for Korngold, someone at Warner Brothers saw fit to match the 'ghostly' atmosphere of the film with a ghostly quality to the sound recording, which rendered the glorious music muffled and fuzzy. There were weaknesses in the script absent from the play – the situation of the characters (that they are dead) is made clear to viewers from the start, hence abandoning much of the original's mystery. The conventional and judgemental attitudes towards heaven, hell and suicide probably helped to date it quickly and make it uninteresting to future generations of film buffs, although the film was well reviewed at the time for its superb acting, 'superior achievement' and 'class entertainment'.

*Of Human Bondage*, on which Korngold worked over the winter of 1944–5, was hailed with no such happy words. This remake, starring Eleanor Parker and Paul Henreid, was ill-fated from the beginning. A film of Somerset Maugham's novel had been made over a decade earlier, starring Korngold's favourite actress Bette Davis. Crossing the lot after watching the original film, he bumped into her and stopped to say hello. He had just watched her film of the same title, he told her, and had been impressed. Of course, he added, some aspects of it were starting to look a little dated ten years on. 'But we,' he added, 'are already ten years out of date!' The story was censored out of all sense by the Hayes Commission and part of the rationale in asking Korngold to write the music was a vain hope that a brilliant score would help to rescue what was a really lousy film. The brilliant score materialized – lush, romantic, melodic in Korngold's most

chocolaty mode, including music such as Nora's theme, which has
survived to be much enjoyed in performance and recording. The
rescue of the film did not materialize, however. The score was even
more of a hindrance than a help; as the film was so obviously weak,
the music virtually overbalanced it.

Korngold's misgivings and 'I can't do it' agonizings at the start
of each film project were increasing. He turned the shift in his
Hollywood fortune to his advantage in his public image as jester. One
popular anecdote runs like this: Max Steiner was teasing him about
how Korngold's film music had declined in quality while his own had
improved. 'Maxie, you're absolutely right,' declared Korngold. 'And
I'll tell you why – I've been stealing from you and you've been stealing
from me!' His wit was a form of armour against such comments
and against the silly demands of ignorant executives, such as the invitation from David O. Selznick to him, Franz Waxman and Miklós
Rosza to score sample scenes for a movie before it was assigned to one
of them. Waxman and Rosza were furious, but Korngold shrugged
and refused with the comment, 'Suppose I should win?' And when he
finally came to leave Hollywood and was asked why, Korngold
remarked glumly: 'When I first came to Hollywood, I could not
understand the dialogue – now I can.'

*Escape Me Never* (1946–7) was none the happier for anybody
understanding the dialogue, but it drew from Korngold one of his
most beautiful and quintessentially Viennese scores. Casting Errol
Flynn as a composer was the first mistake; having a baby die during
the story was the second. Based on Margaret Kennedy's novel *The
Fool of the Family* and the play of the same story, *Escape Me Never*
could have been moving. It tells of a composer's turbulent and misguided love life and the footloose but loyal Gemma (Ida Lupino) who
is devoted to him. She is, however, a widowed mother and when her
baby dies due to neglect, her devotion is broken – after which he
begins to appreciate her at last. Korngold's waltz melody for the
song 'Escape Me Never', which the anti-hero ultimately dedicates to
Gemma, was an integral part of the plot. Its soaring melodic leaps and
swinging cross-rhythms are memorable and songful. The love music
for Gemma and her composer is sweetly ecstatic, and the whole has an
Austro-Bohemian flavour beautifully matched to the romantic
European settings. The film also contained the nearest thing Korngold

Ida Lupino and Errol Flynn
in the bohemian love-story
*Escape Me Never*; the film's
score was composed in
1946, the première followed
a year later.

ever wrote to a popular song: a simple, folk-like ballad, 'Love for
Love', sung by Gemma, which did very well in record sales.

Christmas and birthdays in the Korngold household were always
major events, at Erich's pedantic instigation. 'I took him Christmas
shopping once,' his daughter-in-law Helen told me, rolling her eyes
affectionately heavenwards. He set off with a lengthy list and
would not be satisfied until every item on the list was purchased and
wrapped perfectly. Come Christmas Day, small tables would be
spread with white cloths and piled high with gifts – one such table for
every family member – and, most theatrically, each year would be
'the year' of a different person, highlighted by extra special presents
and announced by Erich only on the day. His generosity was as lavish
as ever. Helen remembered how her legs had ached after standing up
for so long to open her Christmas presents. In 1945, Luzi unwrapped
her pile of gifts to discover something very, very special: the
finished sketch of a new string quartet, his third. 'Erich had come
back to himself,' she wrote.

Now and then Julius had suggested to his son that such-and-such a
passage of music was particularly good and might usefully be

preserved outside the score of the film in question. Korngold had always felt that the music he wrote for films was worthy of a life of its own, and as the wheels of his personal creativity began slowly to turn once again he based much of his output on music that he had already written for movies. The third movement of the D major String Quartet which he gave Luzi for Christmas was based on the sombre, dark-hued score of *The Sea Wolf*, and much of the four-movement work showed him returning to his old love of dramatic bitonal effects.

What had made Korngold begin to compose concert works again? Was it his deep disillusionment with the film world? 'A film composer's immortality stretches all the way from the recording stage to the dubbing room,' he said. Was it increased optimism over the European situation? Or was it an increasing awareness that life is too short not to strive to fulfil one's deepest longings? His experience of mortality had been heightened by two world wars, by the death of Reinhardt and now by the death of his father. Julius Korngold died in 1945, after eighty-five years of turbulent life in which he had seen the transformation of the magnificent Austro–Hungarian Habsburg Empire into part of a Europe divided and devastated by its most horrific war, and the transformation of his son from a boy wonder following in Mahler's footsteps into a fat, lazy, witty scribbler of film scores. Julius's death brought home to his son a sense of guilt at having let down his father's expectations – and the knowledge that now it was too late for his father to see his triumphant return to his rightful status as one of Vienna's foremost composers.

'A man like he,' read one letter of tribute to Julius received by Erich and Luzi, 'whose knowledge and judgement of music was based upon a profound love for this art, such a man should have lived earlier and longer in this country.' The letter came from Arnold Schoenberg, who was great-hearted enough towards his one-time adversary to express sorrow that they had not known one another better.

'I will be fifty next May,' Korngold explained to Warner Brothers when he decided not to renew his contract in October 1946. 'Fifty is very old for a child prodigy. I feel I have to make a decision now, if I don't want to be a Hollywood composer for the rest of my life.'

# 8

The Albertine palace in
Vienna after bomb damage
during the war

*I believe that my newly completed symphony
will show the world that atonality and ugly
dissonance at the price of giving up inspiration,
form, expression, melody and beauty will result
in ultimate disaster for the art of music.*

Letter from Korngold to
Hermann Lewandowsky, 1952

# '... es träumt sich zurück ... ' 1946–57

The distinguished violinist Bronisław Huberman, founder in 1937 of
the Palestine Orchestra (later the Israel Philharmonic), had been an
occasional dinner guest at the Korngold home for many years. There
was a standing joke between him and Korngold: Huberman would say
to the composer, 'So, Erich, where's my violin concerto?' This had
gone on for around thirty years – so that when Huberman arrived one
evening in 1945 and posed the usual question, it was quite a surprise
for him when Korngold promptly sat down at the piano and played
its opening to him: a glorious and touching melody, songful and
perfect for a solo violin. According to one newspaper interview,
Korngold had had this work in mind as early as 1937, when he
composed the score of *Another Dawn*. Enthusiastic, Huberman made
him promise to complete the piece; so Korngold set to with a will,
writing two beautiful, lyrical movements based on themes from
*Another Dawn* (that same opening theme derived from Korngold's
Cheerful Heart motif), and from *Juarez* and *Anthony Adverse* (the
sorrowful romance of the second movement).

A portrait of Bronislaw
Huberman, the violinist who
enthusiastically encouraged
Korngold in writing his
Violin Concerto, though
he ultimately did not give
the première.

But the concerto's progress was not to be simple. Huberman would
not commit himself to a firm performance date, and Korngold
suffered a further setback when he tried to test out the work. Ernst W.
Korngold traces the chequered history of the concerto thus: 'He had
finished the first two movements when he decided to invite a violinist
friend, who shall remain nameless, to his home to sight-read them
with him. The result was devastating. The violinist … produced a
gruesome mishmash of false starts and screeching cacophony.
Korngold put all work on the third movement, which was already
firmly in his mind, aside, his demands for technique too difficult.'

The dedicatee of Korngold's Violin Concerto was Alma Mahler
Werfel, whose husband Franz Werfel had died in 1945. She was
distraught and Korngold's concerto was offered by the composer she
had known since his sailor-hat days by way of a condolence gift,
in memory of his friend. The dedication also recalls Korngold's

admiration for and debt of gratitude to Alma's first husband, Mahler, and those childhood experiences which he had now left so far behind. How did he feel now about his child prodigy years? He remarked to his family one day: 'It's as if it all happened to somebody else.'

It was none other than Jascha Heifetz who finally gave the Korngold Violin Concerto its première, on 15 February 1947 in St Louis. Heifetz was probably the most influential violinist of the twentieth century (after Fritz Kreisler), idolized by generations of string players who longed to emulate his technical and musical wizardry. His clarity, cool demeanour, exceptional virtuosity and complete musical integrity became an inspiration to thousands of musicians. Heifetz's manager, Rudi Polk, was an acquaintance of the Korngolds; he had heard of Korngold's new concerto and soon Heifetz invited the composer to show it to him. Heifetz helped to restore Korngold's faith in the concerto, and insisted that the composer *increase* the technical demands of the final movement, which was

Franz and Alma Mahler Werfel were among the Korngolds' closest friends in Hollywood. Korngold dedicated the Violin Concerto to Alma, following Franz's death in 1945.

The great violinist Jascha Heifetz gave the première of Korngold's concerto; his recording has done much to popularize the work.

based on the main theme from *The Prince and the Pauper*. Not long after their meeting, Korngold met Huberman and told him: 'I haven't betrayed you. I'm not engaged yet, but I've flirted.' Huberman, on learning that Korngold had been flirting with Heifetz, of all people, was apparently eager to clear up misunderstandings and bad feelings and, according to Luzi's book, promised to play the piece even if Heifetz gave the première. But Huberman never did play it; and he and Korngold never met again.

Heifetz's first performance of the concerto, under the conductor Vladimir Golschmann, was a triumph. A review spoke of 'the most enthusiastic ovation in the history of the auditorium' and prophesied a lifetime for the work equal to that of the Mendelssohn Violin Concerto. But Korngold was nervous, knowing that the New York critics were likely to tear the piece to shreds. He wrote a letter to the critic Josef Reitler, an old friend from Vienna days, begging for any help that he could give by way of preview and build-up before the New York performance. 'I am helpless and deserted here,' he told Reitler. 'I have no manager, no agent, not even a publisher in

America.' Although Schott's would publish the work from their London office, they had no American base and no direct means of influence in New York.

Of course, Korngold was partly responsible for that situation himself. When urged to seek the services of an agent a few years before, he had refused, saying that if anyone wanted to play one of his pieces, they could ask him in person. He had expected a return to the success of his Viennese days to be relatively easy; it was already clear, however, that it would not be.

Korngold's fears of the New York critics were justified, although Chicago was kinder and the audiences themselves were enthuasiastic in both cities. Korngold, a critic's son, unfortunately had never learned to shrug off the opinions of the press, and some of these really were nasty. *The New York Times*: 'This is a Hollywood concerto. The melodies are ordinary and sentimental in character, the facility of the writing is matched by the mediocrity of the ideas.' And the *New York Sun* had to coin that immortal phrase: 'More corn than gold.'

Korngold's Cello Concerto was written at almost the same time as the Violin Concerto – but in a very different context. It was an important feature of Korngold's last Hollywood film score, for *Deception*, which starred Bette Davis, Paul Henreid and Claude Rains in an unlikely love triangle between a pianist, a cellist and a composer. The film was based on the Louis Verneuil play *Jealousy*, but, as usual, the story – which Korngold liked very much in its original form – was censored out of all recognition. Bette Davis's character could not be 'punished' in the plot for having had out-of-wedlock relationships, so she had, in the commission's view, to be punished for something else. Hence she rather unconvincingly murders the composer.

Korngold's Cello Concerto was written as the work which the fictional composer creates for the cellist; the composer is 'modern' and therefore Korngold's one-movement concerto is comparatively discordant, although there are some striking melodies as well. Korngold expanded it for concert performance, though at eleven minutes it remains short as concertos go – brief but emotionally intense and requiring a virtuoso technique. In the film it serves as 'film-music' as well as a straight concerto, co-ordinating beautifully with the action: there is a lyrical blossoming in the melody as the cellist (Henreid) glances up in mid-performance to see his beloved

Bette Davis with Korngold on the set of *Deception* (1946). The Cello Concerto which Korngold wrote for the film served superbly as the work of its fictional modern composer, Hollenius, yet remained essentially Korngoldian.

Bette Davis taking her seat in the audience. 'My greatest inspiration,' said Korngold, 'came from the expressive voice, and movements of [the film's] star, Bette Davis.'

Again, Korngold's influence is very much present in the script. At the start of the film, Henreid's character, interviewed by journalists about his favourite composers, cites: 'Stravinsky when I think of the present, Richard Strauss when I think of the past,' and then the film's fictional composer, Hollenius, who 'unites the rhythms of today with the melodies of yesterday'. Aside from the concerto, the rest of the film score was largely based on the expansive theme of the main title (and Korngold's Death motif puts in another appearance as Bette Davis paces about silently considering the murder). The short and lovely Romance Impromptu for cello and orchestra (which also exists in an arrangement with piano accompaniment) was likewise written for the film. Bette Davis took piano lessons for her role, but the Beethoven 'Appassionata' sonata was dubbed in by a young pianist named Shura Cherkassky (who later became one of the century's great pianistic forces). As for Henreid, he could not play the cello, so he was cleverly filmed with a helper on each side, one providing the bowing arm and the other the left hand. The concerto was actually played by Eleanor Aller.

Against medical advice, Korngold accepted an invitation from the Light Opera Company to conduct *Rosalinda* in Los Angeles and San Francisco. He was stubborn in his refusal to curtail his activities on health grounds – whether conducting or eating sweets. If the dinner table held a dish of sweets, chocolates or crystallized fruit, he would distract Luzi's attention and 'sin', quickly picking up a sweetmeat while she was looking the other way. He also insisted on taking a driving holiday to Canada despite the dangers of high altitudes. It was on 9 September 1947 that he was repaid for his stubbornness with a severe heart attack that landed him in hospital, forbidden so much as to move, for two weeks. That was followed by another month of bedrest at home. Lying on his back with nothing to do, he began to think out a new piece, which became the Symphonic Serenade, Op. 39.

The Serenade (in B flat major, as was Marietta's Lute Song) is one of Korngold's most affable and charming works, scored for string orchestra. Its four movements lilt along with all the warm colours of a Viennese autumn: an *allegro semplice* (rapid, simply), intermezzo, *lento religioso* (very slow, religiously) and *allegro con fuoco* (fast, fiery) finale. There is little in it to suggest the turbulence and discordance of his two greatest operas and symphony: it is essentially diatonic in harmony, light and graceful in atmosphere, most akin to the genial *Much Ado* music and the irresistible charm of the operetta completions. It is certainly deserving of a place in the repertoire alongside the popular string serenades by Tchaikovsky, Dvořák and Elgar. Significantly, there is little film music in this piece; it is one of the few works of Korngold's late compositional flowering that is wholly new and it took him nearly a year to complete it. He dedicated it to his wife.

Another serenade had occupied Korngold from 1946: his first musical comedy of his own, named *Die stumme Serenade* ('The Silent Serenade'), with lyrics by Bert Reisfeld and William Okie and scoring for an eight-piece instrumental ensemble and two pianos. The work was not exactly Korngold's masterpiece; although the music abounded in Korngoldian lightness and melodic flow, it made little impact.

Korngold had never ceased to miss Vienna. In 1948, in tribute to his lost home, he wrote a setting of a poem by Hans Kaltneker, author of *Die Heilige*, entitled *Sonett für Wien* (Op. 41). The melody was

The Vienna Opera House was badly damaged by fire during the war, much to Korngold's grief.

the soaring waltz theme from *Escape Me Never*, transformed into a more sedate duple time (two units rather than the usual three), but ecstatic in atmosphere, capturing with much longing Kaltneker's portrait of the great city's churches, saints, processions and fountains – 'You city, you psalm resounding from the mouth of God ...' This quasi-mystical vision was the city Korngold missed – not the anti-Semitic, scandal-ridden hothouse that had banished him. And it was his ideal vision of Vienna that enabled him to consider returning to Europe to resume his old career where the war had interrupted it.

In May 1949 Luzi, Erich and George Korngold set sail for Europe for the first time in eleven years. They were, at last, going home. Or so they thought. George (whose name now had an American *e*) drove the family across the continent and they approached the Austrian border with anxiety as well as excitement, but Luzi wrote of how delighted they were to find that so little seemed to have changed as they approached Gmunden. But their Schloss Hüselberg had been requisitioned for refugees and they were distressed by the state of chaotic disrepair in which they found it.

Neither did they feel welcome in their home city of Vienna. The world that had been theirs was a world that was theirs no more. Although the damage was in general less bad than they had feared, Vienna was now a 'dead city' itself. The opera house, which Korngold so loved, had been bombed; only the façade was still standing. All their relations and most of their friends had either emigrated or been murdered in the Holocaust. They began the fight to get their Sternwartestrasse house back and made contact with the few people they knew who were still there, such as Julius Bittner's widow Emilie, and Helene Thimig, who had returned soon after her husband's death. Korngold was deeply saddened by the opera house bombing and the loss of so many old associates. People they met at concerts would say to them: 'You were clever to leave,' or, 'How nice to see you, when are you leaving again?' and all assured them that they had had no part in 'that'. Now the quality of nostalgia and longing for a better world of the past, which had been powerfully and almost prophetically present in Korngold's music for most of his life, came into its maturity.

At first it seemed that the Korngold comeback would take place according to plan. Korngold wrote to Wilhelm Furtwängler about the Symphonic Serenade; as in bygone days the conductor immediately agreed to perform it, without even seeing it first. Furtwängler had been ostracized by many members of the musical community for remaining in Europe and having held a post in Goebbels's Reichs-musikkammer (from which he was ousted for speaking up on behalf of Jewish artists). But Korngold, idealistic as ever, even now valued artistic excellence ahead of political affiliation. Furtwängler conducted the strings of the Vienna Philharmonic in Korngold's new serenade on 15 January 1950. A succession of near-disasters almost scuppered the première: Furtwängler was snowbound out of Vienna and could not get back for the first rehearsal. Korngold, who was not supposed to conduct because of his heart condition, temporarily took his place. He attributed the success of the performance to the superb musicians of the Vienna Philharmonic itself. 'All in all, a worthy occasion,' was his opinion of the evening.

Just under one month later *Sonett für Wien* and the Five Songs for middle voice, Op. 38, were given their first performances in Vienna as well. Dedicated to Maria Jeritza-Seery (as Korngold's beloved Marietta and Violanta was now called), these songs were partly derived from Korngold's film music: the *Alt-Spanisch Lied* ('Old Spanish Song') was drawn from *The Sea Hawk* and *Glückwunsch* sets a tender Richard Dehmel poem with the principal melody from *Devotion*. The *Alt-Englisch Lied* ('Old English Song') and the last of the five, *Kein Sonnenglanz im Auge* (a setting of the Shakespeare sonnet 'My mistress' eyes are nothing like the sun') spring from the same world, if not the films themselves; the odd one out is *Der Kranke* ('The Invalid'), a melancholy and chromatic setting of an Eichendorff poem.

Korngold visited the administrators of the Viennese state theatres and met with positive responses to the ideas of staging *Die Kathrin* and reviving *Die tote Stadt*. He arranged a private play-through of part of *Kathrin* for some of the committee and after he had performed his opera on the piano for some two hours it was agreed that it would be produced the following season. Meanwhile the State Opera, now playing at the Theater an der Wien, agreed to put on *Die tote Stadt*. Encouraged, Korngold began work on a new composition. For the first time ever, he was writing a symphony.

Korngold's Symphony, in his favourite key of F sharp major (an extremely awkward key for most orchestral instruments), is one of his most deeply felt works. Some of it is based on his film music – for example, *Elizabeth and Essex* and *Anthony Adverse* both put in appearances in the funereal slow movement. Its musical language carries not only his love of lyricism and melody but also a harsh, bitter quality that emerges beneath Korngold's usual optimism – not modernistic but discordantly individual. The language of the whole work is concentrated, incisive and gritty. Brendan Carroll described the opening as 'one of the most arresting to any symphony' and Burkhard Schmilgun called the first movement 'a dance of death'. It is full of tension, brilliant orchestral colouring, the drama of fanfares contrasting with darkness lurking just beneath the surface. Korngold makes use of the Cheerful Heart motif in the celebratory finale, which recalls cyclically a number of the symphony's earlier themes; while the Death motif from *Die tote Stadt* is closely related to the Scherzo's trio with its spirals of descending chromatic lines. The orchestration is characteristic of Korngold too, including piano, marimba, harp and celeste, instruments which give the timbre that Korngoldian extra edge of percussiveness and luminosity.

The symphony's dedication – to the memory of President Franklin D. Roosevelt who had died, like Julius Korngold, in 1945 – is a tribute to the USA, which had saved the lives of the composer and his family and which had, unlike Europe, continued to offer him recognition and respect.

The year 1950 was a strange time for any composer to be producing a full-blown romantic symphony. For it was in 1950 that Stravinsky was completing his opera *The Rake's Progress*; it was the year that John Cage, an off-beat ex-student of Schoenberg, discovered the I Ching, which he subsequently used to create music out of chance operations; and a strange, spiritual and artistic young man studying in Cologne, named Karlheinz Stockhausen – later one of the leading experimental electronic composers of the mid-twentieth century – was beginning to take composition seriously. With a very few notable exceptions, music of this period was lean, terse, mostly 'atonal', mostly tuneless; serialism, the twelve-note system first developed by Schoenberg, was becoming the norm, rather than the exception, in new composition. 'Atonality' was still in the ascendant and over the ten years that followed it increasingly gained a stranglehold on new composers around the world. The music of Korngold the child prodigy had been regarded as new, daring, harmonically innovative; and although his style had refined and concentrated with the years, it had not changed inherently while, in the words of one critic writing of the Violin Concerto, 'composition has travelled a long way from the idea of just writing some warm, romantic tunes'.

Korngold was fully aware of what was happening. He was making a conscious stand for the musical values he believed in. In 1952 he wrote to Dr Hermann Lewandowsky: 'I believe that my newly completed symphony will show the world that atonality and ugly dissonance at the price of giving up inspiration, form, expression, melody and beauty will result in ultimate disaster for the art of music.' One programme note writer described the symphony as a 'despondent but defiant scream'.

Korngold's return to Vienna, the city of cakes and pastries, did nothing to help the diet which he was supposed to be following. He found a confectioners which he patronized regularly for his supply of chocolate. A little while afterwards, he found a shop he liked better. The first shop wrote him an obsequious letter to try to tempt back his custom. When she found the letter, Luzi remarked that he must have been buying a very great deal of chocolate to warrant such an appeal. Rather than giving up eating sugar, he attempted to hide it from his wife. He locked his supply of chocolate and crystallized fruit away in his music cabinet and it was only when Luzi saw their little dog sitting up begging beside the cupboard that she realized what was inside.

Plans for the performances of Korngold's operas were not progressing well. The state theatres were blacked out by a strike by technical workers. Juch, the director, hoped that if the strike were resolved soon, Korngold's *Die Kathrin* could be mounted in April 1950; in the end the performances could not take place until October. This meant that the Korngolds had to extend their stay in Vienna for far longer than they had intended. Now all three of them were home-sick again – this time for the USA. In Vienna they had started to feel that 'we do not belong here any more'.

Other aspects of the arts besides music were moving in a direction with which Korngold did not feel in sympathy. He saw the set design for *Kathrin* – a sparse, symbolic room which came under the category of 'implied' scenery. 'Where's the ceiling?' Korngold asked the designer, Walter von Hoesslin, who explained that a contemporary member of the audience would be able to imagine the ceiling for him or her self. Hoesslin owned a country house in the Tyrol and a few weeks later Korngold wrote to him: 'I am coming to spend the day with you to have another talk about the scenery. Please book me a hotel room. If possible, with ceiling.'

The rehearsals too got off to a bad start. Many of the musicians, not least the conductor, were hostile to the light, warm and traditional romanticism of the opera and when the evening of the première came, the opera house was not full. 'I am forgotten,' declared Korngold. But the performance improved: Maria Reining as Kathrin and Karl Friedrich as François acquitted themselves excellently and at the end there were forty curtain calls. The anxious composer was counting them.

Despite the enthusiasm of the audience, Korngold found, as he expected, that critics were less receptive. *Kathrin* was called 'old-fashioned'. Korngold in general was considered *passé*. And with the hostility of the papers and an indisposed singer combining against the opera, *Kathrin* did not run for more than six performances.

A further disappointment was in store over *Die tote Stadt*. The production was all but under way when the Vienna State Opera's administration sent out a press release stating that one famous tenor was to take the role of Paul. Another tenor, who actually had been booked and had learned the role, instantly refused to sing. The fiasco resulted in the cancellation of *Die tote Stadt*.

Korngold's hopes had been well and truly dashed. In April 1951 a concert of his music was organized by the Gesellschaft der Musikfreunde; Korngold played his own D minor Passacaglia from his first Piano Sonata, and the programme also featured the String Sextet, Third String Quartet and the Psalm. But the hall was far from being full. Even though the concert was well received by those present, including the critics, Korngold was convinced he had been forgotten. He was now looking forward to the family's imminent return to Hollywood.

Schott's, the once supportive publishers, had drawn away from Korngold, as he found when he stopped in Mainz on the way west across Europe. His old friends Ludwig and Willy Strecker showed no interest at all in reintroducing his works. Schott's had become the leading and favoured music publisher of Germany under the Third Reich – but apart from that, the world had changed too much while Korngold's music had scarcely changed at all.

Korngold returned to California with his wife, his son George and George's new Viennese wife Monika. At home he busied himself with family matters. He divided up the house at 9936 Toluca Lake so that George and Monika would have their own self-contained wing. Ernst too was married; his wife was a young American woman named Helen. Soon Korngold was a grandfather, to George's first son Gary, whose godmother was Alma Mahler-Werfel.

Grandfatherhood suited Korngold and helped to lift his spirits considerably. He renewed his interest in the symphony, which had lain uncompleted since the disappointments of Vienna; and he began to rework the *Silent Serenade*, which had been given its première on the radio in Vienna, to make it stageable. He was also called on to add some numbers – twelve in all – to *The Great Waltz* for a new production by the Light Opera Company, starring Dorothy Kirsten and John Charles Thomas.

At the same time, however, he was writing letters to performers and conductors, desperately trying to stimulate some interest in his serious

Korngold coaches Alan Badel in conducting for *Magic Fire* (1955). The ailing composer still shows more genuine strength and alertness in his hands alone than is evident in all the actor's dynamism!

concert works. Conductor after conductor turned down the idea of giving the first performance of the symphony; even Bruno Walter, who expressed enthusiasm for the piece but declared himself too old to perform it – he called it a work 'of real musical substance, masterly written, modern in language and yet generally accessible'. A young pianist called Gary Graffman responded to Korngold's letter berating him for giving yet another performance of Rachmaninov's Second Concerto when his own concerto had remained unplayed for the better part of thirty years, by saying that his options were 'far too extensive to permit side-tracking for twentieth-century trivia'. Korngold was not to know that in later years Graffman would be forced to eat his words when deprived of the use of his right hand. To be dismissed as 'twentieth-century trivia' must have been hard indeed for a man who had been dubbed a genius by Mahler.

The year 1953 brought an unexpected return to the world of film.

William Dieterle, Korngold's erstwhile colleague at Warner Brothers, was planning to make a film biography of Richard Wagner, which he would shoot in Munich. Although Korngold was unwilling to have anything further to do with films, he was swayed by the idea of working again with his old friend. 'I did it to protect Wagner,' he added. He also enjoyed the challenge he set himself: not to change a note of Wagner and not to add anything of his own to the score. But he could not help but feel somewhat put out when, after he had reduced the entire 'Ring' cycle to four minutes, the producer decided that the film was still too long and cut it by half an hour, thereby losing a quarter of what remained of the 'Ring'.

Korngold was officially too ill to conduct himself, so Aloys Melichar, a composer, conductor and author, was called in to wield the baton. Korngold did, however, coach Alan Badel, who was to play Wagner, on conducting techniques. A photograph from one such session shows Korngold looking tired, ill and despondent. However, he did make his own first and last movie appearance in this film, *Magic Fire*, as the conductor Hans Richter at Wagner's podium in Bayreuth. And he enjoyed the sessions, happy to be working once again with good musicians in a sympathetic atmosphere and managing to conduct one eight-hour session of non-exertive music.

Something else which spurred Korngold to take on the German film was the chance it would offer him to be in Europe for a performance of the Symphony, which was planned for October 1954. An American performance in Pittsburgh, which William Steinberg was to have conducted, had already fallen through and the Gesell-schaft der Musikfreunde in Vienna also rescinded on the plan to per-form it in the Musikverein. In the end the première was undertaken by Viennese Radio. The performance was a disaster. The symphony had been under-rehearsed and Korngold's plea to Heinrich Kralik, musical director of the radio station, to cancel the broadcast was ignored.

Although the Symphony was not received as badly as Korngold expected, given the poor quality of the playing and the tape, it would not be performed again in the composer's lifetime. Even after Korngold's death the Symphony was ill-starred. Dmitri Mitropoulos wrote of it in 1959: 'My whole life long I have searched for the ideal modern work. I have found it in this symphony.' He planned to conduct it the following season, but died before he could do so.

The Korngolds were ready to return to Hollywood once more when they heard quite unexpectedly of a new production of *Die tote Stadt* that was to be mounted at the Prinzregent Theatre in Munich in May. They prolonged their stay in Germany and all promised well, with Hans Hopf as Paul, Marianne Schech as Marietta, superb (and not too modern) stage designs and Robert Heger, an old acquaintance of Korngold's from Vienna, conducting, in thorough consultation with and deference to Korngold himself.

For the première the theatre was packed and the Lute Song drew frantic applause. But Richard Strauss's son Franz remarked to Luzi, 'Now they cheer him, tomorrow they'll tear him apart.' He was right. '*Die tote Stadt* remains dead,' declared one newspaper, ignoring the popular success of the evening. Although Korngold had seen with his own eyes that his opera made an impact, he was upset, as ever, by bad reviews. 'He had to forget all hope of a come-back,' wrote Luzi.

Korngold bade farewell to Europe by visiting two places very close to his heart: the Hüselberg at Gmunden, which he was selling to the village of Gschwandt; and, finally, probably for the first time, Bruges itself. 'We stood, like Erich's Paul, on the Minnewater ...' wrote Luzi. 'We heard the bells of the innumerable churches ... On this dull and grey day, Erich's dead city came to life for us.'

In Hollywood there were both deaths and births to greet Erich and Luzi. That year Luzi's sister and mother both died, while Ernst and Helen, the former now a drama teacher in a high school, had a new daughter, named Kathrin after her grandfather's operatic heroine. George, who was working as a music editor at the Walt Disney studio, had a second son, named Leslie.

In the spring of 1955 the music critic Karl Schumann interviewed Korngold and found him in a sorry state.

*He had an anachronistic effect with his obligatory bow tie, old-fashioned courtesy and broad Viennese German. His years in the United States did not seem to have left a mark on him. Speaking with him was like being taken back thirty years in time. He seemed to be appallingly weary, this man who had been through emigration and the mill of the film studio. That he was suffering from heart disease was obvious; so was his heartsickness. In the end he died ... more so of a broken heart. He*

*never reconciled himself to the fact of his expulsion from Vienna, from the
good old days, from the* fin-de-siècle *atmosphere, art nouveau, symbolism,
the cult of music, worship of the opera, and the coffeehouse.*

Korngold received two commissions from a publisher looking for
small orchestral pieces suitable for performance by school orchestras.
The second of these was entitled *Straussiana*: a homage to Korngold's
favourite Waltz King, consisting of arrangements of the master's less
famous melodies, many drawn from the operetta *Ritter Pazmann*.
Here, in barely seven minutes, it is clear that Korngold had lost none
of his feel for the music of Strauss; and the simplicity of both this
piece and its companion, Theme and Variations, demonstrates the
sympathy and affection that the composer held for the young people
who would play the works, as well as his adaptability. The supreme
craftsman wrote exactly what he had been asked for.

The Theme and Variations, the melody marked 'like an Irish
folk song', was Korngold's last original work. Its lightness of touch
harks back to his childhood works like the *Märchenbilder*, and its
seven variations each transform the melody in a concise and sharply
characterized manner. The musical language, as was fitting for a
school orchestra, was very much simpler and more diatonic than that
of the symphony; and there is a mood of quiet resignation that
shines through the little rising and falling theme.

*Straussiana* was published without an opus number. But the Theme
and Variations was Korngold's opus 42, which held a peculiar
significance for the composer. He told his wife: 'From the time I was
a boy I knew I would not make it beyond Op. 42.' Luzi pointed out
that if he counted those works with no opus number and the film
scores, he had actually written a great deal more. And he was preparing sketches for opus 43 – a second symphony – as well as a sixth
opera to be based on a story by Franz Grillparzer. But his superstition
was to be proved correct.

On 17 October 1956 the Korngolds spent the evening with Ernst
and Helen. When they arrived home, Korngold remarked to his wife
that he thought there was something wrong with his language and
that he could not express what he wanted to say. The following day he
seemed to be better, but after another day he found he could not read
the newspaper. Korngold had had a stroke to the left side of his brain.

His condition became gradually worse until symptoms of paralysis set in soon afterwards in hospital. He could not speak, move his right side, or remember the names of his family – though strangely, as Luzi recorded, he could still recall the names of composers and musicians. She cared for him at home and although coming home helped him to feel a little more positive, and although he was able to walk again by Christmas, the extent of his depression and pessimism was clear: he refused to read or do any of the recommended writing exercises to stimulate the nervous system. He could enjoy listening to music, but showed no interest in composing any himself.

His sixtieth birthday on 29 May 1957 was celebrated with broadcasts on a number of radio channels and the ailing but delighted composer received telegrams from many old associates – Bruno Walter, Maria Jeritza and, especially welcome, 'Your Vienna Philharmonic'. Luzi in the meantime had been doing her utmost to stir interest in possible birthday celebrations elsewhere, since her husband was too ill to write himself. Via the publishers Weinbergers, she wrote to Mark Lubbock of the BBC, who was planning a Korngold programme for the event, encouraging him to play some of Korngold's recordings of his own music as part of it and quoting comments by Bruno Walter and Mitropoulos about the Symphony.

Korngold lived on, partially disabled, for exactly another six months. On the morning of 29 November he suffered a cerebral haemorrhage. He died in the North Hollywood Hospital that afternoon. His funeral service was held on 2 December at the Hollywood Cemetary Chapel.

Korngold's death was much mourned and commemorated in America and even in the Europe that had failed to welcome him home. The Vienna Opera House flew a black flag at half mast in his honour. 'It's a little late,' sighed his wife. In June 1959, a memorial concert was held in Los Angeles in his honour – in the Schoenberg Hall (ironically enough). The husband and wife violin-and-piano team Louis and Annette Kaufman, the Kaufman String Quartet, contralto Eva Gustavson and others performed some of his chamber music and songs, a tribute from Bruno Walter was read to the audience and the programme carried messages from a number of musicians including the violinist Fritz Kreisler, the singer Lotte Lehmann and the conductor William Steinberg. The review in the *Los*

*Angeles Examiner* was a fitting tribute to Korngold and his music:

> *A memorial concert to Erich Wolfgang Korngold ... brought to our attention a musical voice which may be regarded, when the smog of controversy rolls away, as one of the most civilised and gracious of the twentieth century.*
>
> *Thirty years ago Korngold's idiom seemed advanced. Then came the schools of atonalism, polytonality and general chaos, and Korngold was suddenly placed in the category of the reactionaries.*
>
> *Among those who discarded him, there are a few survivors. Korngold spoke forth last night with a richness of melody and a luxuriance of harmony that marked him for survival.*
>
> *There is no defeatism in Korngold's music. He loved life, he accepted life and he gave back in music the wonder that he found in it.*

Luzi Korngold survived her husband by only a few years. She died in 1962, in her will exhorting her sons to preserve the memory of their father: 'I beg my sons to do their very best to keep alive their father through his works, and not to grow weak in the struggle. I shall leave this world without any regret because, since my husband has predeceased me, life has lost for me its meaning and purpose.'

Julius Korngold, who did not live to witness the last twelve years of his son's life, must nevertheless have the final word:

> *Erich Wolfgang Korngold, as man and artist, has retained not only the truthfulness and modesty peculiar to the child, but also a certain child-like nature. A kind fate has given him optimism, humour and pleasure in harmless witticisms. He became an ideal husband and father, awakening and enjoying loving attachment. He also remained a good son.*

# Classified List of Works

Korngold's earliest published works, written during his child prodigy days, were printed privately by agreement between his father and Universal Edition and bear no opus numbers. Therefore Korngold's Op. 1 is his Piano Trio, published by Schott's, which published the vast majority of his concert works thereafter. Works such as the Cello Concerto and the short tone-poem *Tomorrow* which were created for films but exist as concert works in their own right are listed with their individual first performance dates although they would already have been heard on film sound-tracks. Film scores are for Warner Brothers unless otherwise stated.

The following list of Korngold's works attempts to be comprehensive. To this end, it includes works that have either remained unpublished or unperformed, sometimes both – an asterisk is used to indicate works that were not published. Wherever possible, dates of composition and first performance are given (fp denotes both 'first performance' and, for the film scores, 'film première'). I am very much indebted to Bernd O. Rachold's edition of Julius Korngold's memoirs, *Die Korngolds in Wien*, for details.

### Stage Works

*Der Schneemann,* ballet-pantomime in two scenes for piano, orchestration by Zemlinsky (1908–9). fp Vienna, April 1910 (piano version); Vienna, 4 October 1910 (orchestrated version)

*Der Ring des Polykrates,* Op. 7, opera in one act, libretto by Leo Feld and Julius Korngold after comedy by Heinrich Teweles (1914, shortened version 1919). fp Munich, 28 March 1916

*Violanta,* Op. 8, opera in one act, libretto by Hans Müller-Einigen (1914–15, orchestrated 1915–16). fp Munich, 28 March 1916

*Die tote Stadt* (The Dead City), Op. 12, opera in three acts, libretto by Julius and Erich Korngold after Georges Rodenbach's novella *Bruges-la-Morte* (1892) and play *Le Mirage,* translated as *Das Trugbild* by Siegfried Trebitsch (1916–19). fp Hamburg and Cologne, 4 December 1920

*Das Wunder der Heliane* (The Miracle of Heliane), Op. 20, opera in three acts, libretto by Hans Müller-Einigen after *Die Heilige* by Hans Kaltneker (1923–7). fp Hamburg, 7 October 1927

*Die Kathrin,* Op. 28, opera in three acts, libretto by Ernst Decsey after Heinrich Eduard Jacob's novel *Die Magd von Aachen* (1932–7). fp Stockholm, 7 October 1939

*Die stumme Serenade*, Op. 36, musical comedy in two acts and overture, lyrics by Bert Reisfeld and William Okie (German translation by Raoul Auernheimer) after Viktor Clement's novel (1946–50). fp Vienna, 26 March 1951 (radio); Dortmund, 10 November 1954 (stage)

### Incidental Music

*Viel Lärm um nichts* (Much Ado About Nothing), Op. 11 (1918–19). fp Vienna, 6 May 1920; Suite for Orchestra: Vienna, 24 January 1920; Suite for Violin and Piano (optional horn): Vienna, 21 May 1920

*Der Vampyr,* play by Hans Müller-Einigen (1922). fp Vienna, 3 February 1923*

### Film Scores

*A Midsummer Night's Dream,* arrangements of Mendelssohn's incidental music, directors: Max Reinhardt, William Dieterle (1934–5). fp New York and London, 9 October 1935

*Give Us This Night* (Paramount), lyrics by Oscar Hammerstein II, director: Alexander Hall (1935–6). fp New York, April 1936

*Rose of the Rancho* (Paramount), two sequences (1935)

*Captain Blood*, director: Michael Curtiz (1935)

*Anthony Adverse*, director: Mervyn LeRoy (1936). fp Los Angeles, 29 July 1936

*Hearts Divided*, two sequences, director: Frank Borzage (1936)

*Green Pastures*, two sequences and background music, directors: William Keighley, Marc Connelly (1936)

*Another Dawn*, director: William Dieterle (1936–7). fp June 1937

*The Prince and the Pauper*, directors: Michael Curtiz, William Keighley (1937)

*The Adventures of Robin Hood*, directors: Michael Curtiz, William Keighley (1938). fp 12 May 1938

*Juarez*, director: William Dieterle (1938–9)

*The Private Lives of Elizabeth and Essex*, director: Michael Curtiz (1939). fp 27 September 1939

*The Sea Hawk*, director: Michael Curtiz (1940). fp July 1940

*The Sea Wolf*, director: Michael Curtiz (1941). fp March 1941

*King's Row*, director: Sam Wood (1941)

*The Constant Nymph*, director: Edmund Goulding (1941). fp 23 July 1942

*Devotion*, director: Curtis Bernhardt (1943). fp New York, 5 April 1946

*Between Two Worlds*, director: Edward E. Blatt (1944). fp 20 May 1944

*Of Human Bondage*, director: Edmund Goulding (1944–5). fp Los Angeles, July 1946

*Escape Me Never*, director: Peter Godfrey (1946). fp 1947

*Deception*, director: Irving Rapper (1946). fp October 1946

*Magic Fire* (Republic Production), director: William Dieterle, arrangement by Korngold of music by Wagner (1954–5). fp 15 July 1955

**Orchestral**

*Schauspiel Ouvertüre*, Op. 4 (1911). fp Leipzig, 14 December 1911

*Charakterstudie für großes Orchester* (c.1911)*

Sinfonietta in B major, Op. 5 (1911–13). fp Vienna, 30 November 1913

Military March in B flat, for military band (1917)

*Tanz im alten Stil* (Dance in the Old Style), for small orchestra (1917)*

*Sursum Corda*, symphonic overture, Op. 13 (1919). fp Vienna, 24 January 1920

Piano Concerto in C sharp major for the left hand, in one movement (1923). fp Vienna, 22 September 1924

*Babyserenade*, Op. 24 (1928). fp Vienna, 5 December 1932

Violin Concerto in D major (1937 and 1945). fp St Louis, 15 February 1947

Cello Concerto in C major, in one movement, Op. 37 (1946, for film score *Deception*). fp Los Angeles, 20 December 1946

Romance-Impromptu, for cello and orchestra (1946, for film score *Deception*)

Symphonic Serenade in B flat major, for string orchestra, Op. 39 (1948). fp Vienna, 15 January 1950

Symphony in F sharp major, for large orchestra, Op. 40 (1949–52). fp Vienna, 17 October 1954

Theme and Variations, for school orchestra, Op. 42 (1953). fp Inglewood, 22 November 1953

**Choral**

*Nixe, Gold*, cantata for soloists, chorus and piano (1906)*

*Der Sturm*, for chorus and large orchestra, text by Heinrich Heine (1913)*

*A Passover Psalm*, for solo, chorus and orchestra, Op. 30, text from the Hagadah (1941). fp Los Angeles, 12 April 1941

*Prayer*, for tenor, women's chorus, harp and organ, Op. 32, text by Franz Werfel (1941). fp Los Angeles, 1 October 1941

*Tomorrow*, tone poem for contralto solo, women's chorus and orchestra, Op. 33, text by Margaret Kennedy (1942, for film score *The Constant Nymph*). fp 10 May 1944

**Vocal**

*Knabe*, for voice and piano (1905)*

*Einfache Lieder* (Simple Songs), for voice and piano: *Abendgebet; Vesper; Waldeinsamkeit; Nachklänge; Die Geniale; Andenken; Reiselied* (texts by Eichendorff); *Nachts* (Siegfried Trebitsch) (1911–13)*. fp Frankfurt, 15 February 1912

*Sechs einfache Lieder* (Six Simple Songs), for voice and piano or orchestra, Op. 9: *Schneeglöckchen* (text by Eichendorff); *Nachtwanderer* (Eichendorff); *Ständchen* (Eichendorff); *Liebesbriefchen* (Elisabeth Honold); *Das Heldengrab am Pruth* (Heinrich Kipper); *Sommer* (Siegfried Trebitsch) (1911–13). fp Frankfurt, 15 February 1912 (Nos. 1–3 only)

*Österreichischer Soldatenabschied* (Austrian Soldier's Farewell), song for voice and piano (1915). fp Vienna, 11 March 1917

*Zita-Hymne*, for solo voice and piano, text by Baronin Hedda von Skoda (1916). fp Vienna, 9 May 1917

*Die Ganzleber im Hause Duschnitz* (Goose Liver in the Duschnitz's House), a festive setting for voice and piano in celebration of 40th wedding anniversary (1919)*

*Vier Lieder des Abschieds* (Four Songs of Farewell), Op. 14: *Sterblied* (text by Christina Rosetti/Alfred Kerr); *Dies eine kann mein Sehnen nimmer fassen* (Edith Ronsperger); *Mond, so gehst du wieder auf* (Ernst Lothar); *Gefaßter Abschied* (Ernst Lothar) (1920–21). fp Vienna, 5 November 1921 (piano version); 14 January 1923 (orchestral version)

Three Songs on poems by Kaltneker, Op. 18: *In meine innige Nacht; Tu ab den Schmerz; Du reine Frau* (1924). fp Vienna, 11 March 1926

Three songs for voice and piano, Op. 22: *Was du mir bist?* (text by Eleanor van der Straten); *Mit dir zu schweigen* (Karl Kobald); *Welt ist stille eingeschlafen* (Karl Kobald) (1928–9). fp Vienna, 9 December 1928 (No. 1 only), 1 January 1930 (complete)

*Unvergänglichkeit* (The Eternal), song cycle, Op. 27, text by Eleanor van der Straten (1933). fp Vienna, 27 October 1937

*Narrenlieder* (Songs of the Clown), Op. 29: *Come Away, Death; O Mistress Mine; Hey, Robin!; Adieu, Good Man Devil; The Rain It Raineth Every Day*, text by William Shakespeare (1937). fp Los Angeles, 28 June 1941

Four Shakespeare Songs, Op. 31: *Desdemona's Song; When Birds do Sing; Blow Thou Winter Wind; Under the Greenwood Tree* (1937, 1941). fp Los Angeles, 28 June 1941

Five songs for middle voice and piano, Op. 38: *Glückwunsch* (text by Richard Dehmel); *Der Kranke* (Eichendorff); *Alt-Spanisch Lied* (Howard Koch, from film score *The Sea Hawk*); *Alt-Englisch Lied; Kein Sonnenglanz im Auge* (William Shakespeare) (1940, 1947). fp Vienna, 10 February 1950

*Sonett für Wien,* song for woman's voice and piano, Op. 41, text by Hans Kaltneker (1948). fp Vienna, 10 February 1950

**Chamber**

Trio in D major, for piano, violin and cello, Op. 1 (1909–10). fp Munich, 4 November 1910

Sonata in G major, for violin and piano, Op. 6 (1913). fp Berlin, 21 October 1913

String Sextet in D major, Op. 10 (1914–16). fp Vienna, 2 May 1917

Quintet in E major, for piano and strings, Op. 15 (1920–21). fp Hamburg, 16 February 1923

String Quartet No. 1 in A major, Op. 16 (1922–3). fp Vienna, 8 January 1924

Suite, for two violins, cello and piano left hand, Op. 23 (1930). fp Vienna, 21 October 1930

String Quartet No. 2 in E flat major, Op. 26 (1933). fp Vienna, 16 March 1934

String Quartet No. 3 in D major, Op. 34 (1945). fp Los Angeles, 1946

**Piano**

*Beim Grossmütterschen,* waltz (1908)*

Piano Sonata No. 1 in D minor (1908–9)

*Don Quixote: Sechs Klavierstücke* (1909)

Piano Sonata No. 2 in E major, Op. 2 (1910–11). fp Berlin, 13 October 1911

*Sieben Märchenbilder,* for piano, Op. 3 (1910, instrumental arrangements, 1911). fp Berlin, 13 October 1911

*Vier kleine, fröhliche Walzer,* for piano duet, 'Op. 5': *Gretl; Margit; Gisi; Mitzi* (1911–12)*

*Vier kleine Karikaturen für Klavier,* Op. 19 (1926)*

Piano Sonata No. 3 in C major, Op. 25 (1930). fp Vienna, 3 March 1932

Waltz for Luzi, in the style of Chopin (1948)*

**Arrangements (instrumental)**

Mendelssohn: B minor Scherzo, instrumentation (1917). fp Vienna, 1 February 1922*

Schubert: *Kindermarsches,* instrumentation (1917)

*Rosenkavalier Variations*, from Richard Strauss (date unknown)

*Geschichten von Strauß,* for piano, Op. 21 (1927)

*Nebeltanz* from Mendelssohn's *A Midsummer Night's Dream* (1935, for Reinhardt film *A Midsummer Night's Dream*)*

*Hell Waltz* from Offenbach's *Orpheus in the Underworld* (1941)*

*Prologue to Max Reinhardt's 70th birthday* on a theme from Offenbach's *La Belle Hélène*, text by Erich Wolfgang Korngold (1943)*

*Urlicht* from Mahler's Symphony No. 2, arrangement for contralto and piano for Max Reinhardt's memorial concert (1943). fp 14 December 1943*

*Straussiana* for orchestra, after Johann Strauss (1953). fp Inglewood, 22 November 1953

**Arrangements (operetta)**

Johann Strauss: *Eine Nacht in Venedig,* original text by Friedrich Zell and Richard Genée, new text for Korngold's arrangement by Ernst Marischka (1923). fp Vienna, 25 October 1923

Johann Strauss: *Cagliostro in Wien,* original text by Friedrich Zell and Richard Genée, text for Korngold's arrangement reworked by Dr Ludwig Herzer (1926–7). fp Vienna, 13 April 1927

Leo Fall (completed by Korngold): *Rosen aus Florida,* text by Dr Alfred Maria Willner and Heinz Reichert (1928–9). fp Vienna, 22 February 1929

Johann Strauss: *Die Fledermaus,* text by C. Haffner and Marcellus Schiffer after Henri Meilhac and Ludovic Halévy (1929). fp Berlin, 8 June 1929

Johann Strauss: *Walzer aus Wien,* text by Dr Alfred Maria Willner, Heinz Reichert and Ernst Marischka (1930). fp Vienna, 30 October 1930

Offenbach: *Die schöne Helena* (La Belle Hélène), original text by Henri Meilhac and Ludovic Halévy, reworked for Korngold's arrangement by Egon Friedell and Hans Sassmann (1931). fp Berlin, 15 June 1931

Johann Strauss: *Das Lied der Liebe,* text by Dr Ludwig Herzer (1931). fp Berlin, 23 December 1931

Leo Fall: *Die geschiedene Frau,* original text by Victor Léon, reworked for Korngold's arrangement by Victor Léon, Heinz Reichert and Erich Wolfgang Korngold, couplets by Max Colpet (1932–3). fp Berlin, 1 Feb 1933

Johann Strauss: *Die Fledermaus ('Rosalinda'),* text by Gottfried Reinhardt and John Meehan, lyrics by Paul Kerby. fp New York, 28 October 1942

Offenbach: *La Belle Hélène ('Helen Goes to Troy'),* new text in English by Gottfried Reinhardt. fp New York, 24 April 1944

Johann Strauss: *Walzer aus Wien ('The Great Waltz'),* adapted for Los Angeles Civic Light Opera by Erich Wolfgang Korngold. fp Los Angeles, 1949

Rossini: Selections of Music for Goldoni's *Servo di Due Padrone,* text by William Okie (1939). fp Los Angeles, 31 May 1939

# Further Reading

Books on Korngold himself are regrettably few. Those that exist, at the time of this publication, are in German and remain untranslated. Korngold's first biography was written in 1922 – when the composer was all of twenty-five years old! The pamphlet-sized *Child Prodigy* by Julius Korngold was published in America in 1945 but is long out of print. A short monograph, *Erich Wolfgang Korngold: His Life and Works*, by Brendan Carroll (president of the Erich Wolfgang Korngold Society), is available in English and provides short musical analyses of several of the composer's works as well as an outline of his life. Carroll is currently preparing a large and scholarly biography of the composer, due for publication around the time of Korngold's centenary in 1997. For those adept in German, Luzi Korngold's biography of her husband and Julius Korngold's memoirs make fascinating reading.

Korngold's contemporaries and colleagues from his Viennese days are much better chronicled in English-language biographical format than Korngold himself. There are interesting books available on Max Reinhardt, Lotte Lehmann, Ernst Krenek, Mahler, Schoenberg, and many others.

Korngold is, however, extremely well served in books on film music. The titles by Tony Thomas and Christopher Palmer are very informative and readable. For Viennese background scene-setting, George Clare's *Last Waltz in Vienna* is a powerful and harrowing portrait of a decaying society and the Nazi Anschluss. Literature on *fin-de-siècle* Vienna is plentiful. An astonishing amount of it contains no mention whatsoever of Korngold.

This list is not intended as a comprehensive bibliography but as a guide to some starting points for those wanting to investigate Korngold further.

## Life and Times

**Carroll, B.** *Erich Wolfgang Korngold, 1897–1957: His Life and Works* (Paisley, Wilfion Books, 1985)

**Clare, G.** *Last Waltz in Vienna* (London, Macmillan, 1981) [originally published in German translation as *Das Waren die Klaars* (Verlag Ullstein GMBH, 1980)]

**Flesch, C.** *The Memoirs of Carl Flesch*, translated by H. Keller (Harlow, Centenary Edition, Bois de Boulogne, 1973)

**Flesch, C. F.** *'And Do You Also Play the Violin?'* (London, Toccata Press, 1990) [originally '*... Und Spielst Du auch Geige?'* (Zürich, Atlantis Musikbuch Verlag, 1990)]

**Heyworth, P.** *Otto Klemperer: His Life and Times, Vol. 1, 1885–1933* (Cambridge, Cambridge University Press, 1983)

*Conversations with Klemperer*, edited by P. Heyworth (London, Gollancz, 1973)

**Hoffmann, R. S.** *Erich Wolfgang Korngold*, in German (Vienna, Carl Stephenson Verlag, 1922)

**Jefferson, A.** *Lotte Lehmann, 1888–1976: A Centenary Biography* (London, Julia McRae Books, 1988)

**Korngold, J.** *Child Prodigy – Erich Wolfgang Korngold's Years of Childhood* (New York, Willard, 1945)

**Korngold, J.** *Die Korngolds in Wien: Der Musikkritiker und das Wunderkind – Aufzeichnungen von Julius Korngold* (Zürich/St Gallen, M. & T. Verlag, 1991)

**Korngold, L.** *Erich Wolfgang Korngold*, in German (Vienna, Lafite-Verlag, 1967)

**Levant, O.** *A Smattering of Ignorance* (New York, Garden City Publishing Co. Inc., 1942)

**Levi, E.** *Music in the Third Reich* (London, Macmillan, 1994)

**Mahler-Werfel, A.** *Gustav Mahler: Memories and Letters* (New York, Viking Press, 1946)

**Mahler-Werfel, A.** *Mein Leben* (Frankfurt am Main, S. Fischer, 1960)

**Prawy, M.** *The Vienna Opera* (London, Weidenfeld & Nicolson, 1970) (German edition Wien-Munchen-Zürich, Verlag Fritz Molden, 1969)

**Reinhardt, G.** *The Genius: A Memoir of Max Reinhardt* (New York, Alfred A. Knopf, 1979)

**Saerchinger, C.** *Artur Schnabel* (London, Cassell, 1957)

**Schnabel, A.** *My Life and Music* (London, Longmans, Green & Co., 1961; Gerrards Cross, Colin Smythe, and New York, Dover Edition, 1988)

**Schoenberg, A.** *Style and Idea* (New York, Philosophical Library, 1950; London, Faber & Faber, 1975)

**Slonimsky, N.** *Music since 1900* (4th edition: New York, Charles Scribner's Sons, 1971)

**Stewart, J. L.** *Ernst Krenek: The Man and his Music* (Los Angeles, University of California Press, 1991)

**Tuggle, R.** *The Golden Age of Opera* (New York, Holt Rinehart and Winston, 1983)

**Walter, B.** *Theme and Variations: An Autobiography*, translated by J. A. Galston (New York, Alfred A. Knopf, 1946)

**Weingartner, F.** *Buffets and Rewards: A Musician's Reminiscences*, translated by M. Wolff (London, Hutchinson, 1937) [originally *Lebenserinnerungen* (Zürich, Orell Füssli Verlag, 1928)]

**Zweig, S.** *The World of Yesterday* (London, Cassell, 1943)

## Film Music

**Darby, W. and Du Bois, J.** *American Film Music – Major Composers, Technique, Trends, 1915–1990* (North Carolina & London, Mcfarland & Co., Jefferson, 1990)

**Palmer, C.** *The Composer in Hollywood* (London, Marion Boyars, 1990)

**Thomas, T.** *Music for the Movies* (London, Tantivy Press; New Jersey, A. S. Barnes & Co., 1973)

## Selected Articles

**Bechert, P.** 'Korngold, Strauss and others: subjective criticism', *Musical Times*, February 1922

**Behlmer, R.** 'Erich Wolfgang Korngold established some of the Filmusic basics film composers now ignore', *Films in Review*, 1967

**Bernstein, E.** 'Interview with Hugo Friedhofer', *Film Music Notebook*, Vol. 1, Fall 1974

**Graffman, G.** 'Korngold was more than a movie composer', *New York Times*, 15 September 1985

**Korngold, Erich W.** interviewed in 'It's On The Sound Track', *Overture*, November 1946

**Rachold, B. O.** 'Vom Genie zum Talent', *Stimmen, Die um die Welt gingen*, 1986

## Sleeve Notes

**Carroll, B.** 'The Background to Korngold's Magnum
Opus *Das Wunder der Heliane*', '*Das Wunder
der Heliane* – an appraisal'; notes to *Das Wunder der
Heliane*, DECCA

**Korngold, Ernst W.** Special note to Korngold
Violin Concerto, DORIAN

**Palmer, C.** '*Violanta*', also forewords by Marcel Prawy
and Karl Böhm; notes to *Violanta*, CBS

**Schmilgun, B.** 'Erich Wolfgang Korngold:
A Composer between the Times'; notes to Korngold
Orchestral Works, four volumes, WDR

# Selective Discography

As I was working on this book, Korngold was becoming increasingly favoured in the new releases lists. Initially very few recordings of his music were available at all and what there was was not always of sterling quality. But more and more recordings have been emerging and among them have been some very sympathetic interpretations – notably the young American violinist Gil Shaham in the Violin Concerto and a superb *Das Wunder der Heliane* conducted by John Mauceri. Even if Korngold is still not the most extensively recorded composer of his generation, it is now possible to hear the majority of his works on CD (with the regrettable exception of complete versions of the pantomime *Der Schneemann* in its orchestral form or the operas *Der Ring des Polykrates* and *Die Kathrin* – all of which are long overdue for attention from recording companies).

Korngold's orchestral music – not including the Violin Concerto or the *Abschiedlieder* – is available on four WDR discs with the Nordwestdeutsche Philharmonie conducted by Werner Andreas Albert. In many cases, these are still the only available recordings, but two recent discs by the BBC Philharmonic – the *Abschiedlieder* and the Symphony conducted by Edward Downes, and the Sinfonietta and *Sursum Corda* conducted by Matthias Bamert – are both to be very highly recommended. The Violin Concerto is the most widely recorded of Korngold's orchestral works. The recording by Jascha Heifetz is superlative and the closest available to 'authentic' Korngold, but the recording by Gil Shaham, conducted by André Previn, is as warm and loving a performance as one could hope to find. Itzhak Perlman has also recorded the work with much success.

Korngold's three most famous operas, *Violanta*, *Die tote Stadt* and *Das Wunder der Heliane*, are all available in fine, complete performances. There is a marvellous selection of extracts from historical performances by the Austrian State Radio Orchestra (1949), in several cases conducted by Korngold himself. Singers include Gundula Janowitz, Ilona Steingruber, Rosi Schwaiger, Anton Dermota, Alfred Poell and others, on 'From the Operas of Erich Wolfgang Korngold', and for the historically eager, recordings of original artists such as Maria Jeritza and Richard Tauber in Korngold arias can be easily found.

## Stage works

*Violanta*
Eva Marton, Walter Berry, Siegfried Jerusalem, Horst R. Laubenthal, Gertraut Stoklassa, Ruth Hesse, Manfred Schmidt, Heinrich Weber, Paul Hansen, Karin Hautermann, Renate Freyer; Bavarian Radio Chorus, Munich Radio Orchestra conducted by Marek Janowski
CBS MK 79229

*Die tote Stadt*
René Kollo, Carol Neblett, Benjamin Luxon, Rose Wagemann, Hermann Prey, Gabriele Fuchs, Patricia Clark, Anton de Ridder, Willi Brokmeier; Bavarian Radio Chorus & Boys Choir, Munich Radio Orchestra conducted by Erich Leinsdorf
RCA GD87767 (2 CDs)

*Das Wunder der Heliane*
Anna Tomowa-Sintow, Hartmut Walker, John David de Haan, Reinhild Runkel, René Pape, Nicolai Gedda, Martin Petzold; Rundfunk Chor Berlin, Radio Symphony Orchestra Berlin conducted by John Mauceri
DECCA 436 636-2 (3 CDs)

## Operatic Extracts

*From the Operas of Erich Wolfgang Korngold*
Various solo artists and conductors; Austrian State Radio Orchestra (1949 recording)
CAMBRIA CD 1032

Richard Tauber and Lotte Lehmann in extracts from
*Die tote Stadt* (1924 recording).
EMI CDH7 64029-2; also on NIMBUS NI7830

Maria Jeritza in *The Lute Song*
RCA 09026 6 1236-2 (1922 recording); PREI 89079
(1927 recording)

**Orchestral Works**

Korngold Orchestral Works: Vol. 1
*Der Schneemann*
*Prelude and Serenade*
*Entr'acte*
*Schauspiel Overtüre, Op. 4*
*Sinfonietta, Op. 5*
Lajos Farkas (violin, Prelude and Serenade)
Nordwestdeutsche Philharmonie conducted by Werner
Andreas Albert
WDR CPO 999 037-2

Korngold Orchestral Works: Vol. 2
*Viel Lärm um nichts, Op. 11*
*Sursum Corda, Op. 13*
*Piano Concerto for the left hand*
Steven de Groote (piano)
Nordwestdeutsche Philharmonie conducted by Werner
Andreas Albert
WDR CPO 999 046-2

Korngold Orchestral Works: Vol. 3
*Babyserenade, Op. 24*
*Cello Concerto, Op. 37*
*Symphonic Serenade, Op. 39*
Julius Berger (cello)
Nordwestdeutsche Philharmonie conducted by Werner
Andreas Albert
WDR CPO 999 077-2

Korngold Orchestral Works: Vol. 4
*Symphony, Op. 40*
*Theme and Variations, Op. 42*
*Straussiana*
Nordwestdeutsche Philharmonie conducted by Werner
Andreas Albert
WDR CPO 999 146-2

*Sursum Corda, Op. 13*
*Sinfonietta, Op. 5*
BBC Philharmonic conducted by Matthias Bamert
CHANDOS CHAN 9317

*Violin Concerto, Op. 35*
Jascha Heifetz (violin), Los Angeles Philharmonic
conducted by Alfred Wallenstein
RCA GD 87963

*Violin Concerto, Op. 35*
Itzhak Perlman (violin), Pittsburgh Symphony
Orchestra conducted by André Previn; with Goldmark
Violin Concerto
EMI CDC-7 47846 2

*Violin Concerto, Op. 35*
*Sinfonietta in B major, Op. 5*
Ulrike-Anima Mathé (violin), Dallas Symphony
Orchestra conducted by Andrew Litton
DORIAN DOR 90216

*Violin Concerto, Op. 35*
*Incidental music for Much Ado About Nothing, Op. 11*
(violin and piano arrangement)
Gil Shaham (violin), London Symphony Orchestra
conducted by André Previn; with Barber Violin
Concerto
DG 439-886-2GH

*Symphony, Op. 40*
*Abschiedlieder, Op. 14*
Linda Finnie (soprano), BBC Philharmonic conducted
by Edward Downes
CHANDOS CHAN 9171

## Songs

*Liebesbriefchen, Op. 9, No. 4*
*Three Songs, Op. 18*
*Glückwunsch, Op. 38, No. 1*
*Old Spanish Song, Op. 38, No. 3*
*Sterblied, Op. 14, No. 1*
*Gefaßter Abschied Op. 14, No. 4*
*Sonett für Wien, Op. 41*
Anne Sofie von Otter (mezzo-soprano), Bengt Forsberg
(piano); with songs by Richard Strauss and Alban Berg
DG 437 515-2

*Unvergänglichkeit, Op. 27*
*Lieder, Op. 38, Nos. 1 and 2*
Steven Kimbrough (baritone), Dalton Baldwin (piano);
with songs by Schoenberg, Weigl and Schreker
Koch Schwann 3-1094-2

*The Lute Song* (from *Die tote Stadt*)
*The Page's Song* (from *Viel Lärm um nichts*)
*Liebesbriefchen, Op. 9, No. 4*
*Come Live With Me* (from *The Private Lives of Elizabeth
and Essex*)
*Old Spanish Song, Op. 38, No. 3* (from *The Sea Hawk*)
*Song of Bliss* (from *Die stumme Serenade*)
*The Prayer and the Letter Song* (from *Die Kathrin*)
*Without You* (from *Die stumme Serenade*)
*The Diary Song* (from *Der Ring des Polykrates*)
*Entr'acte*
Polly Jo Baker (soprano), George Calusdian (piano)
ESCD 6502

## Chamber Music

*Piano Trio, Op. 1*
Beaux Arts Trio; with Zemlinsky's Trio, Op. 3
Philips 434 072-2

*Piano Trio, Op. 1*
*String Sextet, Op. 1*
Göbel Trio, Berlin Sextet
Etcetera KTC 1043

*Piano Trio, Op. 1*
*Violin Sonata, Op. 6*
Glenn Dicterow (violin), Alan Stepawsky (cello), Israela
Margalit (piano)
EMI Classics CDC 5 55401 2

*Violin Sonata, Op. 6*
*Piano Quintet, Op. 15*
Ilona Prunyi (piano), András Kiss (violin), Danubius
Quartet
Marco Polo 9.223385

*String Sextet, Op. 10*
The Raphael Ensemble; with Schoenberg's
*Verklärte Nacht*
Hyperion CDA66425

*Incidental music for Much Ado About Nothing*
Gil Shaham and André Previn; violin and piano
arrangement (see Violin Concerto above)
DG 439-886-2GH
(Several recordings of Jascha Heifetz in this work are
also available, on the RCA and EMI labels

*String Quartet No. 3, Op. 34*
Angeles String Quartet; with Kreisler's String Quartet
Koch International Classics 3-7325-2HI

## Solo Piano

*Piano Sonatas Nos. 1, 2 and 3*
Geoffrey Tozer (piano)
Chandos CHAN 9389

*Piano Sonatas Nos. 1, 2 and 3*
Mathijs Verschoor (piano)
Etcetera KTC 1043

*Piano Sonata No. 2, Op. 2*
*Märchenbilder, Op. 3*
*Viel Lärm um nichts, Op. 11 (excerpts)*
*Piano Sonata No. 1*
Ilona Prunyi (piano)
Marco Polo 8.223384

## Film Scores (excerpts unless otherwise stated)

*Between Two Worlds*
*The Constant Nymph*
*Escape Me Never*
*The Prince and the Pauper*
National Philharmonic Orchestra conducted by
Charles Gerhardt
Varèse Sarabande VSD5207

*The Adventures of Robin Hood*
*King's Row*
National Philharmonic Orchestra conducted by
Charles Gerhardt
Chesky CD71

*Captain Blood*
*The Private Lives of Elizabeth and Essex*
National Philharmonic Orchestra conducted by
Charles Gerhardt
RCA GD82792

*The Adventures of Robin Hood*
*Captain Blood*
*The Sea Hawk*
National Philharmonic Orchestra conducted by
Charles Gerhardt
RCA GD80912

*The Adventures of Robin Hood (suite)*
Warner Brothers Studio Orchestra conducted
by E. W. Korngold
FACET 8104

*The Adventures of Robin Hood (original film score)*
Utah Symphony Orchestra conducted by Varuyjan
Kojian
Andante ACD 85706

*King's Row (original film score)*
National Philharmonic Orchestra conducted by Charles
Gerhardt
Andante ACD 85707

## Miscellaneous

*Viel Lärm um nichts (suite)*
*Piano improvisations on Violanta, Die tote Stadt and Die*
*Kathrin*
Korngold Plays and Conducts Korngold; Austrian State
Symphony Orchestra (1951 recording)
Varèse Sarabande VC 81040

# Index

Page numbers in italics refer to
picture captions

**Photographic
Acknowledgements**

Courtesy of the Academy of
Motion Picture Arts and
Sciences, Beverley Hills,
California: 187
Aquarius Picture Library, Hastings:
162, 174, 214
Archiv für Kunst und Geschichte,
London: 52, 54–55, 64, 69,
80–81, 110–111, 141
Bildarchiv Peter W. Engelmeler,
Munich: 199
Bildarchiv Preussischer
Kulturbesitz, Berlin: 15, 16, 98
Bridgeman Art Library, London/
© Marlborough Graphics,
London; self portrait 1910, litho
by Oscar Kokoschka
(1886–1980): 19
Courtesy of Jessica Duchen,
London: 132
The Ronald Grant Archive,
London: 125, 156, 159, 166, 169,
179, 190, 191, 196
Hulton Deutsch Collection,
London: 208
Interfoto Pressebild, Munich: 18,
82, 146, 189
Courtesy of the Korngold Estate:
46, 62, 65l, 71, 75, 90, 91, 104,
105, 121, 137 , 144, 182
Courtesy of Leslie G. Korngold,
California: 44
Lebrecht Collection, London: 11,
14, 23/© Emil Orlik Estate:
32–3, 35, 56, 59, 66, 67, 74/
B. Schott's Söhne, Mainz: 79,
92, 113, 118, 185r, 204
Library of Congress, Washington
D.C./Courtesy of the Erich
Wolfgang Korngold Estate:
24–5

Österreichishe Nationalbibliothek,
Vienna: 2
Österreichisches Theater Museum,
Vienna: 77, 133
Popperfoto, Northampton: 39, 50,
61, 119, 151
Range/Bettmann, London:
101/UPI: 129, 149, 153, 171
Roger–Viollet, Paris/Harlingue-
Viollet: 13
B. Schott's Söhne, Mainz: 47, 65r,
73, 122–3, 127
Courtesy of Gerald Stonehill: 103
Süddeutscher Verlag Bilderdienst,
Munich: 109, 124, 177, 185,
202, 203
Courtesy of Anthony Thomas,
USA: 193, 206
Ullstein, Berlin: 89, 95, 114–15, 201
Courtesy of Universal Edition,
Vienna: 28, 29l, 40